Pride, Politics, and Humility in Augustine's *City of God*

This book is the first to interpret and reflect on Augustine's seminal argument concerning humility and pride, especially in politics and philosophy, in *The City of God*. Mary M. Keys shows how contemporary readers have much to gain from engaging Augustine's lengthy argument on behalf of virtuous humility. She also demonstrates how a deeper understanding of the classical and Christian philosophical-rhetorical modes of discourse in *The City of God* enables readers to appreciate and evaluate Augustine's nuanced case for humility in politics, philosophy, and religion. Comprised of a series of interpretive essays and commentaries following Augustine's own order of segments and themes in *The City of God*, Keys's volume unpacks the author's complex text and elucidates its challenge, meaning, and importance for contemporary readers. It also illuminates a central, yet easily underestimated, theme with perennial relevance in a classic work of political thought and religion.

Mary M. Keys is Associate Professor of Political Science at the University of Notre Dame, Indiana. The author of *Aquinas, Aristotle, and the Promise of the Common Good*, she has contributed to numerous journals and books, including *The Cambridge Companion to Augustine's "City of God."*

D1453324

Pride, Politics, and Humility in Augustine's *City of God*

MARY M. KEYS
University of Notre Dame

CAMBRIDGE
UNIVERSITY PRESS

Shaftesbury Road, Cambridge CB2 8EA, United Kingdom

One Liberty Plaza, 20th Floor, New York, NY 10006, USA

477 Williamstown Road, Port Melbourne, VIC 3207, Australia

314–321, 3rd Floor, Plot 3, Splendor Forum, Jasola District Centre, New Delhi – 110025, India

103 Penang Road, #05–06/07, Visioncrest Commercial, Singapore 238467

Cambridge University Press is part of Cambridge University Press & Assessment, a department of the University of Cambridge.

We share the University's mission to contribute to society through the pursuit of education, learning and research at the highest international levels of excellence.

www.cambridge.org
Information on this title: www.cambridge.org/9781009201087

DOI: 10.1017/9781009201049

First published 2022
First paperback edition 2023

A catalogue record for this publication is available from the British Library

Library of Congress Cataloging-in-Publication data
NAMES: Keys, Mary M., 1966– author.
TITLE: Pride, politics, and humility in Augustine's *City of God* /
Mary M. Keys, University of Notre Dame, Indiana.
DESCRIPTION: Cambridge, United Kingdom ; New York, NY, USA : Cambridge University Press, 2022. | Includes bibliographical references and index.
IDENTIFIERS: LCCN 2021062738 | ISBN 9781009201070 (hardback) | ISBN 9781009201049 (ebook)
SUBJECTS: LCSH: Augustine, of Hippo, Saint, 354–430. De civitate Dei. | Humility – Religious aspects – Christianity. | Pride and vanity – Religious aspects – Christianity. | Christianity and politics. |
BISAC: RELIGION / Philosophy
CLASSIFICATION: LCC BR65.A65 K49 2022 | DDC 239/.3–dc23/eng/20220215
LC record available at https://lccn.loc.gov/2021062738

ISBN   978-1-009-20107-0   Hardback
ISBN   978-1-009-20108-7   Paperback

For my sister Elizabeth

Contents

Acknowledgments

It's a joyful task to thank all who helped me write and complete this book. Since I've been working on this project for several years and there have been many persons and organizations involved, I'd like to begin by thanking from the heart any whom I forget to include here by name. Many thanks are due to Cambridge University Press publisher Beatrice Rehl, a model of professionalism and sage advice during the manuscript completion and review phases. I'm also grateful to the two anonymous reviewers of the book manuscript, for their helpful comments and suggestions. Back in graduate school at the University of Toronto, the late Edward Synan introduced me to Augustine's *City of God* in a directed readings course lasting an academic year. I now appreciate even more what a gift of time that course entailed, and how significant it would be for my scholarship and teaching.

For their generous support of my research, I thank the National Endowment for the Humanities, the Notre Dame Institute for Advanced Study, the Center for Citizenship and Constitutional Government of the University of Notre Dame, the Earhart Foundation, the Strake Foundation, the Martin Marty Center of the University of Chicago, the Program on Constitutional Government at Harvard University, the Institute for Humane Studies Hayek Fund for Scholars, the de Nicola Center for Ethics and Culture at the University of Notre Dame, and the University of Notre Dame Institute for Scholarship in the Liberal Arts. Portions of the book manuscript and related papers were presented at Emory University, the University of Nebraska at Omaha, the workshop on Augustine and Political Theory at Princeton University, the Notre Dame Political Theory Colloquium, the Yale Political Theory

Workshop, the Wheaton College Workshop in Political Thought, the de Nicola Center for Ethics and Culture Conference on Justice, the Notre Dame Institute for Advanced Study Fellows Seminar, the Association for Political Theory Conference, and the Midwest Political Science Association Annual Meeting; on each occasion, I benefited greatly from the participants' comments and questions. The students in many iterations of a graduate seminar on Augustine and Contemporary Political Thought at the University of Notre Dame have taught me much. I'd like to acknowledge seminar papers by Tae Huhn Ahn, Justin Brophy, O.P., Catherine Sims Kuiper, and Jakub Voboril as enlightening in ways contributing directly to this book. Graduate student research assistants Melody Grubaugh, Robert McFadden, C. S. C., Colleen Mitchell, Jakub Voboril, and Zhuoyue You helped the project along in many ways, as did undergraduate assistants Madeleine Filak, Michael Roesch, and Marcilena Schaeffer. Conversations with Evelyn Behling of Notre Dame and Michael Giles of Michigan State University also provided helpful insights.

My sister Elizabeth C. Keys edited the book with professionalism and precision, offering suggestions for substantive as well as stylistic improvements. Vicki Spencer and Michael Zuckert generously read and commented on drafts of various chapters, with wit, wisdom, and candor. John Cavadini's lectures and writings on Augustine have contributed much to my understanding. The family members and friends who buoyed me with their encouragement over the years of work on this project are too many for me to thank them all by name. I'll mention just a few: my mother Elizabeth N. Keys, my father Bertram L. Keys, Jr., who passed away before this book was completed, my sister Elizabeth, and colleagues and friends Ruth Abbey, Yurdagül Adanali, Sarah Byers, Monica Caro, Paul Carrese, Susan Collins, Patrick Deneen, Solwyn Hart, Alisa Hubbard, Eileen Hunt, Catherine Kustner, Alasdair MacIntyre, Ashleen Menchaca-Bagnulo, Susannah Monta, Hildegund Müller, Phillip Muñoz, Veronica Roberts Ogle, Clifford Orwin, Daniel Philpott, Sidney Reed, John Roos, William Rucker, David Solomon, Deborah Tor, Jue Wang, Paul Weithman, and Catherine Zuckert.

Finishing this book has helped me recall how my life and work have been blessed with many wonderful people. This awareness remains a source of deep gratitude and joy.

Note on the Text

Quotations from *The City of God* are from R. W. Dyson's translation (1998), with occasional modifications, and are given by standard book and chapter numbers, followed by page numbers from the Dyson edition. Where given, Augustine's Latin text from *The City of God* and other works is from the *Opera Omnia CAG: Corpus Augustinianum Gissense* (2000).

I

Introduction

Augustine's City of God *on Humility and Pride*

I know ... what efforts are needed to persuade the proud how great is that virtue of humility which, not by dint of any human loftiness, but by divine grace bestowed from on high, raises us above all the earthly pinnacles which sway in this inconstant age.

Augustine, *The City of God* I, preface

In a remarkable way, therefore, there is in humility something which exalts the mind, and something in exaltation which abases it.

Augustine, *The City of God* XIV.13

Augustine's masterwork *The City of God* is the first major text in the history of Western thought to give humility and pride pivotal roles in its analysis. Written for Augustine's own tumultuous age, the book transcends its time as an enduring classic, engaging our human condition in ways that prompt readers to return to it in every era and amid a great variety of political societies and cultures. *The City of God* has exerted a profound influence on medieval, renaissance, modern, and contemporary thought, especially concerning politics, religion, and philosophy.

In this little book written about a great one, I invite students of politics and political philosophy – and all interested in human excellence, peace, and happiness – to explore with me Augustine's *City of God*, whether returning to it anew or encountering it for the first time, and to consider with special care its defense of virtuous humility (*humilitas*), an ennobling trait for humans rather than a humiliating condition. Augustine crafts his case in favor of humility's excellence, against the seductive pitfalls of pride (*superbia*), through a nuanced argument and narrative,

spanning twenty-two books and over a thousand pages. Elucidating and
following the golden thread of humility amid the rich, variegated tapestry
of *The City of God*, enabling the reader better to grasp humility's import
and to weigh Augustine's copious argument on its behalf, is the humble,
heartfelt task undertaken in this new book.

Augustine began writing *The City of God* about two years after Rome
was sacked by Alaric and the Visigoths in AD 410, in response to his
friend Flavius Marcellinus's request. Marcellinus was a government official stationed in North Africa. A Christian, he was finding it difficult to
reply convincingly to arguments that the new religion had weakened the
empire internally and left it without resources to resist growing external
threats. This view of Christianity stood as an obstacle in the path of
pagans otherwise open to considering the Gospel and the church; a case
in point here was the distinguished Roman patriot Volusianus, another
friend of Marcellinus and a refugee from Rome living in North Africa.[1]
Augustine undertook Marcellinus's challenge by writing *The City of God*
over some twelve years in his spare time as the busy bishop of the African
port city of Hippo Regius. Augustine wrote for the sake of perplexed
Christians in the Roman Empire, shaken as were their pagan fellows at
the polity's palpable vulnerability. He wrote also for his pagan compatriots, whom he hoped to persuade to seek citizenship in the "heavenly
city" – the city of God – and to show them that this was not incompatible
with or prejudicial to their civic duties in an earthly polity. Augustine
completed *The City of God* in AD 427, about three years before his death
in AD 430, during the Vandals' assault on Hippo. Augustine succumbed
then to illness that may have been brought on by famine and stress provoked by the protracted siege of his city.[2]

---

[1] On Volusianus, Marcellinus, and Augustine's decision to write *The City of God*, see
Brown (2000, 297–302), Busch (2008, 9–13), and Lancel (2002, 391–96).

[2] As Lancel writes:

> In the third month of the siege Augustine fell ill. He would have been seventy-six in
> the autumn, and privations and difficulties of all kinds undoubtedly hastened his end.
> Attacked by fever he retired to his room and did not move from it again.... At the start
> of the siege he had philosophically consoled himself by repeating these words of Plotinus
> which had already come to his lips at the time of the sack of Rome: "No great man would
> be greatly affected by the fact that stone and wood are collapsing and mortals dying."
> But at the hour of his death philosophy no longer sufficed. He asked for copies to be
> made of a few psalms dealing with penitence, so that when they were placed against the
> walls of his room he could read them from his bed. At last, on August 28, 430, Augus-
> tine rejoined Monica, Adeodatus, Nebridius, Severus, and several others in "Abraham's
> bosom." (Lancel, 2002, 474–75)

In penning *The City of God* as a lengthy apology (*apologia*, defense speech) for the Christian religion and indeed for the entire heavenly city against charges that they are prejudicial to social and civic life in this world, Augustine gives pride of place to a defense of virtuous humility. By the heavenly city, he refers to the society, anagogically (*mistice*) speaking, of those in whom, thanks to the unmerited gift of divine love that they have freely welcomed, the love of God (*amor Dei*), rather than self-love (*amor sui*), acts as their chief motive and guide, if imperfectly so in this life (*CG* XV.1, 634, and XIV.28, 632).[3] Augustine's emphasis on humility is apparent already in the preface:

In this work, O Marcellinus, most beloved son – due to you by my promise – I have undertaken to defend [the city of God] against those who favor their own gods above her Founder. The work is great and arduous; but God is our helper. I know, however, what efforts are needed to persuade the proud how great is that virtue of humility.... Thus, when the nature of the work here undertaken requires us to say something of it, and as occasion arises, we must not pass over in silence the earthly city also: that city which, when it seeks mastery, is itself mastered by the lust for mastery even though all the nations serve it. (*CG* I, preface, 3)[4]

In framing his "long and arduous" *City of God* as a defense speech and task of persuasion, Augustine employs the ample liberal arts and rhetorical education he received in his youth and polished in his first professional posts. These were positions of oratorical instruction, and thence, at the pinnacle of his rhetorical career, as an imperial orator in Milan. From these successes, the next step foreseen by Augustine and his family was a political appointment to a provincial governorship or higher post. With this promotion would come solid social and financial advancement for his family, of impoverished noble stock (*Confessions* [*Conf.*] III.3.6, 40; VI.11.19, 110).[5]

---

3 Cf. *CG* XI.1, 449: "We have learned that there is a city of God, *whose citizens we long to be because of the love with which its Founder has inspired us*" (emphasis added). For an account of the two loves that founded these two cities, emphasizing the relational and divinely given character of *amor Dei*, and so also understanding citizenship in this city in this life as a work in progress, a gift, task, and aspiration, and never an achievement, see Ogle (2021).

4 Quotations from *The City of God* are from R. W. Dyson's translation (1998), with occasional modifications, and are given by standard book and chapter numbers, followed by page numbers from the Dyson edition. Where given, Augustine's Latin text from *The City of God* and other works is from the *Opera Omnia CAG: Corpus Augustinianum Gissense* (2000).

5 Quotations from Augustine's *Confessions* are from F. J. Sheed's translation, Michael P. Foley, ed. (2006), and are given by standard book, chapter, and paragraph numbers, followed by the page number(s). For a study of "Pride and Humility" in Augustine's *Confessions*, see Baumann (2020).

Yet, as the tale Augustine tells in his *Confessions* clarifies, the liberal arts and rhetoric were not the sole content of his education.[6] In his teenage years, reading Cicero's now-lost dialogue *Hortensius* enflamed the young Augustine with a desire for philosophical inquiry and wisdom (*Conf.* III.4.7–8, 40–41).[7] The sophistical aspects of rhetoric in his era increasingly left him yearning for something more fulfilling and meaningful.[8] At Milan, where he had to write discourses flattering imperial pride, Augustine read "some books of the Platonists" (*Conf.* VII.9.13, 126). These philosophical works led him to an abiding awareness of the excellence of the Platonic school and to a new conviction concerning the existence of spiritual being (see *Conf.* VII.7.11–17.23, 124–33). His disillusionment with sophistry and the rhetorical imperial politics of his day drew Augustine to the life of the mind, while his reading of Platonic philosophy led him beyond his previously held materialism (cf. *Against the Academicians* I.1.3–4). After an unforgettable incident in a garden adjacent to his lodging, when he heard a child's voice chanting *tolle et lege* (take and read) and chanced upon a passage of scripture that proved for him a channel of conversion and grace (*Conf.* VIII.12.28, 159), Augustine embarked on a months-long retreat of contemplation, discussion, and writing in the company of family and friends at a friend's villa in the town of Cassiciacum (*Conf.* IX.3.5, 166).[9] He resigned his post as court rhetor and teacher of rhetoric, returning to Milan to prepare for and receive baptism "from Ambrose's hands" at the Easter Vigil in 387 (Lancel, 2002, 114; *Conf.* IX.5.13–6.14, 171–72). Augustine as we know him had been (re)born.

Decades later, just before he completed *The City of God*, Augustine elaborated a revised understanding of rhetoric, in book IV of his *On Christian Teaching* (*De doctrina christiana*, completed c. AD 426).[10] In his view, the classical oratorical aims of delight and persuasion should be subordinated and ordered to rhetoric's third traditional task,

---

[6] For studies of Augustine's thought reflecting on both *The Confessions* and *The City of God*, see Bathory (1981), Versfeld (1990), and Dodaro (1994).

[7] See also *De trinitate* (*The Trinity*) XIV.5.26, and *Against the Academics* I.1.4.

[8] The period in which Augustine studied and taught rhetoric became known as the Second Sophistic. On oratory and its practice in this era, see Farrell (2008, 268) and Kennedy (1999, 47–52).

[9] On Augustine's stay at Cassiciacum and the import of the dialogues he wrote there, see Boone (2016), Brown (2000, 108–20), Foley (1999, 2003), Lancel (2002, 99–111), and McFadden (2018).

[10] For a volume that includes book IV of *De Doctrina Christiana* together with essays of scholarly commentary from various perspectives and disciplines on Augustine's rhetoric, see Enos et al. (2008).

teaching: speaking what is not merely pleasing or moving, but also, to the best of the speaker's knowledge, true, and with the ultimate goal of revealing and sharing truth as far and effectively as possible with one's interlocutors or audience (Fortin, 2008; Kabala, 2020).

With this in mind, and reflecting on Augustine's style of writing in *The City of God*, we may term his method and form of expression here *rhetorical dialectic*, understanding dialectic in a broadly classical sense.[11] As a work of rhetoric, *The City of God* aims explicitly at persuasion and so is rhetorical in a nonpejorative manner, at least in its author's aspiration. It aims also at defense and so takes on a courtroom context reminiscent of that in Plato's *Apology of Socrates*. As steeped also in dialectic,[12] rigorous inquiry starting from the shared perceptions inherent in common views and speech, giving rise to dialogue and debate examining presuppositions, unmasking errors, discerning definitions, and educating in truth, *The City of God* reflects and expresses the philosophical life as Augustine came to understand it. For him, philosophy comprises a love of wisdom that undertakes profound rational inquiry and opens ultimately to revelation and true religion.[13] Dialectic is not a science with a specific

---

[11] For Augustine's specific mentions of dialectic (*dialectica*) in *The City of God*, see VIII.7, 322, and especially XXII.5, 1113:

> Indeed, we shall find, if we consider it, that the manner in which the world came to believe is itself even more incredible [than the miraculous doctrine taught]. A few fishermen, uneducated in the liberal arts ... with no knowledge of grammar, *not armed with dialectic, not adorned with rhetoric*: these were the men whom Christ sent out with the nets of faith into the sea of the world. And in this way He caught all those fish of every kind, including – more wonderful still, because more rare – even some of the philosophers themselves. (Emphasis added)

> Augustine judged it opportune to enlist his training in the liberal arts, grammar, and rhetoric, and his appreciation of dialectic, in the mammoth task of writing *The City of God*. He doubtless considered it a motive for humility that the evangelical fruits of his labor were sure to be much more modest than those of the far less educated and erudite apostles and disciples of the first Christian generation.

[12] For discussions of Cicero's understanding and uses, political and philosophical, of dialectic, which undoubtedly influenced Augustine's, see Crosson et al. (2015, 101–3) and Smith (2018, 140–41, 226–30). Crosson underscores parallels between Aristotelian and Ciceronian dialectic, while Smith emphasizes continuity between dialectic in its Socratic and Ciceronian forms. On Platonic dialectic, see Van Ophuijsen (1999, 292–313).

[13] In his early dialogue *De ordine* (*On Order*), written during his stay at Cassiciacum, Augustine describes dialectic as the academic "discipline of disciplines.... Dialectic teaches how to teach and how to learn. In her, Reason shows herself and makes clear what she is, what she wants, what she is capable of. Dialectic knows what knowing is; it alone not only wants to make people know but is also able" (*De ordine* 2.38; quoted in Kenyon [2018, 118–19]). Kenyon notes that at Cassiciacum Augustine wrote a now-lost

subject matter, commencing from foundational rational principles; it is rather a mode of inquiry akin to an art and applicable to any subject matter. It is an essential form of conversation and study for politics and philosophy alike (Smith, 2018, 230). As Aristotle wrote, "[A] syllogism is ... dialectical (*dialektikos*) when it reasons from beliefs that are generally accepted (*endoxa*) ... which seem true to everyone or to the majority or to the wise (*sophoi*)" (Crosson et al., 2015, 101, quoting Aristotle, *Topics* 1.1, 100a25–100b23). As we will see, this mode of inquiry and exposition well describes Augustine's in *The City of God*.

In defending the heavenly city and its founder, Augustine endeavors whenever possible to begin from Rome's and other ancient polities' civic experience, history, culture, poetry, and epic narratives. From commonly held views, past and present, as well as from definitions and rational arguments accepted by prestigious philosophers of his and earlier eras, Augustine aims to establish a meaningful dialogue with pagan and Christian readers of the late Roman world. In our contemporary era, when tensions between secularist and religious, elite and "common" worldviews too often accompany and feed political polarization, Augustine's defense of virtuous humility and prosecution of vicious pride offer an example of a scholarly discourse during a troubled time that endeavors to bridge religious, intellectual, and cultural divides.[14] How successful he was is a matter of debate, certainly, and how helpful he will be for us remains to be seen. Yet his was a worthy effort that impacted political, philosophic, and religious thought for centuries after his death, and continues to do so today. We might well, then, choose to accompany Augustine on his long trek across history, earth, and cosmos in *The City of God*, and see what in the end we can learn from this journey about humility and pride as they pertain to politics, philosophy, and religion. Such is the invitation offered to readers of this book.

Recent decades have seen a remarkable renewal of scholarship on Augustine's political thought and on his *City of God*. At the same time,

---

dialogue, *De rhetorica*, and may have planned or even begun another dialogue, *De dialectica* (Kenyon [2018, 129]). See also another of Augustine's Cassiciacum dialogues, *Against the Academics* (2019): "And by joining [the study of moral, natural, and divine matters] under dialectic, the foundress and judge, as it were, of those parts (dialectic is either wisdom itself or that without which wisdom can in no way be), Plato is said to have compiled the complete discipline of philosophy" (III.17.37; cf. III.29, 13, and trans. Michael Foley's commentary, ibid., 184, 194–95).

14 For essays exploring what benefits contemporary citizens and scholars might gain from engaging Augustine's works in our current contentious era, see Kabala et al. (2021). For an earlier work on *The City of God and the Politics of Crisis*, see Brookes (1960).

several insightful studies have been published that treat humility and pride in political theory and the history of political thought. Why then this new book? Article-length studies on the topic wisely limit their studies to a particular aspect or angle of the theme: for example, pride vis-à-vis the common good (Markus, 1990); humility and true religion (Bobb, 2010); or Christ's humility and its impact on Augustine's account of humility in *The City of God* (Fitzgerald, 2014). To the best of my knowledge, no book-length study of *The City of God* has focused on its defense of humility against pride, a theme which, as we have seen, Augustine indicates in his preface to be crucial to his overarching intent. A recent monograph, *The Greatness of Humility: St. Augustine on Moral Excellence*, incorporates a broad range of sources, especially Augustine's *Sermons* and including *On Christian Teaching, On the Trinity, Confessions,* and other works, as well as *The City of God*, in its interpretation and argument (McInerney, 2016).[15] Major recent works on humility and pride in the history of political theory have tended to highlight modern political philosophy rather than the late classical political thought of Augustine's era (Brooke, 2012; Cooper, 2013; Jacobson, 1978).

Two of these recent monographs, those by Julie E. Cooper and Christopher Brooke, commence their narratives of modern political theories of pride and humility precisely from Augustine and *The City of God*, indicating the milestone in the history of political thought that Augustine's defense speech on behalf of humility against pride constitutes, and its enduring import in the early modern era. These studies highlight problems perceived in Augustine's view (and/or those of his early modern interpreters), which some of the greatest modern minds in political theory have sought to isolate and address. In *Secular Powers: Humility in Modern Political Thought*, Julie E. Cooper argues that Augustine leaves readers with a choice between stark binaries – philosophical pride versus Christian humility and human agency versus divine agency – that we would do well to overcome via new genealogies of humility and pride. As Cooper writes, "The humility/pride antithesis [in Augustine's *City of God*] tracks a series of oppositions.... Making subjection to God and self-direction mutually exclusive, these oppositions deny human sufficiency and discredit human initiative" (Cooper, 2013, 2; see also 23). On

---

[15] Dodaro (2004) and Ogle (2021) also consider humility and pride in Augustine's political thought. Dunnington (2018, 29–46) offers an interpretation of Augustinian humility based on a reading of *Confessions*, and in dialogue with contemporary moral and religious philosophy.

Cooper's reading, Augustinian thought "conflates human agency with pride" (Cooper, 2013, 4).

In *Philosophic Pride: Stoicism and Political Thought from Lipsius to Rousseau*, Christopher Brooke engages Augustine's debates in *The City of God* with the Stoics on themes including human sinfulness and self-sufficiency (see Brooke, 2012, 1–11). Brooke writes:

> The obvious mistake the Stoics make, from this Christian point of view, is to think that postlapsarian humans can live without being troubled by the disturbances [of irrational passion], and therefore without sin. Christians have it as an article of faith that they cannot, and therefore that the claim of the Stoics appears ridiculous, impious, and prideful, insofar as it denies human dependence on God. (Brooke, 2012, 10)

Although Brooke notes shortly after this quote that Augustine provides a philosophic challenge to these and related aspects of Stoicism (see Brooke, 2012, 11), the passage just quoted suggests a rather fideistic reliance on revelation in Augustine's critique.

These thoughtful accounts, each eminently worth engaging, draw their synopses of Augustine's views mainly from book XIV of *The City of God*,[16] which together with book XIII investigates the primordial sin or fall of Adam and Eve narrated in the book of Genesis, and its enduring impact on humanity. The root of human evil evident in the Fall, argues Augustine in book XIV, is precisely vicious pride, *superbia* (CG XIV.13, 608–9; cf. XIV.14, 611).

Augustine indeed has much to say about pride and humility in the fourteenth book of his *City of God*. Book XIV constitutes a climax of Augustine's discussion of these themes, and so is an excellent choice of focus for brief treatments of the bishop of Hippo's thought on humility and pride, such as Brooke's and Cooper's.[17] If we wish more fully to understand Augustine's thought on these crucial characteristics as expressed in his *City of God*, however, we need to read and consider the work as a whole. Augustine's magnum opus, we have noted, is comprised

---

[16] Though not exclusively: Brooke refers to *The City of God* XII.22, ff. (see Brooke, 2012, 3), XIII.24 and XVIII.1 (3 and 210, notes 8–9), XIII.15 and XXII.30 (10–11 and 211, notes 47–48), and XXII.24 (95 and 228, note 99). Cooper also refers to a passage found in book XII of *The City of God* (see Cooper, 2013, 167, note 10).

[17] McInerney (2016) also adopts this approach: "Although the theme of pride and humility is announced in the prologue of *The City of God* and runs throughout the course of that work, the relationship between the two receives its most explicit and systematic treatment in book XIV. In Chapter 4, I will provide an analysis of this text to highlight the themes Augustine presupposes and develops in relation to his understanding of humility and greatness" (12; cf. McInerney, 2016, 111–24).

of twenty-two books and more than a thousand pages. While readers have complained of Augustine's digressions and the seemingly random nature of some of the work's content, a close, sustained reading suggests a clear ordering and a unified argument in all its multiplicity – though perhaps with an occasional tangent! The work thus comprises a single, highly complex defense speech, and so we may reasonably expect that understanding Augustine's rhetorical dialectic concerning humility, pride, politics, and philosophy requires considering *The City of God* in its entirety.

The task of this book is to offer an interpretation of a crucial aspect of the argument of *The City of God*, considered in its entirety, through the lens of Augustine's defense of humility and prosecution of pride. Among the benefits of considering Augustine's rhetorical dialectic as a whole are an increased sense of the complexity of the "two cities" as they exist in this world or age and their intermingling, thus complicating the rigid binaries that scholars such as Cooper have noted; an appreciation of Augustine's emphasis on the relational, social nature of humility, before and beyond its epistemic aspects,[18] and of humility's salubrious effects on human agency and action; and an increased appreciation of the natural, philosophical, and human-experiential components of Augustine's *apologia* for humility against pride.

At this juncture, readers may be wondering how Augustine defines humility and pride. After all, these concepts have had and do have varied, contested meanings within and across languages and cultures, and throughout the history of ethical, religious, and political thought. Augustine's own rhetorical dialectic in *The City of God* acknowledges a variety of versions of humility. One might say, paraphrasing Alexis de Tocqueville, that Augustine is interested in defending virtuous humility, "rightly understood," distinguishing it along the way from counterfeits or mistaken iterations. Augustine seeks to persuade readers that, paradoxically, a virtuous, ennobling form of this lowly quality does exist, and that it is wise to seek and cultivate it, in place of humility's demeaning variants. To borrow from Aristotle, one might say that, for Augustine, the quality known as humility is susceptible to excess and defect (see

---

[18] Mark Button in his 2005 article offering an intellectual history of humility and arguing for its place in contemporary democratic theory and practice presents Augustine's humility as essentially a "virtue of self-knowledge" (Button, 2005, 850; cf. 843). While it is true that humility has crucial epistemological dimensions for Augustine, his account of this virtue (and of its foil, vicious pride) highlights even more deeply its metaphysical-existential and social-relational aspects, as this book will illustrate.

Nicomachean Ethics, 1104a11–26). Its excess – often, as Augustine suggests, still called "humility," at least in Christian settings – consists of a disposition to lower oneself below people or other beings to whom or which one is in fact equal or superior. Humility's defective condition veers by contrast toward, and at its extreme comprises, vicious pride.

What then is truly virtuous humility? Augustine does not offer readers a succinct or proper definition in *The City of God*, nor to the best of my knowledge, in any other work. Yet based on what he says about this trait throughout this long and arduous work, we can construct a provisional definition. Augustine's humility is the virtue or excellence by which human beings willingly acknowledge their dependence on God and their essential equality with their fellow human beings and strive to live accordingly with right worship, justice, moderation, and mercy. As such, and as Augustine writes elsewhere, humility is the "dwelling place" of charity, of divinely given, freely received love of God and neighbor.[19] Moreover, since the Christian religion affirms that "God is love" (*Deus caritas est*; 1 John 4:16), Augustine indicates in his preface and at various other points in *The City of God* that virtuous humility expresses and opens itself to the gifts of grace, godliness, and true deification or divinization.

Vicious pride, by contrast, resists rightful subordination to God and disdains equality with one's fellow human beings. Pride is a desire for a "perverse kind of elevation" (*CG* XIV.13, 608), the "vice of exaltation" or "elation" (*CG* XIV.13, 609; XII.1, 498), whereby one makes oneself, individually or collectively, into an absolute principle or foundation of one's being, and one's own *telos*. Pride expresses at its core a seduction by and an aspiration to false or perverse forms of imitating God or divinization (cf. *CG* XIX.12, 936). Vicious pride propels to domination, war, and oppressive, inequitable peace (cf. *CG* XIX.12, 936). Humility well understood and practiced, by contrast, conduces to just rule and righteous forms of peace (see *CG* V.24, 232; XIV.28, 632; XIX.14, 940–42). Humility allows people to perceive better, appreciate affectively, and live

---

[19] *Holy Virginity* 51, in Augustine (1999, 207). Augustine's Latin reads: *non ergo custodit bonum uirginale nisi deus ipse, qui dedit, et deus caritas est. custos ergo uirginitatis caritas; locus autem huius custodis humilitas* (chapter 52 in the CAG text of *De sancta uirginitate*). Augustine writes so extensively about humility in this work, that at the beginning of chapter 51, just before the passage quoted above, he observes, "At this point someone will say, 'But this is not to write on virginity, but on humility'" (Augustine, 1999, 206). See also Augustine, *The Trinity* IV.1.2: "[God arranged things] so that the power of charity would be brought to perfection in the weakness of humility."

more consistently in the truth – truth about humanity, polity, cosmos, and divinity. It opens the imagination and mind to wonder; to amazement at creation, beings, and human beings; to a constantly renewed appreciation for the miracle of nature, as well as for showier miracles worked by God in history (*CG* X.12, 411; XXI.7, 1057–60; XXII.8, 1120–34). Pride, by contrast, constricts imagination and intellect, even as it appears at times to exalt them. It deceives its possessors and prompts people to promulgate and perform falsehoods in the personal, philosophic, social-civic, and religious dimensions of their lives (inter al. *CG* IV.32, 184). It is the origin of all sin and injustice. Vicious pride's evil issues readily in envy, the resentment of goods of others, and the desire to deprive them of what one cannot enjoy oneself (*CG* XIV.3, 586; XV.5–7, 640–47); in vanity and vainglory, foolish or excessive pleasure in one's real or presumed excellences or honors (see *CG* IV.3, 147; X.1, 390; XII.1, 498; and XV.21, 678); and, at an extreme, in total apathy, imperviousness to the needs and sufferings of others (*CG* XIV.9, 602).

These are, of course, big, contentious claims. To understand and assess them, it is worth the effort to "[assume] the character of an enquirer" (cf. *CG* X.11, 407, 410) and engage with openness Augustine's difficult rhetorical dialectic in his *City of God*. This book aims to assist readers in this task and to make its inception easier, inviting them to accompany me as I undertake it on my own part, in the knowledge that other readers of Augustine may well see farther and better in interpretation, evaluation, and critique.

This book on Augustine's defense of humility closely follows the contours and content of *The City of God*. Augustine provides his readers with ready outlines and reminders of his roadmap, at intervals throughout *The City of God* itself and also in his letter to Firmus, discovered in the mid-twentieth century. *The City of God* comprises twenty-two books, of which books I–X constitute the first major part, and books XI–XXII, the second. In books I–X, Augustine aims to refute arguments that the spread of Christianity and its adoption as the official imperial religion prompted Rome's decline and recent sack. He does so directly in book I, examining pagan arguments to this effect and endeavoring to rebut them. In books II–V, Augustine continues his critique by contesting the case that Rome's previous, polytheistic public cult had caused happiness for the polity and the personal well-being of its citizens in this life. Books VI–X examine the prospects of pagan polytheism, practiced in and interpreted by civil religion and philosophic theology and theurgy, for leading people to happiness in the afterlife. Books I–X thus form a veritable tour de force of the classical world that Augustine inherits as a Roman citizen and scholar. Its narrative ranges from social, religious, and political history, through learned commentary on Rome's ancestral civil religion, to natural theology, or philosophy about divinity, and to Jewish and Christian revealed religion.

While the first part of *The City of God* comprises mainly critique, the second main part of Augustine's magnum opus is chiefly constructive. In this second part, Augustine develops the overarching theme that he has introduced in the work's preface and circled back to numerous times already, that of the two cities built by two loves (see *CG* XIV.28, 632): in the earthly city, love of oneself, personal and/or collective, above God; and in the heavenly, love of God above oneself and all one's earthly fellowships. In book XV, Augustine clarifies that these two "cities" or "societies" are so called analogously or anagogically (*mistice*; *CG* XV.1, 634) and therefore do not neatly map onto the visible aspects of what we would term church and state (see Ogle, 2021, 14–18). In describing the heavenly city, or city of God, and its pilgrimage in this world, Augustine begins from the person of Jesus Christ and from the scriptures of the Old and New Testaments. Throughout his argument, he refers as well to secular works penned by pagan poets, statesmen, and historians, and to classical philosophy as taught by its various schools, again indicating that he hopes not to forget his pagan readers or talk past them, while addressing his perplexed fellow Christians. Books XI–XIV chronicle the beginnings of the two cities; books XV–XVIII, their development and histories; and books XIX–XXII, "their merited ends" (*CG* XI.1, 450).

The rhetorical dialectic of Augustine's *City of God* thus comprises five chief segments: the first two, of five books apiece, and the following three, of four books apiece. Each chapter of my book endeavors to read one segment (or, in a few cases, half a segment) of Augustine's magnum opus in light of his stated concern to defend virtuous humility and prosecute vicious pride.[20] The chapters offer a series of interpretive essays and commentaries, endeavoring to unpack Augustine's complex rhetorical dialectic and elucidate its meaning, import, and challenge. The narrative follows Augustine's *City of God* from the political pride of ancient

---

[20] For other works commenting on *The City of God* following the order of its books, see Meconi (2021), O'Daly (1999a), Rickaby (1925), and Versfeld (1958). For thematically and historically organized studies of *The City of God*, both monographs and edited volumes, see Brookes (1960), Curbelié (2004), Donnelly (1995), Figgis (1921), Ogle (2021), Ruokanen (1993), Vessey et al. (1999), and Wetzel (2012).

Rome, republican and imperial, to the prospects he sees in pagan philosophy for a theistic modesty analogous to humility. The very real advance toward truth he finds in classical philosophy nonetheless appears tarnished in his eyes by its aptness to cultivate and justify its own versions of vicious pride and to rest content with an unbridgeable gap between the few and the many and their diverse prospects for happiness. From this critique of philosophic pride and vanity, Augustine's constructive exploration of the two cities embarks, considering in succession numerous "great" and "most difficult questions" concerning creation, being, nothingness, good, evil, sociability, sin, life, death, happiness, history, *res publica*, justice, and peace (see *CG* IX.14, 376; XII.22, 533; XIII.1, 541; XV.1, 634; XX.28, 1035).

In a sermon, Augustine bishop of Hippo once inquired of his congregants, "Do you wish to grasp the exaltedness of God?" Anticipating an affirmative response, he continued by exhorting them, "Grasp first the humility of God" (Hill, *Sermons*, in Rotelle, 2001 III/4, 220).[21] The way to transcend the inconstant paths and pinnacles of this world, even as we tread them as well as we can, is for Augustine the path of virtuous humility (*CG* I, preface, 3; cf. Fitzgerald, 2014, 258). If we wish for true exaltation of mind and heart, and even a share in divinity, humility is said by Augustine to be the marvelous means (*CG* XIV.13, 609). If we long for a worthy, nondomineering peace, one based on a just "fellowship of equality under God," humility as pride's antithesis again appears to constitute the key (*CG* XIX.12, 936). How then can we humans understand humility aright and cultivate it in our lives? Augustine's ultimate answer is a religious one: by learning to know and love Jesus Christ, in whose incarnation, life, and death the astounding and inspiring humility of God is fully revealed. Allan Fitzgerald (2014) argues helpfully that Augustine's heightened appreciation for and attention to humility, evident especially in his later writings, such as *The City of God*, has its roots in Augustine's contemplation of Christ and Christ's great humility. Augustine's account of virtuous humility and vicious pride as its foil is thus theistic and specifically Christian.

If this is so, as it clearly seems to be, then why might those professing faiths other than Christianity, or no faith at all, choose to continue

---

[21] *vis capere celsitudinem dei? cape prius humilitatem dei* (*Sermones*, PL 38.671). For a fuller discussion of this passage in the light of the *Christus medicus* (Christ the physician) motif, see Meconi (2013, 101). See *CG* XIV.13, 608, on pride as "an appetite for a perverse kind of elevation" (*[appetitus] perversae celsitudinis*). For notes on humility in Augustine's sermons and letters, see Clair (2016, 71–72, 141, 162).

along this intellectual journey with Augustine? There are, I think, many possible reasons. It seems common for citizens and scholars in our contemporary world to value certain forms of humility and modesty in themselves, friends and colleagues, and government officials, even as many find excessive pride and arrogance causes for concern. In the West at least, it was through Judaism and Christianity that humility entered the catalogue of the virtues. Though its inclusion has been rejected or questioned by some prominent modern philosophers and political leaders, if we find in humility even a potential ally in the search for justice, peace, and meaning, then an open-minded consideration of its canonical treatments such as Augustine's in *The City of God* may help us understand it more deeply. We might find ourselves persuaded by Augustine at key points in his long study, and even if we do not, we may find some areas of agreement or consensus, and can learn where and why we dissent from his views and so sharpen our own, as intellectuals as diverse as Hannah Arendt (Arendt et al., 1996), Albert Camus (2007), and William Connolly (1993) have done.[22]

Augustine is well aware that in addressing readers who are not Christian together with those who are, he ought early and often to begin with and incorporate arguments accessible to unaided human reason (*CG* XIX.1, 909). He does so frequently at the beginning of major sections of *The City of God*: for instance, in books I–V, his politically focused analysis of Roman history, rooted in the classic writings of pre-Christian historians and philosophic statesmen; in books VI–X, where he engages philosophic supporters of Rome's pagan civil cult and Platonic arguments concerning God, soul, and afterlife; and again in book XIX, the most famous portion of *The City of God*, in which Augustine offers an extensive survey and assessment of leading philosophic judgments, concerning the nature of human happiness and the ways of life that conduce to it. Whether Augustine concurs with specific philosophic opinions or dissents from them, he acknowledges the high dignity of philosophy's enterprise and the great difficulty and import of the questions it takes up (*CG* VIII.1, 312).[23] His respect for the philosophy of the Platonic school is especially elevated and palpable (*CG* X.1, 390), while not exclusive of other schools and approaches, and philosophers of any nation, whether known or unknown to him (*CG* VIII.11, 327).

[22] For studies bringing Camus and Augustine into dialogue, see Carlson (2014), Lavere (1985), and Smith (2020).

[23] On Augustine on the nature and import of philosophy, see Rist (2012).

One oft-repeated concern about Christian humility, and one that Augustine's analysis suggests may have troubled certain Platonists living in Christian times, is that it appears opposed to greatness of soul or magnanimity, a classical virtue informing political life and arguably also philosophic life at their pinnacles (cf. *NE*, 1123a35–1125a35). Augustine too, throughout his life and writings, is preoccupied by greatness and inspired by great human beings: by the *exempla* or exemplars of the Roman tradition (*On Order*, 20.53; *CG* I.22–23, on the greatness of Plato and Cato); and by the martyrs, apostles, and other saints in Jewish and Christian context (*CG* X.21, 423, on the martyrs as heroes; XX.17, 1004, on Saint John).[24] In *The City of God*, as we see in its preface, Augustine offers an account of humility understood *precisely as a form of and path to greatness*, and as itself a tremendous excellence or power (*virtus*; cf. McInerney, 2016).[25] This paradox, the exalted character of a virtuous form of lowliness, of closeness to the earth (*humus*), that enables humans to receive divine gifts without obstacle and even to become "partakers of the divine nature" (2 Peter 1:4) without loss of their humanity or personality, offers readers of the rhetorical dialectic of *The City of God* a refreshing, hopeful, and challenging perspective that we may well wish to consider – and even to rejoice in – if at our journey's end we were, like Augustine, to find it true.

---

[24] On Augustine on Roman heroism and Christian martyrdom, see Dodaro (2005); on Augustine in dialogue with classical and modern philosophers on greatness and humility, see McInerney (2016).

[25] On *virtus* and politics in the works of the great Roman historians, see Balmaceda (2017). On Roman virtue and political thought, see Harding (2008) and Hammer (2014).

2

The City of God I–V

Political Pride against Natural Right

In books I–V, the opening segment of *The City of God*, Augustine aims to address and refute arguments that Christianity bears responsibility for Rome's decline and recent sack, whereas the pagan cult previously fortified, defended, and glorified the city and its empire. This section of his magnum opus presents considerable difficulties for interpretation, as the subject matter ranges widely from the crisis of Augustine's own era in the empire back to the legendary foundations and over the whole history of Rome, especially its political history, intertwined with a panoply of religious, artistic, and philosophic motifs. In this chapter, I show the unity of Augustine's complex rhetorical dialectic in these books, precisely by focusing on our themes of humility and pride, as they enter Augustine's narrative and rhetorical dialectic in this long and arduous work (see *CG* I, preface, 3). These books seek to persuade readers that vicious pride, *superbia*, rises up against what is by nature right in human affairs, leaving a trail of misery in its wake. Faced with this realization, readers who have no initial affection for humility may begin to appreciate its value, intimated also in Augustine's defense of a related virtue, moderation, in civic affairs, and undergirded by the Platonic natural theology and the example of Christ, which together comprise the climax of this segment. At the close of this opening section, near the end of book V, Augustine calls those in positions of leadership to shun pride and cultivate a modest, magnanimous humility for the common benefit and their own deep welfare.

An earlier version of this chapter was published as "Augustinian Humility as Natural Right," in Ann Ward and Lee Ward, eds. (2013), 97–113.

PRIDE AND HUMILITY IN BOOKS I–V

Books I–V comprise a microcosm of Augustine's overarching argument in *The City of God* for the excellence of humility (*humilitas*) and the shameful folly of pride (*superbia*). In books I–III, Augustine's analysis follows some of pagan Rome's great historians, embarking from the very great pride – apparently strong and glorious, but actually enslaving and enfeebling – of political power and polities.[1] Such civic *superbia* is enslaving, not liberating, for humans *precisely because it is unnatural*, comprising a mere creature's individual or collective usurpation (and also distortion) of the place of God vis-à-vis his or her fellow humans. Political pride therefore paves the path to unwitting, yet quite real, bondage to human finitude, folly, and moral weakness. Augustine's argument against pride peaks in book IV with his introduction of a metaphysics or natural theology of creation, coupled with a significant intimation of the superiority of worshipping one God, revealed most perfectly in Christ, who is "meek and humble of heart," over honoring a "swarm" of often proud pagan divinities (*CG* IV.16).[2] In book V, Augustine continues this contrast, with special reference to the characteristics of citizens and rulers in this world: King Tarquin the Proud, succeeded by the proud Roman people in the republic and empire, and the ideal of a Christian emperor who cultivates the gift of humility in the imitation of Christ. Together, these five initial books seek to establish divine governance as the only fully just and liberating form of rule, yet one on a far higher plane than free human jurisdictions, undergirding and guiding rather than usurping and undoing them.

Throughout this chapter, I aim to show how in defending virtuous humility Augustine seeks to defend not only the Christian religion and divine grace but also a new account of natural right, or justice according to nature.[3] The concept of natural right played a crucial role in earlier Greek and Roman ethical and political philosophy, with which Augustine is in dialogue throughout *The City of God*. Classical natural right theories seek to identify the foundation of justice for and among human beings in

---

[1] On the moral and civic vision of Rome's great historians, see Balmaceda (2017), Earl (1966), Hammer (2014), chapters 3, 5, and 7; and Harding (2008), chapter 2.

[2] On the link between God's humility and justice, manifested most perfectly in Christ's sacrifice on the cross, and on "the question of humility" as "the backbone" (*l'épine dorsale*; 204) of *The City of God* and Augustinian thought generally, see Curbelié (2004, 201–5); quoted in Fitzgerald (2014, 246).

[3] Others who read Augustine as in some significant respect a natural right (justice according to nature) thinker include Peter Busch (2019), and John von Heyking (2001, 1).

accord with their common nature, and Augustine's *City of God* continues this critical quest. In its first five books, comprising an inquiry into the pagan religious cult's contributions to happiness in this life, *The City of God* as a matter of course considers the nature of right or justice and of human flourishing more broadly, together with key causes supporting or undermining them. Alasdair MacIntyre (1988, 160) advances an argument similar to mine, concerning humility and the nature of Augustinian justice, although in *Whose Justice? Which Rationality?* he does not elaborate on the textual basis for his conclusions. MacIntyre presents humility's foundational nature for Augustine in terms of the postlapsarian human will "returning to freedom" by countering the evil of pride, the root of injustice. "The fundamental human vice is of course pride; correspondingly the fundamental human virtue is humility (*humilitas*). … Justice, therefore, cannot inform an individual's character unless that character is also informed by humility, and the rootedness of injustice in pride entails that injustice consists in disobedience" (1988, 157). MacIntyre puts Augustine's understanding of humility in stronger positive terms a bit later, commenting on the Augustinian nature of the theological-political thought of Gregory VII. MacIntyre writes: "The virtue underlying and required for justice is humility. It is at once clear that it is indeed Augustine's scheme of the virtues, presupposing Augustine's psychology, which is being expressed in political terms" (160). Robert Markus (1990, 251–53) also notes that Augustine considers pride to countervene a right order of love's and human nature's social dimension, ordered to community and common good. Questions concerning nature generally play a much greater role in Augustine's *City of God* than is often recognized; indeed, *natura* (nature) and its variants occur far more frequently in this work than *gratia* (*qua* divine grace) and its variants, critical as grace certainly is from Augustine's point of view.[4]

In the background of Augustine's rhetorical dialectic in books I–V is the surprising humility of God, known to an extent through contemplation of nature and far more fully through revelation, especially in the person

---

[4] Rhetorical-dialectical discussion of nature – divine, creaturely, and specifically human – will continue to guide much of Augustine's inquiry in books VI–X, examined in Chapters 3 and 4 of this book. Books VI–VII explore the classical philosophical theme of nature and convention in political life through the lens of civil religion and its Roman philosophical (re)interpretations. Books VIII–X find Augustine's rhetorical dialectic in dialogue with pagan natural theology, or philosophy concerning divinity. As in books I–V, Augustine's rhetorical dialectic in these later books takes up, implicitly and explicitly, questions of what is right or wrong in a foundational sense, according to nature and human nature. Augustine's concern with nature continues with many manifestations through books XI–XXII.

of Jesus. As we will see in this and subsequent chapters, Augustine's argument in *The City of God*, encapsulated and foreshadowed in these first five books, accompanies its political-philosophic readers on a rhetorical-dialectical journey, from political power and domination to a recognition of pride as an unnatural wrong, and thence via moderation, creation, and Christ, to the natural and divine right of humility.

POLITICAL PRIDE, HUMAN NATURE, AND JUSTICE

In *The City of God*, Augustine undertakes to defend the work's namesake and its founder – and with him the virtue of humility – from contemporary and, we may assume, future critics. Augustine makes it apparent from his preface that he considers humility a strong and splendid virtue, conferring on its possessors a transcendent, divine loftiness and power, and a serene stability amidst the tempestuous temporal world. God's delight in humility and displeasure with pride reflect a "maxim of the divine law" promulgated "in the Scriptures of His people" (*CG* I, preface, 3). Augustine relies on divine assistance and employs copious human argument on humility's behalf in this "great and arduous" rhetorical dialectic (cf. *CG*, I, preface, 3). Yet, as we have already noted, an important part of Augustine's endeavor is to persuade those who do not accept scripture's authority of the excellence of humility and so invite them to seek citizenship in the city of God (see *CG* II.29, 91–93). Since he undertakes this task despite what he admits to be its daunting difficulty, Augustine must consider humility to have a foothold or a foundation of some sort in human nature, notwithstanding what he takes to be its fallen condition.

As the end of his preface indicates, an epistemic and experiential foothold for humility accessible to all humans is the misery and injustice caused by human pride, reaching a pinnacle in politics when pride claims divine honors and attributes in the service of its insatiable "lust for mastery" (*dominandi libido*; *CG* II.29, 91–93). Augustine is famous for this phrase, yet its literary origins are in the writings of the pagan historian Sallust, who was as Augustine emphasizes "noted for his veracity" (*CG* I.5, 9).[5] Augustine may not be able to appeal effectively, as his first step, to the natural and graced goodness of humility for human beings, yet he can, he hopes, begin to demonstrate to the jaded earthly city that "when it seeks mastery, [it] is itself mastered by the lust for mastery even though all the nations serve it" (*CG* I, preface, 3). Pride thus fails to ground or comprise

---

[5] On Sallust in Augustine's thought, see Burns (1999).

a reliable foundation for human freedom, happiness, and greatness, if Augustine is correct. In making these and similar arguments, Augustine intimates that he recalls for his readers, especially for those with a liberal education, what they already know through experience, history, and the writings of leading philosophic statesmen, but might not have articulated or acknowledged fully, even to or within themselves. Someone persuaded of the socio-political pathology of vicious pride, as Augustine depicts it in these opening books of *The City of God*, can begin to investigate with its author his fuller, constructive case for humility's justice and goodness.

After the preface, in the main body of book I Augustine commences what we might term his *apologia pro humilitate*, his defense speech on behalf of humility, with a rhetorical-dialectical critique of political pride. Civic and cultural *superbia*, he first aims to show, obscures an honest social and civic vision. Augustine observes how in recent years pride has blinded certain pagan citizens to the mitigation of the horrors of war, which the spread of Christianity among the "barbarians" appears to have effected during Alaric's sack of Rome (*CG* I.1–7, 4–11). Many Roman pagans, together with their Christian neighbors, escaped slaughter or slavery through the kindness of some Arian Christian Goths. Romans of all religions sought refuge in Christian churches, respected by the invaders as "places of mercy and humility" and so of life and liberty (*CG* I.4, 9). Recalling a poignant scene from Virgil's *Aeneid*, Augustine contrasts this respect of persons, at least dimly reflecting divine justice and pity, with the Greeks' selection of Juno's temple as a place to heap up booty and imprison captives. This pagan temple was presented not as a scene of "mercy and humility," but rather of "avarice and pride" (*CG* I.4, 8–9). Why then, Augustine asks liberally educated Roman citizens, who should be aware of and sensitive to this contrast, do some still fail to clearly perceive the cause of their comparatively good fortune: the coming of Christ and the impact of the Christian religion on the outlook and actions of those who believe in him? Augustine's answer is "ungrateful pride," precluding for people held in its grip a just recognition of Christian mercy's ameliorating effects in this time of war (*CG* I.1, 5; cf. V.23, 230–31).[6]

---

[6] That (some of) the barbarian troops' restraint regarding *some* customs and "rules of war" (*CG* I.2, 4), chiefly in the churches, is not enough for a true Christian military ethic becomes clear later in book I:

> [Christians] are bound by no military authority, nor by an oath of military service, to smite *even a conquered enemy*. Who is so grievously in error, then, as to suppose that a man may kill himself because a foe has sinned against him, or for fear that a foe may sin against him, *yet may not kill the foe himself who has sinned, or will in the future sin, against him*? (*CG* I.24, 37; emphasis added)

As Augustine's rhetorical dialectic develops, it appears that prideful callousness has also led some pagan contemporaries to blame Christian women who were victims of sexual assault during the city's pillaging, instead of rightfully acknowledging their dignity in the face of grave injustice and consoling them for the crimes perpetrated against their persons and their will (*CG* I.16, ff.). This harsh, iniquitous response to violence of humiliating and blaming the victims, betrays the noblesse of Roman righteousness, as described by Virgil, requiring of the virtuous great and their civic community that they "spare the humble and subdue the proud" (*Aeneid* 6,853; *CG* I, preface, 3).[7] In Virgil's poetic praise of ancient Rome, Augustine finds profound evidence of the city's unjust pride – its hubris in attributing to human beings and a human city a task of judgment and retribution that only God can rightly and equitably fulfill (*CG* I, preface and I.6). Augustine invites his readers instead to "reflect humbly" with him on the sins, including "horrible pride," that human beings commit, and on the chastisements that ensue and that divine justice could reasonably impose in consequence (*CG* I.9, 13). Augustine indicates that such humble reflection leads to a recognition of "the duty of teaching and admonishing, and sometimes even of rebuking or correcting, sinners. We [ignore] this either when we weary of the effort, or when we hesitate to offend their dignity, or because we wish to avoid enmities" (*CG* I.9, 13). In this spirit, Augustine's *City of God* book I undertakes to point out and correct the moral and civic blindness caused by vicious pride, so that readers may have the chance to expand their outlooks and recover clearer civic vision for their own benefit and that of many among whom they live.

In this portion of his rhetorical dialectic, Augustine the bishop clarifies that his key concern is not only to defend but also to console the many Christian women who suffered sexual assault during Alaric's sack of their city, and who may have been taunted as guilty of unchastity by some among the pagans (*CG* I.16, 26). Against the backdrop of their suffering is Roman culture's powerful image of the noble Lucretia, the legendary exemplar of womanly fortitude and virtue (see Livy, *History* I.58). After she suffered sexual assault by the tyrant Tarquin the Proud, she killed herself in witness to her unwillingness to suffer so, as well as to underscore the good for the community of female marital fidelity. Her memory became a rallying cry for her family members and fellow citizens who overthrew the king and established the republic, and her final deed was thus immortalized as an icon of virtue for Roman women. In such

---

[7] For a study of the place of Virgil in Augustine's thought, see MacCormack (1998).

a cultural milieu, how could Roman women – Christians and pagans alike – overcome the temptation to end their own lives in witness to their chastity of mind after this illustrious Roman lady's example?

Once again in this discussion pride and humility come to the fore in Augustine's rhetorical dialectic. In Rome's glory-idolizing culture – about which Augustine will soon have much more to say, especially in book V – Lucretia would appear to have internalized her city's customs and idols (see Ogle, 2021, 62–66). Augustine thus imagines her as "a Roman lady excessively eager for praise," as her polity encouraged its leading citizens to be, and thus unable to bear public shame, suspicion, or reproach, even when she knows it is levied unjustly (CG I.19, 31; O'Daly, 1999a, 78). Augustine would have Lucretia profess her innocence and Tarquin's guilt and then stand firm in her proper dignity, refraining from harming herself. The victims of sexual assault should cry out for justice, and if that cannot be given them, uphold the untarnished value of their life and future. Augustine next considers Cato's suicide in resistance to Caesar, arguing that to take one's own life under horrible duress or threat, while deserving of any decent person's compassion and pardon, still falls short of righteous freedom of spirit and true greatness of soul (CG I.23, 35–36; cf. I.16–17, 26–27; I.22, 34–35; and I.24, 36–37).[8] Augustine suggests that the legendary Roman general Marcus Regulus evinced a truer greatness in his death than Cato's at the end. Regulus chose to die under Carthage's cruelest tortures for the sake of his fatherland and in fidelity to an oath, not taking his own life when he could have done so (CG I.24, 36–37).

To bear wrongs bravely with perseverance and patience – including the myriad injustices inflicted during the sack of Rome – reflects a true strength of mind, Augustine encourages his readers to consider. Christians have even greater motivation to follow this course of action than had the ancient pagan heroes, aware as they should be that "they will not be forsaken in this humiliation by the Most High, Who for their sakes so humbled himself" (CG I.24, 37). Pagan divinities gave no such assurance or example. Even in the wake of the admittedly atrocious (howsoever mitigated) recent events in Rome, Augustine holds out hope for the healing of injured persons by means of humility and compassion and through them for the healing of their civic culture from its unjust, damaging attachment to vainglory, reputation, and pride.

---

[8] For a discussion of Augustine's philosophical and theological treatment of suicide, see Dougherty, "St. Augustine and the Problem of Political Ethics in *The City of God*," in Dougherty (2019, 14–21).

In books II and III, Augustine continues to encourage humbler, more realistic readings of pre-Christian Roman social and civic life, employing renowned historians and statesmen whose works educated pagans knew well against naïve or falsifying claims that the old pagan days were good or even significantly better. Roman pride is chastened first through Augustine's survey of ancient historians' accounts of the moral evils and injustices that occurred as far back as the founding of the city and in its monarchy and early republic. In book II, Augustine follows the Roman historian Sallust (Gaius Sallustius Crispus, 86–c. 35 BC) in considering the possibility of locating natural right or natural justice in the early Roman citizenry and their polity. At least three times, Augustine quotes Sallust's claim concerning the epoch immediately following the expulsion of the Tarquins that "'[j]ustice and goodness prevailed among [the Romans] as much by nature as by law'" (*Catil.* 9, 1, quoted in *CG* II.17, 69, and II.18, 71). Augustine questions the truth of this praise by referencing Sallust's own account of events, including the abduction of the Sabine women by Rome's men and the war waged afterward against their parents and patria; the removal from the magistracy and exile of Lucius Tarquinius Collatinus, Lucretia's husband, for no other reason than that he shared a name with the hated former king; the trumped-up charges and civic ingratitude that led to the exile of Marcus Camillus, a general to whom Rome owed a critical military victory; and the domineering, unjust actions of the patricians vis-à-vis the plebeian class and the resultant civil strife (*CG* II.17–18, 69–72; Dodaro, 1994, 82–84).

Roman moral rectitude and civic harmony reached their high point between the second and final Punic Wars, but not because of any natural goodness or justice. Rather, the chief cause, as Sallust himself indicates and Augustine emphasizes, was the fear of foreign invasion, just as in earlier periods of relatively "equitable and moderate [rule of] law" (*CG* II.18, 72).[9] After Carthage was destroyed and fear of foreign might

---

[9] Wood (1995) explores this foregrounding of fear in political analysis and its integration into early modern political thought. Wood's perspective differs from Augustine's in reading Sallust's analyses, especially as reflecting the socio-economic conditions of his times and expressing a "a prudential commonplace" prevalent among Sallust's contemporaries. "On the contrary, my position is that Sallust's Theorem developed out of and was intimately related to the precapitalist social and political conditions of Western Europe from classical antiquity to the early modern era" (Wood, 175; cf. 188–89). For Wood's discussion of Augustine's commentary on Sallust and its import, see 179–81. Wood observes, "St. Augustine proves to be a discerning commentator on these crucial passages in Sallust's *Histories*, two (I, 10, 13) of which have survived only because they are reproduced in the *City of God*, and a third (I, 12) is preserved in that work and by Gellius" (179).

assuaged, "'the morals of our forefathers were swept away, not by slow degrees, as formerly, but as if by a torrent'" (*CG* II.18, 73, quoting Sallust, *Hist. frag.*, I, 16).[10] Augustine indicates in this chapter that "love of justice" for its own sake belongs to human nature when it is right (whether unfallen or as justified after the Fall) more properly than does "fear of uncertain peace" (*CG* II.18, 71), yet Rome's civic behavior did not often exhibit such natural love. Augustine opines that the pagan divinities would have benefitted the city tremendously by giving it laws to supplement and educate nature, "laws of right living," yet they apparently failed to do so (*CG* II.16, 69; cf. II.6, 56–57). So the Romans borrowed legislation from Solon's Athenian constitution while prudently "endeavoring to improve and amend" these precepts (*CG* II.16, 69). Augustine indicates that the ancient Romans would have done well also to borrow from philosophers like Plato, who tried valiantly to discover and teach virtuous and just modes of living and made great headway at times. Yet these philosophers' arguments lacked the strength of divine authority, which was usurped instead by the pagan divinities who exerted a more profound impact on public customs. Moreover, pagan philosophers like Rome itself and the great Greek cities before it were at times led astray in their study precisely by their pride.[11] In book X, Augustine's rhetorical dialectic will return to develop this theme, during his dialogue with the Platonists on natural theology. His chief example there of the perils of philosophic pride will be Porphyry.

Book III, which focuses on the physical and social afflictions that plagued pre-Christian Rome, continues Augustine's unmasking of pride as an unnatural evil despite its cloak of glory and grandeur. The heart of Augustine's critique here is pride's destructive impact on natural ties of human affection, especially spousal and familial affection. Sallust is again Augustine's chief classical interlocutor and inspiration. The incident most illustrative

---

[10] Augustine makes an overlapping argument earlier near the end of book I, noting how Scipio opposed Cato over the destruction of Carthage "fear[ing] security [and the subsequent absence of fear] as the enemy of weak spirits. ... [T]he outcome proved how truly he had spoken. For when Carthage was destroyed ... *once it had conquered a few of the mightier men*, that *lust for mastery* ... *overcame other men also*, worn out and exhausted as they were by the yoke of servitude" and civil strife (*CG* I.30, 44–45; emphasis added).

[11] "And some of them, insofar as they were aided by God, did indeed make certain great discoveries. When impeded by their own humanity, however, they erred, especially when the *divine providence justly resisted their pride*, so that it might show by comparison with them that *it is through humility that the path of godliness ascends on high*. There will, however, by the will of God, the true Lord, be an opportunity for us to investigate and discuss this later" (*CG* II.7, 58, emphasis added).

of this evil is the war provoked by the Romans against their mother-city Alba (*CG* III.14, 109–12). Despite ties of consanguinity and shared history, Rome embarked on a bloody war to subdue the Albans to their rule and celebrated when the war was won. Augustine begs his readers to realize that the right response for humanity would be mourning and sorrow.

The misery and horror of this military exploit were heightened after its completion when the weeping of a young Roman woman for her Alban fiancé, dead by her own brother's hand, resulted in her victorious brother slaying her. In this woman's pity and grief – for her deceased betrothed, and perhaps also, Augustine suggests, for her brother who slew his future brother-in-law – we find a great measure of *humanitas* (humanity or humaneness), and yet her bellicose brother tragically could not see it (*CG* III.14, 110).[12] We may finally see in her deed, Augustine implies, an action reflecting what is right by nature, in accordance with human nature and the human condition, yet rejected as wrongful by her triumphant brother.[13] And why was it so rejected? It seems that the prideful love of martial glory, merging perhaps already with lust for domination, could not bear a humble manifestation of natural spousal or kindred affection when it interfered with or dampened the triumph of military progress and consequent civic expansion.[14]

Rather than rejoicing at their victory over Alba, Augustine opines, Rome's surviving citizens should have been mourning the death of brothers and kin in the three Alban and two Roman warriors and the great loss of life in the battles leading up to this combat, suffered by a mother or sister city, as well as by their own. But they were rejoicing in victory, and the celebratory background made the sister of the Horatii's grief and tears

---

[12] Cf. Wegemer (2011), inter alia 1–22, for a study of Roman sources (and often, their Greek philosophic referents) on the meaning and political import of *humanitas* in the context of Erasmus's and especially More's renaissance humanism.

[13] Cf. *CG* IX.5, 365:

I do not think that any right-minded person would condemn [well-moderated and justly directed passions]. ... [Yet the] Stoics, indeed, are wont to reproach even compassion. ... [W]hat is compassion but a kind of fellow feeling in our hearts for the misery of another which compels us to help him if we can? This impulse is the servant of right reason when compassion is displayed in such a way as to preserve righteousness.

[14] For other discussions of this incident, especially the tears and fate of the sister of the Horatii, see Livy I.25–26; Jacobitti (1996), on Vico's assessment of Horatia's killing in its historical context, and comparison of Vico's treatment with considerations by Livy, Augustine, and Machiavelli; and Bergel (1970), for analysis of presentations of the Horatians and their sister in the ethical-political and poetic-dramatic works of Augustine, Dante, and Aretino.

stand out. After praising this young woman, "who showed such affection" for evincing "more humanity than the entire Roman people"[15] (*CG* III.14, 110) precisely because she expressed love, pity, and grief, Augustine contests both the justice and the grandeur of Rome's triumph.[16] "Why do our adversaries plead the words 'praise' and 'victory' to me? Take off the cloak of vain opinion, and let such evil deeds be examined naked." He borrows here from Sallust's critique of wars of aggression fueled by the lust for mastery, which the ancient Roman historian attributed first to Cyrus and the Athenians and Spartans in their imperial wars (Sallust, *Catil.* 2,2). Here, in its lust for domination over others, Augustine turns the proud glory of Rome against its own polity and its very humanity. "This 'lust for mastery' disturbs and consumes the human race with great ills. Rome was conquered by this lust when she triumphed over Alba; and, in praising her own crime, she called it glory" (*CG* III.14, 111; cf. preface, 3). The evil of Rome's proud injustice at Alba was only intensified and its horror made manifest by its familial, hence impious, context. "It was because of this wrongful purpose, then, that the great wickedness of war between allies and kinsmen was perpetrated" (*CG* III.14, 111).[17]

---

[15] Augustine's Latin here reads: *humanior huius unius feminae quam uniuersi populi Romani mihi fuisse uidetur affectus.* Augustine's commentary in the same vein, a bit later in the chapter, continues: *quaeso ab humano impetremus affectu, ut femina sponsum suum a fratre suo peremptum sine crimine fleuerit, si uiri hostes a se uictos etiam cum laude fleuerunt. ergo sponso a fratre inlatam mortem quando femina illa flebat, tunc se contra matrem ciuitatem tanta strage bellasse et tanta hinc et inde cognati cruoris effusione uicisse Roma gaudebat* (*CG* III.14; emphasis added).

[16] For commentary pertaining to this contrast, with reference to "the sister of the Horatii" and to the problem of mastery more broadly, see Marshall (2012):

Such discernment [encouraged by Augustine] creates space for critical interpretation of acts of nobility performed by captives, women, and slaves. By recognizing the ethical and political agency of victims of contingency, exilic virtue insists that servitude can be heroic. Augustine calls such heroism under conditions of servitude "greatness of soul": "We might properly call a soul great if it can bear a life full of calamity and not flee from it, and if it can in the light of a pure conscience hold human judgment in contempt: especially the judgment of the vulgar which is so commonly wrapped in the darkness of error." Augustinian exilic virtue thus offers a personal discipline that can improve but not wholly reform the human condition as slaves and potential slaves struggle against the temptations of mastery. (177; cf. Marshall, 2012, note 86)

[17] Augustine continues this critique of rhetorical concealments later in this long chapter:

Away, then, with concealments and deceitful whitewashings! Let these things be examined openly. ... If two gladiators were to enter the arena to fight, one a son and the other his father, who could endure such a spectacle? ... How, then, could the clash of arms between two cities be glorious when one of the cities was a mother and the other her daughter ... and that broader battlefields were filled with the bodies, not of two gladiators, but of multitudes belonging to two peoples? (*CG* III.14, 111–12)

Augustine's theme of political pride versus familial love and *pietas* continues through the central and concluding chapters of book III. Junius Brutus ordered and presided over the execution of his rebel sons and brothers-in-law, according to Virgil, out of "love of country ... and the immense love of praise" (*CG* III.16, 117, quoting Virgil, *Aeneid* 6, 820 ff., and *CG* V.18, 219). This too was during the period of "just and equitable" rule of law in the *res publica*, according to Sallust. In this same era "the Voconian Law was passed, which forbade anyone to make a woman, not even an only daughter, his heir" (*CG* III.21, 130). Augustine comments poignantly concerning this proviso, "I do not know of any law that could be said or thought to be more unjust" (*CG* III. 21, 130). Here again we grasp that natural right, the human nature shared by women and men alike, and familial bonds are closely united in Augustine's mind. Pride demotes or even severs these bonds, while humility acknowledges them gladly. Rome's lust for mastery seeks a disproportionate share of its citizens' loyalty, their whole hearts and wills, and efforts at the expense of other commitments and connections that are also, and even more so, naturally right. At its limit, this perverted desire expresses a false deification of the political community and its exemplar citizens and rulers, a desire for worship that is emphatically not their natural due. When political societies or their rulers turn against the affective and moral ties that give birth to and sustain their citizenry, pride cooperates in and motivates grievous unnatural wrongs, boding ill in the long run for the regime and rulers that perpetrate them.[18]

MODERATION, A HUMBLE HEALER, AND
THE METAPHYSICS OF HUMILITY

Book IV plays a pivotal role in Augustine's rhetorical dialectic against vicious pride and for virtuous humility. In this segment of *The City of God*, Augustine develops his political and moral critique of pride with a rhetorical dialectic favoring an analogue, or close relative, of humility: moderation.[19] Throughout this book, Augustine's reflections on virtuous

---

[18] In this regard, Augustine's thought seems quite close to some ancient poets' and tragedians' views; consider the narrative interrelatedness of familial, civic, and divine right in Sophocles's *Antigone*.

[19] Cf. Origin (*Homily on Luke* viii), as quoted by Thomas Aquinas: "'If thou wilt hear the name of this virtue, and what it was called by the philosophers, know that humility which God regards is the same as what they called [*metriotes*], i.e., measure or moderation'" (*Summa Theologiae* II–II 161, 4, *sed contra*). A closer examination of Aquinas's analysis shows that he, like Augustine, considers moderation and humility closely related but not identical virtues.

moderation prepare the way for him to present a positive appeal of virtuous humility to his fellow Romans, pagans, and Christians alike.

Augustine begins this task with a strategy that inverts Socrates's dialogic methodology in book II of Plato's *Republic* (368c–369b). In his response to the plea of Glaucon and Adeimantus that Socrates defends the goodness of justice in itself and particularly for the people who cultivate and hold fast to justice at the cost of great suffering, Socrates famously suggested that it would be easier to find and understand justice in a big entity like a city than in a small being such as one man. So he constructs *a city in speech* and leads his interlocutors in searching for justice and the virtues in it. Augustine, by contrast, suggests in book IV that virtues and their relation to happiness are likely easier to identify in a single human being's life than in a political society, and so he crafts two *human beings in speech*. As a former professor of rhetoric who had political ambitions of his own in his youth, Augustine is acutely sensitive to the power and splendor of the language connected with politics on a large scale, probably always and everywhere, and certainly in Rome. Sharing Socrates's anti-sophistry, Augustine challenges his readers to look more closely toward reality, to things as they are and as we ought rightly to perceive them,[20] and so to avoid becoming overly impressed by grand phrases and magnificent appearances.

Let us not allow the edge of our attention to be dulled by the splendid names of things when we hear of "peoples," "kingdoms" and "provinces." Instead, let us imagine [*constituamus*] two men (for each individual man, like one letter in a text, is, as it were, an element of the city or kingdom, no matter how extensive it is in its occupation of the earth). (*CG* IV.3, 146; cf. III.14)[21]

One of these men is of moderate means (*mediocrem*), possessing enough to live simply and well. He is beloved by his family and dwells in amicable concord with his neighbors. The other is wealthy but feverish,

---

[20] This formulation is rooted in one by J. R. R. Tolkien, in his essay "On Fairy-Stories." See Tolkien (2001, 57–58):

> Recovery (which includes return and renewal of health) is a re-gaining – regaining of a clear view. I do not say "seeing things as they are" and involve myself with the philosophers, though I might venture to say "seeing things as we are (or were) meant to see them". ... Of course, fairy-stories are not the only means of recovery. ... Humility is enough.

For a study of Augustine, William Shakespeare, and J. R. R. Tolkien on humility and politics, see Kundmueller (2018).

[21] For commentary on this passage in light of the import of interpersonal encounters, friendship, and political good, see von Heyking (2008, 119).

constantly acquiring property, but never free from cares, conflicts, and fears that his adversaries' greed may one day overtake his own and strip him of his gains. Augustine's (again seemingly Socratic) answer to the question of which life and ordering of soul should be preferred, the *moderate* one, extends outward from a single human being along the chain of communities. "[S]o [also in the case of] two families, two peoples, two kingdoms ... and if we use this principle vigilantly, to guide our search, we shall very easily see where vanity dwells, and where happiness lies" (*CG* IV.3, 147). Augustine concludes that the Roman Empire would have been happier – that is, the *human beings* whose *res publica* it is or purports to be would have been happier – if it had remained moderate in size and ambition rather than seeking to extend its dominion throughout the world. As it was, "the Romans always lived in dark fear and cruel lust, surrounded by the disasters of war and the shedding of blood which, whether that of fellow citizens or enemies, was human nonetheless." By nature, then, Augustine indicates, it is right and prudent for human beings to wish for peace and cultivate civic concord and moderation, but not to "glory in the breadth and magnitude of an empire" (*CG* IV.3, 146).

To support this conclusion regarding the natural goodness of moderation and the wrongful harm of greedy overreaching, Augustine again appeals to a Roman historian, now Marcus Junianus Justinus. Justinus claims that, in the world before Rome, kings initially ruled on account of "'the knowledge that good men had of their moderation (*moderatio*). The people were not bound by any laws'" (*CG* IV.6, 149, quoting Justinus's *Philippic Histories*). This all was changed – including the then-customary moderation of military force, employed only or chiefly in defensive causes – by the Assyrian king Ninus. "[A] new greed for empire" led him on a snowballing series of offensive wars (*CG* IV.6, 150, quoting Justinus, *Philippic Histories*).[22] This immoderate love of dominion, Justinus quietly indicates and Augustine shouts for all to hear, is an instance as well

---

[22] Cf. Augustine's earlier citation of Sallust, with diverse culprits (like Justinus's villains, none of them Roman) but a strikingly similar account of the praiseworthiness of (very) ancient civic moderation and the decline caused by those who "'began ... to deem lust for mastery a sufficient reason for war (*libidinem dominandi causa belli habere*), and to hold that the greatest glory belongs to the greatest empire'" (*CG* III.14, 111, quoting Sallust, *Catil.* 2,2.). On Sallust's Thucydidean connection of "political decline" with the "devaluation of language: the use and abuse of important political words to signify new ideas or behaviors," to justify what peoples previously considered unjustifiable, see Balmaceda (2017, 73–82).

as a cause of great injustice: "What else is this to be called than great robbery?" (*CG* IV.6, 150).[23]

The key to Augustine's rhetorical dialectic in this section of book IV is its argument for the greater naturalness and goodness of moderation, compared with prideful acquisitiveness; of temperate self-rule extended also to benefit others, over self-enslaving love of domination over others. At this point in his argument, Augustine reintroduces a theological emphasis, asking whether gods and goddesses whose example stoked immoderation, and whose multiplicity and conflict countered human concord, should be praised for their political beneficence.[24] Augustine's reply once again begins from ancient pagan wisdom as recorded by sages, historians, and statesmen and moves on toward a philosophic monotheism capable of giving a more solid grounding to the virtues of moderation and humility. In the midst of this portion of his rhetorical dialectic, Augustine gestures toward the humble Mediator, Jesus, who alone, he holds, can heal the pathology of human pride.

Starting from popular paganism, which takes the multiplicity of divine beings at face value, Augustine reasonably wonders which (one or many) of these competing gods should be held responsible for the breadth of empire and its duration, and why if their chief aim was the temporal protection and extension of Rome they so often failed in their charge (*CG* IV.7–8, 150–53). From here Augustine follows the interpretation of "the natural order" and its principles offered by various learned Romans (*CG* IV.11, 157), including the great poet Virgil and the scholar Varro, with whose thought on poetic, civil, and natural theology Augustine will engage at length in books VI and VII. These cultural luminaries

---

[23] See also the following chapter of book IV, in which Augustine retells an anecdote from Cicero's *De Republica* 3, 14, 24:

> It was a pertinent and true answer which was made to Alexander the Great by a pirate whom he had seized. When the king asked him what he meant by infesting the sea, the pirate defiantly replied: "The same as you do when you infest the whole world; but because I do it with a little ship I am called a robber, and because you do it with a great fleet, you are an emperor." (*CG* IV.4, 148)

For a study of Augustine's commentary on Alexander the Great, see Harding (2008b).

[24] Later in his survey of ancient Roman divinities vis-à-vis the preservation and expansion of Roman dominion, Augustine notes that while the Romans had set up *pudicitia*, shame or modesty, as a goddess with a temple of her own, they did not choose similarly to honor temperance (*temperantia*). "Why did temperance not deserve to be a goddess – for many Roman chieftains (*principes*) gained no small glory in her name?" (*CG* IV.20, 166). Temperance and its ethos appear much closer than shame to virtuous moderation (*moderatio*), as Augustine, with help from Justinus, presents it in book IV.

concur with Augustine that plain polytheism is untenable. But unlike Augustine, they argue or imply that the cult of multiple divinities only requires reinterpretation by and for the learned. On this account, the many divine beings are thought to be parts of the one god Jupiter or metaphoric expressions of his attributes or natural works. Virgil writes that "[a]ll things are full of Jupiter," and "Varro believes that [Jupiter] is worshipped, though called by another name, even by those who worship one God only, without an image" (*CG* IV.9, 154; cf. IV.10–13, 154–61). Augustine still judges as unpersuasive these sophisticated, pantheistic interpretations of the god Jupiter as the soul of the corporeal world, beginning his challenge to them from the perspective of a pious pagan, who would not wish to trample on a part of god when stepping on a stone or bug (*CG* IV.12–13, 159–61).

Augustine now brings his rhetorical-dialectical critique full circle, returning to plain popular polytheism as the heart of the Roman attribution of its grand empire to Jupiter, the chief god among many, saying it is "only by the king of the gods ... that a kingdom of men could have been propagated and increased" (*CG* IV.13, 160–61). But then, why Jupiter and not the Roman goddess Victory, or why not deify "empire itself" (*ipsum regnum*; more literally, rule or kingdom) officially, since the Romans seem to have done so already in their aspirations and actions (*CG* IV.14, 161; cf. IV.17, 163)? Here again, Augustine pauses his theological-political reasoning to reiterate the critique of imperial expansion and grandeur, considered as intrinsically valuable ends. He echoes and amplifies select pagan histories, which reflect a natural, rational recognition of the wrongness of victory won by aggression against "peaceable neighbors who have done them no harm, in order to extend ... rule" (*ad dilatandum regnum*; *CG* IV.14, 161). Chapter 15 radicalizes this inquiry by asking whether even basically just conquests of iniquitous polities are rightful causes for rejoicing. Augustine rejects such victories as unqualifiedly good but also admits the reasonableness of a moderate, just contentment in an outcome of better peace than might otherwise have resulted (*CG* IV.15, 161–62).[25]

---

[25] In this chapter, Augustine notably indicates the naturalness of some sort of political life, marked by moderation, familiarity, and concord, even absent sin and the Fall. "[I]f men were always peaceful and just, human affairs would be happier and all kingdoms (*omnia regna*) would be small, rejoicing in concord with their neighbors. There would be as many kingdoms among the nations of the world as there are now houses of the citizens of a city" (*CG* IV.15, 161). Cf. also Justinus's "theory," or didactic account, of ancient kingship, based on moderation and freedom (IV.6, 149–50), which Augustine may also have in mind given the proximity of these two passages and similar contexts of argument.

Much less questionable as true goods for human beings than wide rule over others and the "foreign iniquity" that enables empire's just increase (*CG* IV.15, 162) are genuine peace and quiet, as Augustine highlights in the ensuing, brief chapter. Why, asks Augustine, when so many and rather questionable divinities received civil-religious honors, did the temple of the goddess Quiet, "who brings quietude," lie outside the city walls of Rome and receive no public cult? Did this omission underscore Rome's restless spirit? "Or did it perhaps indicate that one who persists in the worship of that swarm … cannot possess that quiet of which the true Physician speaks when he says 'Learn of me, for I am meek and humble in heart, and ye shall find rest unto your souls'"[26] (*CG* IV.16, 163)? This is perhaps the most significant commentary in all of books I–V on the person of Jesus Christ, Augustine's chief exemplar of humility, divine and human. Its brevity and lack of adornment seem reflective of Augustine's aim in these books of disproving the connection between temporal prosperity and pagan worship, and in so doing, preparing for his defense of humility via the prosecution of political pride. As we will see in a later chapter, Christ and his humility become a more explicit and pronounced theme in book X, the climax of Augustine's debate with the Platonists on the right and truly efficacious "way" to eternal life (cf. also *CG* II.7, 58).

After this brief but significant note on Christ as physician, and the wholesome peace and quiet that stem from his meekness and humility, Augustine's rhetorical dialectic continues its passage from the moderation of political pride toward virtuous humility, with an initial consideration of natural or philosophic theology, accessible to pagan and Christian readers alike. This aspect of Augustine's opening defense speech reaches its climax as he challenges those who worship creatures rather than the Creator – who worship gifts of God as if they were God – to acknowledge humbly the gap separating transcendent, infinite being from finite and contingent beings, and the dependence of the latter on the former (*CG* IV.24–25, 173–74). Augustine's argument here applies alike to plain, popular polytheists and sophisticated, philosophic, or poetic pantheists. To the popular polytheists, Augustine argues that their late introduction of Felicity as a goddess indicates they did not think their chief god Jupiter capable of bestowing true and lasting happiness. Yet they did consider happiness to be a gift of a divine being who possesses

---

[26] *ad quam uocat uerus medicus dicens: discite a me, quoniam mitis sum et humilis corde, et inuenietis requiem animabus verstris* (Matthew 11:29).

it and so can bestow it. The name of this being they did not know, so the name of the gift became their name for the unknown giver.

Now ... we shall, perhaps, be more easily able to persuade as we wish those whose hearts are not already too greatly hardened. For human infirmity has now clearly realized that felicity cannot be given except by some god. ... [B]y this argument I prove that they believed felicity to be given by some God whom they did not know. Let that God be sought, therefore; let Him be worshipped, and it is enough. (*CG* IV.25, 173–74; emphasis added)[27]

Augustine's invitation to the popular pagans, intimating that they *are* groping for the true God and so are closer than they might think to finding him, is substantially the same as his word to the sophisticated intellectual Varro and others with a pantheist world-soul understanding of the deity.[28] Augustine's admiration for their achievement of a good measure of truth tempers his critique of their public reticence to teach or even to act consistently with their philosophic monotheism; we will consider this with Augustine at greater length in Chapter 3, covering books VI–VII of *The City of God*. Though Augustine does not give a full account of metaphysics, he unmistakably refers his readers to a Platonic philosophy of soul and divinity that he thinks might have persuaded Varro that the one God is transcendent, distinct from his creation. Augustine's assessment of Varro's theology marks the high point of book IV's philosophic movement and merits quoting at length:

[Varro] ... also says that ... the only men who have truly understood what God is are those who have believed Him to be the soul of the world, governing it by movement and reason. And it appears from this that, though Varro still did not hold the correct view (for the true God is not a soul, but the maker and establisher [*effector et conditor*] of the soul), yet, if he could have been free to resist the prejudice of custom, he would have confessed, and persuaded others, that only one God is to be worshipped. ... The only question then remaining to be debated with him in this connection would be that he had called Him a soul, and not rather the Creator of the soul. ... *[S]o close to the truth, he might perhaps have been easily persuaded of the mutability of the soul, and so have come to understand that the true God is that immutable nature which created the soul itself (quoniam animam condidisset).* (*CG* IV.31, 183; emphasis added; cf. VIII.1, 312–13, and VIII.5–9, 318–25)

---

[27] Augustine's argument here is reminiscent of the apostle Paul's discourse in the Athenian Areopagus: see Acts 17:22–31.

[28] See also the rhetorical plea, strikingly similar to the one Augustine addressed to the popular pagans in *CG* IV.25, made by Augustine to the Platonic philosophers and those who admire their teachings near the outset of book VIII. "Let him be sought, therefore, in whom all things are ordered for us; let him be discerned, in whom all things are certain for us; let him be loved, in whom all things are right for us" (*CG* VIII.4, 318).

Had Varro achieved this final philosophic step, a true ethics of humility, starting from the willing recognition of one's own, one's polity's, and all human beings' creaturely status vis-à-vis the divine Creator, would have been within his reach, and perhaps all Rome's as well. As it was, the common people of Rome were left prey to the proud lust for domination of civic elites, who tolerated and even fomented false faith among the masses, so as to "bind men more tightly ... in civil society ... [and] possess them as subjects" (*CG* IV.32, 184).

PROVIDENCE, PRIDE, AND HUMILITY IN BOOK V

Book V completes the first and – taken as a whole – the most deeply political segment of Augustine's *City of God*. It opens by aiming to demonstrate that Rome's political grandeur, might, and fame are consequences of divine and human causation, fruits of the interplay of providence and human freedom. In this book, Augustine returns to the concerns with which his first book began, and so he principally addresses fellow Christians who, together with the Western Roman Empire's pagan population, are attempting to comprehend and come to terms with the causes of their polity's former greatness and current decline. Augustine again endeavors not to leave his pagan compatriots behind, engaging with their great philosophic statesman Cicero and with the Stoic philosophers on the question of the compatibility of divine providence and human free will. In so doing, Augustine once again outlines his theology of creation and its implicit metaphysics of finite and infinite being, paving the way for his fullest engagement to come in books VIII–X with the Platonic philosophers, to whose arguments we have already seen him appeal. Like Augustine, many pagan Platonists of the late classical era argue metaphysically beyond the pantheism of Varro and the limited theism (or as Augustine suggests in one passage, possibly atheism) of Cicero (see *CG* V.9, 198–204). "[These Platonists] agree that a divine nature exists and concerns itself with human affairs ... a God Who made not only this visible world ... but also every soul whatever, and Who makes the rational and intelligible soul, of which kind is that of human beings, blessed by participation in His unchangeable and incorporeal light" (*CG* VIII.1, 312–13).

According to Augustine's rhetorical dialectic in book V, it is not necessary to choose in human affairs between divine providence on the one hand and human responsibility and freedom on the other once one recognizes that all finite beings, including rational and free human beings, are by nature creatures of an infinitely wise and omnipotent being. God's authority as the "Author and Creator of all nature" (*auctor omnis conditorque naturae*) operates on a transcendent level and poses no competition to human freedom (*CG* V.9, 202). Indeed, the Creator purposefully creates and sustains human creatures, endowed with reason and will and therefore capable of freedom and responsibility. Augustine thus implies that human dignity and humility can and should go hand in hand, and that in their virtuous forms, neither of these human attributes is independent of the Creator's providence. Divine agency and human agency are not mutually exclusive; rather, the former creates, sustains, and perfects the latter.

In this segment of his argument, Augustine also provides evidence supporting the naturalness of social and civic life among humans (see also *CG* IV.15, 161). His rhetorical dialectic presents political life as among the natural human realities created and governed by providence, though now doubtless in forms much changed and marred by sin and *superbia*. Augustine writes:

[T]he supreme and true God, then ... [is the] Creator and Maker of every soul and every body. It is by participation in Him that all are happy who are happy in truth and not in emptiness. He made man a rational animal composed of soul and body. ... Neither heaven nor earth, neither angel nor man, not even the inward parts of the smallest and most inconsiderable animal, nor the feather of a bird, nor a tiny flower of a plant nor the leaf on the tree, has God left unprovided with a harmony and, as it were, a peace among its parts. It can in no wise be believed, then, that He has chosen to exclude the kingdoms of men and their rule and service from the laws of His providence. (*CG* V.11, 206)[29]

After this theological-philosophic prelude, Augustine speculates that Rome's fame and political grandeur were the result of the justice and mercy of God, respecting the choice made by many ancient Romans to pursue human glory and to cultivate justice and virtue in glory's service. Because they did not recognize or worship the one Creator, however, the Romans fell prey by degrees to their own pride, making themselves individually or collectively into self-sufficient gods to whose praise their actions were directed.[30] Love of freedom – natural and noble in itself,

---

[29] Where I translate "rule and service," Augustine's Latin reads *dominationes et servitutes*. I have modified here Dyson's translation, "lordships and servants," since *servitus* refers to a condition or state of affairs of service or servitude, rather than to the persons carrying it out (servants); and so I have read *dominationes* as referring similarly to a *condition* of governance or political power, rather than more specific institutions such as "lordships." The plural forms Augustine uses are awkward in English; hence, "rule and service."

[30] As Dodaro observes (2003, 83, ff.), Augustine implies that the deepest impulse animating this drive for glory was a desire for immortality and the fear of death. "[T]hey sought to find even after death a kind of life in the mouths of those who praised them" (*CG* V.14, 215). Dodaro connects Augustine's treatment of this primordial human fear with questions of hope, justice, and humility in our contemporary world as well.

yet twisted by a proud disdain of humbly serving others – grew into hubristic love of glory. From there, too many Romans plunged headlong into the pit of their individual and collective *libido dominandi*, effecting the intensely proud deification of mere mortals as masters of the fates of others (see *CG* V.12–20, 207–27; and *CG* I, preface, 3). In so doing, they undid by degrees the very freedom Rome had begun by seeking to preserve, becoming enslaved personally and politically to a lie about their identities, and refusing to look up to, or at least to look for, the true source of their being, and so to glimpse and perhaps more fully discern their nature's true right.

While the first eleven chapters of book V aim to establish divine providence and free human agency rather than blind chance or predetermined fate as responsible for Rome's rise, rule, and grandeur, the ensuing chapters offer readers portraits of various citizens and statesmen, a "mirror of princes," to borrow from a later genre. Augustine's rhetorical dialectic here highlights pride, humility, and related traits as personal and public characteristics. Consuls, kings, and emperors rule peoples, while dominant polities or nations govern other peoples; in both cases, one can observe pride and/or humility in play. The relationship between these opposing traits can be complex in political life, Augustine observes. For instance, after the ancient Romans rebelled against King Tarquin the Proud and refused to install another monarch to rule over them in his wake, these same citizens who did not want to be ruled by a proud or arrogant individual became themselves the collectively proud rulers over neighboring peoples (*CG* V.12, 207–8).

How did ancient Rome simultaneously reject and affirm social and civic *superbia*, or pride? On Augustine's account, this was the result of choosing to deify the glory of their *civitas*, to make it the chief object of their personal and common affections and the ultimate end of their political enterprise. The Romans considered two goals paramount in view of their polity's fame and honor: liberty and mastery. Again, a thoughtful observer might sense a contradiction, but to borrow an expression from Aquinas, each is here considered under a different aspect, Rome's *own* freedom and its mastery over *other* peoples. "Royal majesty," regarded as incompatible with liberty, in the republican period at least, "was not regarded [by Rome] as the mark of a proper ruler or of a benevolent counselor, but of a proud master. ... Once they had achieved freedom, however, so great a desire for glory then arose that liberty seemed to them too little by itself, unless they also sought dominion over others" (*CG* V.12, 207–8). Augustine evokes the very poetic praise of the *patria* in Virgil's *Aeneid*, with which he closed his preface to *The City of God* in book I, locating Rome's special genius and mission in rule *over others*, subduing the proud and sparing the humble. Here in book V, Augustine quotes at length from the *Aeneid*, providing readers with context for the brief quote with which he had closed his preface:

> "Even cruel Juno ... shall mend her ways, and with me shall protect the Romans, the people of the toga, the masters of all things. So it is decreed. For, as the years pass, there shall come a time when Assaracus's house shall bring Phthyia to servitude, and great Mycenae too, and be lord of Argos." ... I have ... quoted these words in order to show that, next to liberty, the Romans had so high a regard for dominion that they included it among those things on which they bestowed the highest praise. Hence also it is that the same poet, preferring to the arts of other nations the peculiarly Roman arts of ruling and commanding and subjugating and vanquishing peoples, says: "Let other men with gentler touch ... tell of the rising and falling of the stars. But thou, O Roman, remember that thy task is to subject peoples to thy sway. These arts are thine: to establish ways of peace, to spare the fallen and subdue the proud." (*CG* V.12, 208–9, quoting *Aen.* 1 and 6)

Augustine acknowledges the great difference there is between love of the glory achieved by the praise of good human beings, and so conducing to the choice of just and virtuous means to "glory and authority and lordship," and love of domination, seeking praise and mastery without regard to the character of those who bestow it (*CG* V.19, 224). A man inspired by the latter passion will easily strive for glory "by treachery and deceit, wishing to seem good even though he is not" (*CG* V.19, 224). Even worse is a complete lack of concern for good reputation or glorious fame, when coupled with lust for domination. Nero Caesar is Augustine's prime exemplar of this sort of political persona, even as Augustine notes that in troubled human history their number is legion (*CG* V.19, 224–25). At the opposite extreme from Nero among pagan Roman *principes* or first citizens in this respect is Cato, who seemed relatively unconcerned for his own glory even as he sought the glory of virtue and freedom for his city and fellow citizens (*CG* V.12, 210; but cf. I.23, 35–36).

How did republican Rome arrive at last at imperial rule at home, as well as abroad, beginning with personal-glory-seeking Caesar and declining toward Nero? Augustine's analysis suggests agreement with Sallust and Cicero that the chief cause was a dearth of citizens concerned with seeking glory by the true way through virtue and care for public goods, even at the cost of their private welfare. Sallust observes that the increased extent of the commonwealth after the Carthaginian wars gave greater scope and license to "the vices of its generals and magistrates"

(*Catil.* 52, 21f.; quoted in *CG* V.12, 212). Augustine's political psychology of Rome aims to deepen – or reveal hidden implications of – these analyses. Precisely *because* love of earthly glory was paramount in the hearts of leaders and commoners, even within Rome's walls, the great among them soon began to seek mastery over the common people, their fellow citizens, who like the patricians did not relish losing their liberty. Civic and social upheavals followed, quieted periodically when fear of foreign aggression flared up, and united the people again in a common project (*CG* V.12, 211–12; cf. *CG* II.18, 71–72). Perhaps Augustine's most powerful statement of pride's pathology in Rome's internal strife and civic decline occurred back in book I, near its close:

> [W]hen Carthage was destroyed and the great terror of the Roman commonwealth thereby repulsed and extinguished, the prosperous condition of things immediately gave rise to great evils. ... Finally, once it had conquered a few of the mightier men, that lust for mastery which, among the other vices of the human race, belongs in its purest form to the whole Roman people, overcame other men also [the plebeians], worn out and exhausted as they were by the yoke of servitude. ... But, *once established in the minds of the proudest, how can such lust for mastery rest until, by the usual succession of offices, it has reached the highest power*? (*CG* I.30–31, 45; emphasis added)

In imperial or monarchic polities such as the Roman empire of Augustine's era the education of rulers was a special concern – though of course the education of human beings, specifically citizens who would participate actively in their regime and its rule, had long been a key question for political philosophy, regarding republics as well. Near the middle of book V, Augustine recalls a passage from Cicero's *De Republica*, in which the philosophic statesman considers the proper "education of the city's ruler, who ought, he says, to be nourished on glory" (*De rep.* 5, 7, 9, quoted in *CG* V.13, 213), recalling the marvelous works that glory inspired in the great Romans of old. Augustine acknowledges that Cicero himself has reservations with this civic ethic, in that "in his philosophical works" Cicero considers activities that ought to be sought after for the sake of what is truly good, not on account of human praise. Yet on Augustine's reading, Cicero still seems to concede that in practice glory and honor inspire most noteworthy deeds of human beings. "Honor fosters the arts, and all men are fired in their endeavors by the prospect of glory; whereas men always neglect those things which are held in low esteem" (*Tusc. Disp.*, I.2, 4; quoted in *CG* V.13, 213).

In reality, Augustine's rhetorical dialectic here suggests, what is right and good will often be found among those lowly realities where a proud person will not look, or where he or she would disdain to go. The proud, vainglorious person is not only the ancient pagan, Augustine is at pains to convince his Christian interlocutors; all human beings, even those who ardently desire citizenship in the city of God, are susceptible to these vices to some extent at least.

> It may be that, in this life, [love of praise] cannot be completely eradicated from the heart. After all, it does not cease to tempt the minds even of those who are well advanced in virtue. But let the lust for glory be at any rate so surpassed by the love of justice that, if at any point "those *things which are held in low esteem*" should be neglected *even if they are good and right*, the love of human praise will blush and yield to the love of truth. (CG V.14, 214; emphasis added)

Only in virtuous humility, Augustine's rhetorical dialectic here suggests, can human beings, citizens, and rulers challenge popular or elite opinion and restrain their own desire for praise whenever this is needed in order to discern, love, and pursue what is truly right and just. Humility counters false divinization of self and society, and so strengthens commitment to moderation and justice among human beings. It opens persons up to a love of rightful equality among human beings; to recognition of the true merits in others; to public service performed with personal sacrifice on behalf of others and for the common good; and to the extension of one's natural familial affection and care to include the poor and abandoned of society (see CG V.14, 214–15; V.17, 218; and V.18, 219).

Humility's apparent lowliness, as Augustine intimated already in his preface, is the starting point of all paths that lead to true divinization and immortality, and the early Christian apostles and martyrs taught and trod that path with fidelity.[31] Though they indeed received glory in the church, "They did not rest in that glory as if it were the virtue which they sought as their end. Rather, they referred that glory itself to the glory of God, by whose grace they were what they were ... for their Master had taught them to be good men, but not for the sake of human glory" (CG V.14, 214). Yet, if the princes and heroes, as it were, of the early church could exemplify meekness and humility to a significant extent, can leading citizens and rulers, even emperors, of political societies do likewise? Should they also endeavor to cultivate humility for both their own and the public's welfare? Augustine's rhetorical dialectic indicates an affirmative reply to these queries, as the ensuing chapters illustrate.

---

[31] On Augustine's understanding of heroism and, more specifically, on the martyrs as heroes, see Dodaro (2005) and CG X.21, 423.

Augustine's own portrait of a good citizen and ruler is painted most fully in the final chapters of book V. In these chapters he deepens his critique of pride and defense of humility by reminding Christian citizens how great the deeds of many ancient Romans were; how impressive the greatest pagans' self-overcoming on behalf of temporal, personal, and political glory; and hence how foolish Christians would be to over-rate deeds reflecting great love of God and neighbor, performed by the gift of grace and with an immortal polity and divine glory in view. Recalling awe-inspiring feats of magnanimity, self-sacrifice, and public spiritedness performed by the legendary figures of Rome's founding and early republic, Augustine exhorts his Christian readers, "Let this consideration, then, be useful to us in subduing pride" (*CG* V.17, 218; cf. V.18, 218–23).[32]

In books II–IV, Augustine painted various pictures of proud states-men and emperors and showed the deleterious effects of political pride and lust for domination in the characters of these leading citizens. Now, near book V's finale in chapter 24, he paints a broad, generalizable por-trait of a truly good, happy Christian emperor.[33] Among various traits, this portrait stresses the character traits of justice, humane and reli-gious humility,[34] and righteous mercy (see *CG* V.24, 232). In chapter 25, Augustine highlights Constantine's temporal successes but makes no reference to his humility or to any other ethical trait or virtue. Augustine cautions his readers against misunderstanding Christianity as a gospel of this-worldly prosperity, a path to the "felicity which Constantine enjoyed" (*CG* V.25, 232–33).

---

[32] Among these memorable deeds, Augustine highlights especially Romulus's famed offer of asylum and civic partnership to criminals, which seems to foreshadow "the remission of sins which gathers together the citizens of the eternal country" (V.17, 218). Not all of these deeds are unambiguously praiseworthy in Augustine's estimation, as for instance Brutus's slaying of his rebellious sons, as Virgil imagines it, for "love of country … and the immense love of praise" (*CG* V.18, 218–19; cf. III.16, 117; both passages quote *Aeneid* 6, 820, ff.).

[33] It seems noteworthy that Augustine in *The City of God* speaks of "Christian emper-ors" (*christianos imperatores*; see *CG* V.24, 231–32), and of "Christian times" (*tempora christiana*; see, e.g., *CG* I.1, 4–5, and Rist, 1994, 208), but never of "Christian empire."

[34] [W]e say that they are happy if they rule justly; if they are not lifted up with talk of those who accord them sublime honors or pay their respects with an excessive humility, but remember that they are only men; … if they prefer to govern wicked desires more than any people whatsoever; if they do all these things not from craving empty glory, but from love of eternal felicity; and if, for their sins, they do not cease to offer to their true God the sacrifices of humility and contrition and prayer. We say that, for the time being, such Christian emperors are happy in hope (*CG* V.24, 232).

The last emperor treated – and the one discussed at greatest length – is Theodosius I (347–95), one of the first Roman emperors to profess Christian faith. The portrait in *The City of God* of this Christian emperor emphasizes what Augustine takes to be his just and merciful deeds, peaking with an account of Theodosius's "religious humility" and public penance. The context of this penance was a serious lapse in imperial judgment, administration of justice, and judicious detachment from the opinions of others. A serious offense was perpetrated in Thessalonica, after which Catholic bishops interceded with Theodosius asking for mercy in his treatment of those who had perpetrated the crime. Theodosius promised to honor this request and respond with restraint. Instead, by Augustine's account, "he was compelled to take vengeance *on the people* by the tumult of certain persons close to him" – that is under pressure, he ordered, or at least condoned, not the harsh punishment of the guilty, but a massacre (*CG* V.26, 235; emphasis added). Ambrose, bishop of Milan, confronted the emperor about this incident in a forthright letter. He charged Theodosius with grave injustice, excommunicating him until he could show repentance.[35] Rather than remaining aloof and stubborn, Theodosius admitted to wrongdoing, sought pardon, and performed "penance with ... humility" before the people of imperial Milan (*CG* V.26, 235).

Ambrose, Augustine's former mentor, brought before Theodosius's eyes the example of King David, who repented of his sins with great humility, once true prophets had helped him to recognize them: "Thus, by [David's] humility he became more acceptable to God, for it is not strange that man sins, but it is reprehensible if he does not acknowledge that he has erred, and humble himself before God" (Ambrose, 2001, 23).[36] While Augustine does not draw this connection here in book V, his approval of Theodosius's apparent repentance and humility foreshadows Augustine's later commentary in *The City of God* on David as king. "He is greatly praised by the Divine testimony because his sins were overcome by a piety so great, and a penitence of such wholesome humility" (*CG* XVII.20, 812).

[35] For Ambrose's letter 51, to Emperor Theodosius concerning the massacre at Thessalonica, see Ambrose (2001, 20–26).

[36] From the vantage point of this chapter's focus on humility as natural right, the opening of Ambrose's letter is also significant. There the bishop refers to the "natural right" of members of court to be heard by the emperor (Ambrose, 2001, 20).

FROM POLITICS TO PHILOSOPHY AND CIVIL RELIGION

Augustine's rhetorical-dialectical argument in books I–V for the natural wrong of *superbia* and the natural right of *humilitas* continues and is deepened and developed throughout the remainder of his *City of God*, as we will see throughout the chapters to come. In book XIX, Augustine expresses his case for humility as natural right in this way: "[T]he task of [justice] is to give each his due. … It is for this reason that there is established in man himself *a certain just order of nature*, such that the soul is subordinated to God and the body to the soul, and thus both body and soul are subordinated to God" (*CG* XIX.4, 921, emphasis added; cf. *CG* IX.5, 365).[37] This right or just order, Augustine will argue, has been weakened and indeed nearly undone by the Fall and personal sin (see *CG* XIII–XIV, to be treated in Chapter 6), yet continues to exist still in our nature – at least in its reason and in its yearning for fulfillment and happiness – and may be recovered and renewed with divine grace's assistance and our free acceptance.

Augustine considers that philosophy plays an important part in the human quest to discern and recover natural right; yet in his view, philosophy also is impeded by the threat of pride and the finitude of the human mind and will (*CG* II.7, 57–58; and *CG* VI–X, to be discussed in Chapters 3 and 4). Augustine therefore concludes, both with and against the Platonists of his era, that the quest for justice in and by philosophy must lead the true lover of wisdom beyond the power of his or her own mind to seek a mediator who can purify human beings from the sin of pride and lead both learned and unlearned persons to righteousness, to salvation. Augustine considers that this Mediator has indeed come, in lowly flesh and "humble of heart" (see Matthew 11:29), to point out the right "way of humility"[38] (cf. Fitzgerald, 2014, 258–61, referencing Augustine, *ennarationes in psalmos* 31.1.18) and assist humans to follow

---

[37] *unde fit in ipso homine quidam iustus ordo naturae, ut anima subdatur deo et animae caro, ac per hoc deo et anima et caro* (*CG* XIX.4). It seems significant that in chapter 5 of book IX Augustine explicitly links the teaching of scripture with this naturally right order of human nature. "Scripture, indeed, places the mind itself [*illa ipsam mentem*] under the governance and help of God, and the passions under the mind, so that they may be moderated and bridled and turned to righteous use" (*CG* IX.5, 365; cf. X.5, 398).

[38] Augustine alludes also to *wrong* ways of humility, as for example in *CG* X.4, 396: "Many terms belonging to divine worship are … wrongly used in showing honor to human beings, whether out of an excessive humility or … flattery"; and also *CG* V.24, 232: "Rather, we say that Christian emperors are happy if they rule justly; if they are not lifted up by the talk of those who accord them sublime honors or pay their respects

it, though never with perfection in this life.[39] Augustine's rhetorical dialectic of pride and humility in *The City of God* indicates with hope that
human beings can recover the true order of justice rooted in humility,
written in our common human nature and expressed in Judeo-Christian
scripture. "'He hath shewed thee, O man, what is good; and what doth
the Lord require of thee, but to do justly, and to love mercy, and to walk
humbly with thy God?'" (Micah 6:6–8).[40]

Before we arrive at this conclusion, however, and appreciate better
how Augustine comes to hold it, we have our long rhetorical-dialectical
journey to resume with the author of *The City of God*. The next stages of
this pilgrimage pass through civil religion as publicly practiced and philosophically (re-)interpreted in Rome, and through Platonic philosophic
theology itself, with Augustine once again calling readers to remain
attentive to the perils of pride that attend to both politics and philosophy
in this *saeculum*.[41]

---

with an excessive humility, but remember that they are only men." Augustine also shows
an awareness of the problem of feigned virtue, including the deception wrought by
an appearance of religious poverty, which could mistakenly be interpreted as a manifestation of detachment and humility, but instead is used as a cloak for hidden pride.
"[Beneath a squalid appearance] there can be much bragging; and this is even more dan-
gerous because it deceives under the guise of piety, with the appearance of serving God"
(Augustine, *De sermone Domini in monte* 2).

[39] See Dodaro (2004) for a study of the relationship between *Christ and the Just Society*.

[40] Augustine quotes this passage later, in *CG* X.5, 398. The Latin version of this passage
that he quotes, perhaps from memory, does not include "humbly," however: *aut quid
dominus exquirat? te nisi facere iudicium et diligere misericordiam et paratum esse ire
cum domino deo tuo?*

[41] On pride, politics, and the common good in Augustine's thought, see Markus (1990). For
an influential study of *Saeculum: History and Society in the Theology of St. Augustine*, see
Markus (1988) [1970]. For responses to and developments of the argument of *Saeculum*
and its interpretation of Augustine, see O'Donovan (1996) and Markus (2006).

3

The City of God VI–VII

Nature, Convention, and Rome's Civil Religion

In Chapter 2, we considered Augustine's initial critique in books I–V of *The City of God*, of vicious pride (*superbia*) as unnatural wrong. Such pride calls attention, first and perhaps most forcefully, to the blindness, injustice, and misery it produces in social and civic life. Pride in political power culminates in the false deification of the *civitas* and its founders, rulers, and heroes. Such *superbia* needs chastening – and its possessors, cleansing – through a recovery of virtuous moderation (*moderatio*) and humility (*humilitas*). And yet, political power's pathologies are not the only sign Augustine sees of *superbia* rising up against reason, right, and *res publica*. There is also philosophic pride, which forms a surprising yet strong alliance with false forms of humility in civic life. In books VI–X – the second major segment of *The City of God* and our subject in this chapter and the following – Augustine's rhetorical dialectic contends that pride in human wisdom turns its possessors away from a wholehearted love of wisdom (*philo-sophia*), just as excessive pride in political liberty and civic strength steers the ship of state toward corruption and destruction.

Early in *The City of God*, Augustine offered his readers a prelude to his case for and against philosophy, especially Platonic philosophy. In book II he noted:

[S]ome of [the philosophers], insofar as they were aided by God, did indeed make certain great discoveries [in natural, ethical, and logical science]. When impeded by their own humanity, however, they erred, especially when the divine providence justly resisted their pride, so that it might show by comparison with them

Portions of this chapter were included in "Books 6 & 7: Nature, Convention, Civil Religion, and Politics," in Meconi, ed. (2021).

44

that it is through humility that the path of godliness ascends on high. There will ... be an opportunity for us to investigate and discuss this later. (*CG* II.7, 58)

Augustine's extended dialogue with Plato and his followers will commence in earnest in book VIII. First, however, in books VI and VII, Augustine aims to prepare his readers to enter fruitfully into this dialogue. In this interlude, the topic of this chapter, Augustine engages the thought of Roman intellectual luminaries Varro and Seneca on the meaning and value of Rome's civil religion. With this pair of guides, Augustine considers philosophic interpretations and vindications of the most political dimension of Rome's ancient religion, thus probing the right relationship between nature and convention in civic affairs – regimes and offices, laws and customs, and elite and popular opinion. In this regard, Augustine again continues an investigation central to the Socratic-Platonic school and also to the philosophies of Romans like Varro and Seneca.

As in books I–V, in which Augustine began his dialectical defense of humility with what would, upon reflection, be most obvious to most people among his audience (the pathos of political pride and its concomitant *libido dominandi*), so now, in books VI–X, he adopts a similar strategy. His key contention, one with which he hopes he can persuade at least some of his readers to concur, is that the pagan Romans (together with other polytheistic worshippers), though they view Christian meekness and humility as demeaning to free men and citizens, already practice a version of humility by lowering themselves to worship beings that, if they exist at all, are by nature of lesser or equal *dignitas* to good human beings. Their cult thus constitutes a form of unreasonable or excessive humility – vicious rather than virtuous.[1]

Books VI–X together exemplify Augustine's endeavor to unmask counterfeits of genuine humility and exhort his contemporaries to live and worship only in accord with their great dignity, a dignity that encompasses the human body as well as the soul, and is shared by all human beings, not only by the wise or great. True, virtuous humility – recall from Augustine's preface to *The City of God* – is recognizable by its power to uplift, protect, and ennoble its possessors (*CG* I, preface, 3). To political and philosophic elites alike, Augustine pleads that they cease obstructing common persons from their proper greatness. His arguments

---

[1] "Excessive humility" is used explicitly by Augustine when speaking of subjects flattering their rulers, being overly obsequious in addressing them, or addressing them with words reflective of divine honor: see *CG* V.24, 232, and X.4, 396.

may surprise the political-philosophic great by suggesting that in doing so, they too will find obstacles lifted from their own paths to fulfillment.

Parallel to Augustine's ordering of content in books I–V, we find in books VI and VII an overall structure of ascent that points beyond theater, temple, and philosophic pantheism, toward the Platonic philosophy that will be the focus of books VIII–X, and ultimately what Augustine discerns as "true religion" and the true humility of its Mediator (*CG* VII.3–33; cf. 35). This rhetorical-dialectical ascent mirrors Augustine's understanding of humility itself. Far from consisting of poor self-esteem or an underrated estimate of one's own worth or abilities, virtuous or true humility as Augustine develops and defends it in *The City of God* comprises a metaphysically rich virtue – an existential and relational stance leading humans from lowliness to true and enduring exaltation.

Books VI and VII play three significant roles in Augustine's rhetorical dialectic for humility against pride, despite the fact that this pair of books makes little explicit mention of pride and humility.[2] First, Augustine uses the preface of book VI to consider the sorts of persons his dialectic might profitably engage, those whom he hopes to persuade of the goodness of humility. Second, in this pair of books, Augustine engages writings by Varro and Seneca on Rome's civil theology to prepare his own readers to recognize the rational superiority of the Platonists (and others who might concur with or surpass them in any nation, epoch, and culture: *CG* VIII.9, 324–25) in natural theology, philosophy about the divinity or deity.[3] Third, Augustine emphasizes anew what he takes to be the truth about creation and the Creator's relationship to creatures, in this dialogic *apologia* for humility, including philosophic humility. As Augustine elsewhere opines that humility is the "dwelling place" of charity (*Holy Virginity*, 51), so humility here appears as the home of true *philo-sophia*, the full and free love of wisdom. This theme is stressed more intensely in book VII, as Augustine's rhetorical dialectic runs rapidly toward his critical engagement with the Platonists in books VIII–X.

Indeed, though humility and pride are not mentioned by name in book VI, and occur only rarely in book VII, chiefly near its conclusion, these themes comprise the climax of these books. Their argument can be read as an ascent from the political-religious cave of ancient Rome, where the

---

[2] Book VI is the only book of *The City of God* with no occurrences of *superbia* or *humilitas* or their cognates. Book VII includes three usages of *superbia* and its cognates and two of *humilitas* and its cognates.

[3] Augustine considers Aristotle, and the Peripatetics generally, to be among "the Platonist philosophers": see *CG* VIII.12, 329.

people were left easy prey to the *libido dominandi* of false gods and civic elites alike, along the path upwards paved by the philosophical questionings, insights, and advances of luminaries like Varro and Seneca, and ultimately to the true Creator-God and his humble Incarnation and redemption of humanity (*CG* VII.31–33, 306–8; cf. II.7, 58; IV.31–32, 183–84; and VI.6, 249). This crucial pair of books illustrates afresh how an ascent to full freedom appears attainable only through the lowliness of true, virtuous humility.

THE PROBLEM OF DIALOGUE

The problem of achieving fruitful dialogue, in which persons truly hear one another and seek together to unmask error and draw nearer to truth, is on Augustine's mind from the opening lines of his preface of *The City of God*. Recall that he notes there the difficulty of *persuading* (in his view, a rhetorical and dialectical task requiring divine grace to reach fruition) proud interlocutors of the merits of humility. At the conclusion of the first part (books I–V) of this rhetorical dialectic, Augustine pleads for all too elusive, open-minded, and friendly engagement. He begs his critical reader to "lay aside his empty boasting and ... engage to his heart's content in argument as one earnest for discussion, listening as he should to those with whom he is engaged in friendly debate, as they answer him honestly, gravely and freely, to the best of their ability" (*CG* V.26, 236).[4] Such a plea presupposes, of course, that Augustine also has made and will make an honest effort to *listen* to pagan thought and to assess it open-mindedly, an endeavor to which his life's work and familiarity with the classical writers bear abundant, if not unambiguous, witness.[5]

---

[4] See *CG* VIII.13, 331: "Let the Platonists therefore explain these things to us. ... We will explain it, they say. Let us, then, listen respectfully"; cf. also *De ordine* I.9.27–31, on a group of intelligent, spirited interlocutors and careful, critical readers known to young Augustine.

[5] On paganism in the Roman empire of Augustine's day and the earlier days of his mother Monica, its meanings, and the tolerance of its culture and festivals, even after the legal banning of its sacrifices and public cult, see Gillian Clark (2015, 121–25). Augustine's closest friends as a young man included the reflective, gentle-souled pagan Nebridius, a model of philosophic dialogue and depth of learning (Brown, 2000, 57). On Augustine's connections with the pagan cultural-intellectual circles of Symmachus and Volusianus, the influence of the latter in Augustine's decision to write *The City of God*, and the special care with which he reviewed pagan thought, especially Platonic philosophical texts, in preparation for writing this "great and arduous work," see Brown (2000, 297–311). Although Augustine never endorsed the forced conversion of pagans to Christianity (something that the imperial edicts of his era also refrained from commanding), he may have lacked sensitivity to the obstacle to fully free dialogue *in written form*, on the part of pagan interlocutors, that the legal restrictions on pagans' public practices likely entailed (see *CG* V.26).

Now, at the outset of books VI–X, Augustine pauses once again to reflect on the pagan readers with whose minds and hearts he hopes most to connect, those who can engage his intellectual effort with seriousness and profit. These seem to be the young, and perhaps also the young at heart, serious students of liberal learning who are not yet jaded by immoderate sorrow, fear, hatred, or prejudice.

> There are ... some who understand and carefully ponder what they read without any – or at least without any great and excessive degree – of the obstinacy of long-held error. ... [T]hese more thoughtful readers will be unable to doubt that such [anti-Christian] hatred is entirely without rightful thought and reason (*rectae cogitationis atque rationis*), and is full of shallow temerity and most ruinous enmity. (*CG* VI, preface, 237)

It is critical to note, as this passage demonstrates, that Augustine does not consider all pagans to be fettered by pride, thus calling into question a rigid, "humble Christians versus proud pagans" binary interpretation of *The City of God*. Indeed, Augustine seems to know from experience that many non-Christians possess a good measure of modesty and friendliness, together with habits of reflective reading and truth-seeking, which he hopes will open their minds and hearts to receive "the gift of humility."[6]

Augustine hopes, moreover, to lead such open, philosophic, and youthful-spirited readers to the recognition of the Creator-God, as he himself once was led, with the help of Platonic philosophy. The Platonists and any philosophers like them are excellent dialogue partners in natural-theological matters, the best among those "philosophers who are dissatisfied with the opinions and errors of the people" (*CG* VI.1, 238). Augustine proposes to debate with these thinkers

> the question of whether, for the sake of the life which is to come after death, we should worship not the one true God who has made every creature, whether spiritual or corporeal, but the many gods who (as some of those same philosophers, and they more excellent and noble than the rest, have believed) were made by Him and set on high by Him. (*CG* VI.1, 238)

CIVIL THEOLOGY, PHILOSOPHY, AND FREEDOM IN BOOK VI

The question of civic vis-à-vis natural theology is, in Augustine's thought, bound up with questions posed by classical Greco-Roman philosophy. Not least of these is the right relation in political life between nature

---

[6] I borrow this phrase from Dodaro (2003); see also Fitzgerald (2014, 261).

and convention, with the latter being present and often predominant in human laws, civic customs, and cultural traditions.[7] As naturally social beings, humans flourish in familial and civic settings, but these often give birth to opinions and ways of life that lead away from nature's rhyme and reason and harden humans in those deviations. Augustine sees in Rome's civil theology one such case of "customs and laws" that tend to deform the character of those who follow them, while blinding people to the nature of true divinity and piety (*CG* VI.2, 242; cf. *CG* VI.4–6, 244–51). Philosophy brings to light falsehoods covered by such conventions and so holds out the prospect of freedom from them, for those who truly love and pursue wisdom (cf. *CG* VI.10, 261–64). Has this promise of philosophic freedom been fulfilled in Rome's greatest intellectuals? Augustine begins to seek an answer in the writings and lives of Varro and Seneca, luminaries in the intellectual life of Rome and well-known to all his contemporary, liberally educated readers.

Varro

Marcus Terentius Varro (116–27 BC) is Augustine's chief interlocutor in books VI and VII, as the authority (*auctoritas*) of choice among educated Romans in religious matters (cf. *CG* IV.22, 169; IV.31–32, 182–84). While in his day Varro lacked freedom to speak openly against the "gods of the nations" (*CG* VI.1, 238; VII.33, 307) as represented and worshipped publicly in Rome, Augustine opines that Varro nonetheless managed to communicate his disbelief in and disdain for civil theology to thoughtful, open-minded readers. Varro variously presents Rome's traditional civil religion as framed by its founders for political utility on the one hand and philosophic pedagogy on the other. Civil theology and its rites so understood bind mythic pagan deities and popular views of their intervention on behalf of Rome to a naturalist, pantheistic account

---

[7] For perhaps the *locus classicus* in Greek philosophy on nature and convention in politics, see Aristotle's *Nicomachean Ethics*, book 5, chapter 7, which opens:

> What is just in the political sense can be subdivided into what is just by nature and what is just by convention. What is just by nature has the same force everywhere and does not depend on what we regard or do not regard as just. In what is just by convention, on the other hand, it makes originally no difference whether it is fixed one way or another, but it does make a difference once it is fixed, for example, that a prisoner's ransom shall be one mina, or that a sacrifice shall consist of a goat but not of two sheep, and all the other measures enacted for particular occasions (such as the sacrifice offered to Brasidas) and everything enacted by decree. (1134b18–24)

of God (and/or the gods) as the world itself or its soul. As Augustine interprets Varro, the latter lends his learned, public-spirited support to the civil cult, with its deep roots in convention or custom (*consuetudo*), even while directing thoughtful readers beyond the civil cult to philosophic or natural theology. Varro is thus an indispensable interlocutor for Augustine to complete the political-historical-religious inquiry of *The City of God* books I–V and to prepare for the engagement with Platonic natural theology in books VIII–X.[8]

In explicating Varro's two-part division of his *Antiquities* (*Antiquitates rerum humanarum et divinarum*) into discussions of "things human" and "things divine," and his three-part classification of theology comprising mythic, civil, and natural approaches to the divine, Augustine follows the eminent pagan scholar in broaching the critical question for classical political philosophy concerning the right relation between nature and convention in civic life and institutions.[9] And while books VI and VII constitute Augustine's most sustained reflection on this theme in *The City of God*, as we have noted, the whole work is concerned with the meaning and status of nature vis-à-vis God, goodness, justice or right, evil, and grace.

Varro's method, as Augustine understands it, was first to deconstruct the mythical or fabulous theology popular with the people and inspiring Roman theater, and then quietly to make the essential agreement between fabulous and civil theology apparent, in his independent exposition of the latter. Varro had not achieved full freedom of speech, Augustine observes, yet he "did not wish to remain silent as to those things which disturbed him, and so spoke of them under the guise of commending [civil] religion" (*CG* VI.2, 243). Varro praised Roman civic-religious

---

[8] For an exchange of views on Augustine's analysis of Varro's thought, see Markus (1994) and O'Daly (1994).

[9] On the tripartite theological framework in antiquity, see Klauck (2007) and Lieberg (1984). Commenting on Greek, as well as Latin, sources for the notion of *theologia tripertita*, with special reference to Plutarch, Klauck writes:

[I]t is noteworthy that the triadic pattern can be overlaid by binary oppositions, when, for example, poets and legislators on the one side close ranks against philosophers on the other side. ... Here we may see the much older [than Plutarch's life and works] antithesis of *nomos* (law) and *physis* (nature) or of *thesis* (convention) and *physis* still at work, which has been seen by some as the place of origin of the tripartite theology. (Klauck, 2007, 337)

See also Plato's *Republic* for Socrates's comment that there is "an old quarrel between philosophy and poetry" (607b; cf. 377b–383c, and Plato's *Apology of Socrates*, 20e–22c), and Foley (2015), on this quarrel in the early dialogues of Augustine.

convention as an allegory of physical or natural theology. His arguments to this effect, however, contradicted one another in obvious ways, so that Augustine reads Varro as an esoteric writer who hoped safely to share his philosophic critique with perceptive readers.[10]

In support of this interpretation, Augustine calls our attention to the order of Varro's *Antiquities*, which treats first human things (or, rather, Roman things: *CG* VI.4, 245) and then divine things (*CG* VI.3, 243–44). Augustine interprets this order as reflecting Varro's conviction that in their true nature, as it were, the gods of the empire are merely conventional human institutions and inventions: "[A]s I have mentioned ... [Varro] expressed this more clearly elsewhere. For he says that, if he were himself founding a new city, he would have written according to the rule of nature, but since he found himself to be a member of an old one, he could do nothing but follow its custom"[11] (*CG* VI.4, 246; cf. *CG* IV.31, 182). Varro's ordering – placing human affairs before the divine – might seem at first sight to reflect hubris. Well understood, however, Varro's ordering expresses a form of political-philosophic humility, indicating the impotence of mere human wisdom to counteract or undo powerful civic opinions and customs. Whether such humility is fully virtuous seems, however, still an open question.

Augustine's rhetorical dialectic suggests two causes for Varro's failure to find full freedom through his study of philosophy. The first is ancient philosophy's disdain for, or despair regarding, the pre- or nonphilosophic majority of the population (see *CG* IV.31–32, 182–84). Augustine quotes Varro's saying that "we must keep company more with the philosophers than with the poets." Yet Augustine simultaneously notes Varro's reservation on this score, since "he [also] says that the people are more inclined to believe the poets than the natural philosophers. In the former place, he speaks of what ought to be done; in the latter, of what is done"

---

[10] On esoteric modes of writing, see Strauss (1954), and Melzer (2007 and 2014). On Augustine and classical esotericism, see Crosson (2005), Kries (2010), Russell and Promisel (2017), and Balot (2019). Kries offers this interpretation of Augustine's position on esoteric teaching, before and after the advent of Christ: "Augustine's answer [to ... the question about the accuracy of esotericism's assessment of the relationship between philosophy and society] is that perhaps esotericism had once understood the problem as well as was then possible, but that the problem had changed, and with this change the case for esotericism's understanding of the relationship between philosophy and society had collapsed" (Kries, 2010, 247).

[11] *quod apertius alibi posuit, sicut in quarto libro commemoraui, ex naturae formula se scripturum fuisse, si nouam ipse conderet ciuitatem; quia uero iam ueterem inuenerat, non se potuisse nisi eius consuetudinem sequi.*

(*CG* VI.6, 251). Despairing of converting the plebeians – and perhaps also most patricians – to a life of philosophy, Varro seeks, on the surface of his religious works, to move what he knows to be poetic, theatrical civil religion closer to the truth via naturalistic interpretations of its gods (*CG* VI.8, 255, and VII.5–16). These revaluations reflect Varro's philosophical vision of the world and its soul. For Varro himself and others like him to have full freedom, Varro implies that custom must change, and for that to happen the people must be persuaded of natural theology's truth – something for which Varro apparently holds out no hope.

Varro's pantheistic natural theology itself constitutes a second obstacle to his quest for philosophic freedom. Augustine observes that Varro's thought did not comprehend the distinction between creature and creator, between infinite, immutable spirit and finite, mutable soul. Only this understanding could have freed Varro's mind from bondage to a contingent, mutable cosmos. In speaking of the accounts of civil theology offered by Varro and his followers, Augustine underscores this limitation with an artful play on words: "[A]ll these things, our adversaries say, have certain physical interpretations; that is, interpretations in terms of natural phenomena – as if in this discussion we were seeking physics rather than theology, which is an account not of nature, but of God. For although *the true God is God not by opinion but by nature, nonetheless all nature is not God*" (*CG* VI.8, 255; emphasis added).[12] Varro's God, conceived as the soul of an immense yet still finite cosmos, cannot rescue humans from death and free them for the lasting happiness that by nature they cannot help but desire. Augustine contends that this pantheist understanding of God is not true, and so it comprises a chain for the soul as it seeks to ascend to the One. In book VIII, as we will see, Augustine chooses the late classical Platonists over their pantheist contemporaries as his preferred philosophic interlocutors precisely on this count. Pagan Platonists may not yet be fully free, in Augustine's estimation, but their philosophic freedom runs deeper and farther than Varro's.[13]

Nonetheless, Augustine admires Varro for his immense learning and lauds him for sincerely seeking truth about things divine and human, coming closer to religious truth than did most of his contemporary compatriots. Here in book VI, Augustine underscores how Varro lacked some

---

[12] *quamuis enim qui uerus deus est non opinione, sed natura deus sit: non tamen omnis natura deus est.*

[13] For Tocquevillian reflections on pantheism and modern democratic politics, see Lawler (2001).

of the blessings of liberty, especially full freedom in politically salient speech and writing. Within the bonds that his philosophy and his city's conventions had set for him, however, Varro did what he could in the service of freedom and truth. By his open critique of poetic-theatrical religion and his veiled critique of civil theology and cult, Varro opened for reflective readers a path toward a truer philosophy of deity and religion – a path Augustine himself now follows in his *City of God* and along which seeks to guide his readers. Varro as a scholar and writer thus appears to approximate a virtuous, if imperfect, form of humility, as Augustine understands it, in his service to those seeking truth.

Augustine concludes his discussion of Varro in book VI by observing with approval:

> [T]hus, when Varro so carefully expounds and reveals the civil theology, showing that it is similar to the unworthy and shameful mythical theology, and demonstrating also that the mythical theology is part of the civil, who is so stupid as not to understand that *he is endeavouring to prepare a place in men's minds for the natural theology*, which, he says, belongs to the philosophers? ... Thus, when both [theatrical and civil theology] have been condemned by men of right understanding, the natural theology alone remains as worthy of choice. (*CG* VI.9, 260; emphasis added)[14]

Seneca

While Varro treated Roman civil theology delicately, cloaking it with the respectability of the natural theology he claimed it imaged and criticizing it only indirectly, Augustine writes that Lucius Annaeus Seneca (4 BC–AD 65) openly "hack[ed] [the civil theology] to pieces" (*CG* VI.10, 263). At first sight, then, Seneca's commentaries on Roman religion suggest a freer philosophic soul behind them when compared with Varro's writings. "[I]n the book that he composed against superstitions [Seneca] condemns the civil and urban theology much more copiously and more vehemently than Varro does the mythical and theatrical" (*CG* VI.10, 261). Augustine observes that "the philosophers, as it were, made [Seneca] free"[15] to reveal in his writing truths about Rome's superstitious and ignoble civil religion (see *CG* VI.10, 264). By contrast, Augustine notes, "Varro did not have

---

[14] See also the previous chapter, in which Augustine writes that Varro and learned men like him "proposed the [mythic theology] for blame, and they showed the [civil] to be very like it. This was done ... [so that] that theology which they called natural might find its place in better minds" (*CG* VI.8, 256).

[15] Here rendering Augustine's *iste, quem philosophi quasi liberum fecerunt*.

the freedom to speak thus. He dared to condemn openly only the poetic theology" (*CG* VI.10, 263–64). Perhaps he was inferior in courage to Seneca, and so fell short of freedom, although if Augustine's interpretation of Varro is correct, Varro's indirect yet accessible attack on civil religion may have helped foment an atmosphere of religious skepticism that made such open speech safer for Seneca in his day to dare.[16]

In another respect, however, it is Seneca's conduct that seems inferior to Varro's, in Augustine's estimation. Varro at least gave such philosophic interpretations of the civil religious deities and rites that, when his educated compatriots witnessed him in the temple, they could understand his worship to be directed according to his natural theological lights. The same could not be said for Seneca. His critique of the civil religion debunked it with no ennobling naturalist interpretation offered. Rome's divinities represented only an "ignoble swarm of gods … assembled by the long age of ancient superstition" (*CG* VI.10, 263, quoting from Seneca's now-lost work *Against Superstitions*). In this Seneca thought and wrote truly, and yet he continued to worship these gods publicly in the temples and encouraged others to do so, submitting to the laws of Rome. For the uneducated majority of people, Seneca's actions bespoke sincere beliefs that he did not really hold, and for the educated elite his actions bespoke a higher valuation of the city's laws than of philosophic truth and true worship. This deference seems reflective of a false or excessive form of *humilitas*. As Seneca opined, "[T]he wise man will observe all these things as commanded by the laws, but not as pleasing to the gods"; and again, "let us adore these [false and un-holy gods] … but let us also remember that their worship is more a matter of formality than of reality" (*CG* VI.10, 263, again quoting from Seneca's *Against Superstitions*).

Augustine himself employs and appreciates irony, as his writings and in particular, his discussion of Socrates (*CG* VIII.3, 314–16, to be discussed in Chapter 4) evince. He is not similarly open to hypocrisy, however, and considers Seneca's conduct to have crossed the line from the former to the latter.[17]

[Seneca] worshipped what he condemned, did what he deplored, and adored what he blamed. Philosophy, clearly, had taught him something great: not to be superstitious in the world, but to do in the temple what he certainly would not do in the theatre. It had taught him to imitate the part of an actor for the sake of

---

[16] On this general topic, see Dodds (1991).

[17] For an analysis of "the honesty of humility" as the only effective antidote to hypocrisy in ethical, artistic, and civic life, according to Augustine, see Herdt (2008, 58–61).

the laws of cities and the customs of mankind. This was all the more damnable in that *he acted out his lying part in such a way that the people deemed him to be acting truthfully*. An actor, at least, would rather amuse the people by playing than deceive them by cheating. (CG VI.10, 264; emphasis added)[18]

As Jeremiah Russell and Michael Promisel argue, for Augustine, speech – or any other outward form of human communication – is mendacious when it is deliberate, duplicitous, and seeks to deceive, or even when all of these characteristics are not present, if the speaker has a responsibility to communicate the truth more directly (Russell and Promisel, 2017, 472 and 457–58). "Lying is as much about wanting to convince someone that the speaker believes something as it is about convincing the addressee to believe something. Augustine's discussion of jocose lies is informative here," as for Augustine the intention of this playful sort of falsehood, for instance, in works of fiction, is to "delight" rather than to "deceive," and so it is not per se problematic (Russell and Promisel, 259). Augustine's analysis of Seneca thus circles back to the theme of civic-religious deception of the common people by civic elites. Because of the disparity between Seneca's writings, which only the educated would have access to, and his actions, which would be on display to all people in the temples, civic elites would be "in the know," while the plebeians were left – purposefully, if benevolently – in the dark by Seneca and his philosophic mentors and educated friends.

Augustine thus finds fault with Seneca for failing to *live out the truth* about philosophic theology as he ascertained it, in part because of an insufficient or defective political philosophy. In thought and written word, Augustine's Seneca followed nature (*natura*) according to his best understanding of divinity and humanity; in his public religious activity, he conformed to custom (*consuetudo*) or civic convention – even untenable, and as Seneca himself judges, "ignoble," convention. Seneca's life thus lacked not only full freedom but also coherence, integrity, and unity of existence. "This freedom was present in [Seneca's] writings, ... though it was not present in his life" (CG VI.10, 261). Ryan Balot (2019) notices the particularly pointed critique of Seneca in *The City of God* VI and asks why Augustine would assess his actions so harshly while recognizing that "the systematic conditions of Roman society put pressure on

---

[18] On Augustine on imitation and theatrical performance, see Herdt (2008, 45–71), Herdt (2012, 111–29), and Foley (2014). On Augustine's and Plato's understandings of art and its relationship to politics, see Kries (2019).

Seneca" to conform to its religious conventions (189). Balot concludes, tentatively yet plausibly, that Seneca's public role and responsibility as a senator may have rendered his example particularly blameworthy in Augustine's eyes (Balot, 2019, 189). To this assessment, I would add this Augustinian view: That Seneca's decision *not* to write esoterically on Roman religion made his public worship more harmful than Varro's and that of others who did write esoterically. If one is going to write and publish the truth as one grasps it – unadorned and unvarnished – then one should all the more live according to that truth, in public as well as in private. Unlike Seneca, Varro at least tried on the surface of his writings to reconcile civil religion with rational or natural interpretation, so that in conforming to the former, he could be understood as endeavoring to follow and to live according to the latter. Paradoxically, Varro's less open and forthright form of writing on religious matters may have allowed him to live a life more integrated with truth as he understood it.[19] And this, for Augustine, matters enormously, at all times and especially after the coming of Christ.[20] That Augustine is writing in Christian times and Seneca unlike Varro lived at the dawn of those times may also explain the vehemence of his critique of this great Roman thinker.

The theme of endeavoring to live in truth and to resist pressures from culture and political systems to live according to lies continues throughout the remainder of *The City of God* (see *CG* XIV.4, 586–87; XIV.5, 588–89; XVIII.13–14, 837–39; XVIII.18, 842–45). Augustine's late classical appeal for fuller freedom for truth and for rightful forms of unity and integrity in human life and thought, foreshadows the writings of

---

[19] For a helpful discussion of Augustine's awareness of classical forms of esoteric writing, and of the distinction between such esotericism and Augustine's preferred mode of endeavoring to write responsibly for a diverse readership, see Crosson (2005). Russell and Promisel employ a more capacious definition of "esoteric" communication and argue that in Augustine's view and their own "scholars who characterize all forms of esoteric writing as lies make too sweeping a judgment, as do those who fail to acknowledge any possible mendacity" (2017, 472). In "Esotericism and Living in the Truth" (2015), Peter Lawler argues that in our contemporary milieus, "more effective in countering pervasive inauthenticity than the recovery of the esoteric–exoteric distinction as a public theme is the effort by dissident thinkers such as Solzhenitsyn to get us to live in the truth, to take responsibility for what we really know about who each of us is and what each of us is supposed to do" (199).

[20] See *CG* VI.10, 261, where Augustine notes that "Annaeus Seneca ... flourished at the time of our apostles"; and *CG* VI.11, 264: "[Seneca] ventures to mention the Christians ... only in neutral terms, for fear of praising them against the ancient traditions of his fatherland, or, perhaps, of condemning them against his own will."

Václav Havel and other dissident intellectuals of the twentieth century. Aleksandr Solzhenitsyn's plea to his fellow Soviet citizens – and indeed to all humanity – to "Live Not by Lies!" (Solzhenitsyn, 2006, 556–60) in this regard constitutes a powerful precursor to Havel's exhortations to live by or within the truth (see "The Power of the Powerless" and "Politics and Conscience," in Havel, 1990). Together with other dissident intellectuals, Havel and Solzhenitsyn ascertained that integrity of life is central to humanity and its rightful dignity, and sought to show others that integrity often begins with a simple refusal to speak, act, or live according to a lie, especially one that would exchange truths about humanity and divinity for economically, politically, or scientifically sanctioned idols.

The problem of the disintegrated or "divided" human person, fragmentation or compartmentalization of human existence, and falsified identities or actions, did not begin or come to light only in late modernity, as Augustine helps us recall.[21] It seems as old as the (postlapsarian) human race, and it was powerfully present in classical Rome. In Augustine's account, such dis-integrity is often connected with political pride and with what he deems "an excessive humility" (*CG* X.4, 396; cf. VI.10, 263; X.19, 421) of human beings before public power, civic stability, and progress. "[M]en who are princes – not, indeed, righteous princes ... – have persuaded the people in the name of religion to accept as true those things which they knew to be false: they have done this in order to bind men more tightly, as it were, in civil society, so that they might likewise possess them as subjects" (*CG* IV.32, 184).[22]

---

[21] On this topic, compare Cavadini (2007) and E. J. Hundert (1992). Cf. also Melzer (1980) on Rousseau's alternative account of, and prescriptions for, the problem of the disunity of the human soul. Melzer (1980, 1021, note 10) briefly references *The City of God*, citing Gilson (1960) on Augustine as a philosopher of unified existence.

[22] Cf. *CG* IV.31, 182:

[Varro,] speaking of religion in another place, ... plainly said that there are many truths which it is not useful for the common people to know, and, moreover, that there are many false views which it is expedient that the people should take to be true. ... Here, beyond doubt, he discloses the whole policy of the supposedly wise men by whom cities and peoples are ruled.

See also Dodaro (1994) for a study of Augustine's critiques of lies in political and military matters and consideration of the relationship between Augustine's views and some contemporary ethical theories.

CIVIL-RELIGIOUS ORIGINS, NATURE, AND
CONVENTION IN BOOK VII

The problem of knowledge of the origins of, and therewith of the reasons for, Rome's civil-religious practices is raised by Augustine near the beginning and end of book VI and again in book VII. Augustine first recalls how Varro was lauded by his countrymen for helping them in the task of civic memory and recovery. Cicero's praise of Varro is particularly moving:

> When we were wandering and roaming (*peregrinantes errantesque*) like strangers in our own city, it was as though your books led us back to our home, so that we could at last know who we were and where we were. You have opened up for us the age of our fatherland, the phases of its history, its sacred laws, its priesthoods, the discipline of its domestic and public life … and the names, kinds, offices and causes of all things divine and human. (Cicero, *Acad. Post.* I, 3, 9; quoted in *CG* VI.2, 242)[23]

Near the opening of book VII, Augustine recalls Varro's explanation that those who first invented images, rituals, and even the attributes of their divinities did so in order to bring the vision of "the soul of the world and its parts" to the people – that is, to teach them truths of natural theology as he understood it (*CG* VII.5, 274). At the close of book VII, Augustine again recalls Varro's narration of the origins of Roman civil religion, but this time via the story Varro recounts about King Numa Pompilius, Romulus's successor, who through divination learned and transcribed the origins and meanings of Roman public rituals. Numa buried these writings in his own tomb lest others see them. Generations later, they were unearthed by a plowman. After perusing them, the leading senators decided to burn rather than promulgate them. This they did, according to Varro, precisely as "religious men" (*CG* VII.34, 309, quoting from Varro's nonextant work *De cultu deorum*; cf. *CG* III.9, 102–3, and III.12, 106–7).[24]

---

[23] On travel, migration, and home as broader motifs in Augustine's life and works, see Smith (2020) and TeSelle (1996).

[24] Plutarch offers a similar version in his "Life of Numa Pompilius":

> Valerius Antias writes that the books which were buried in the aforesaid chest or coffin of stone were twelve volumes of holy writ and twelve others of Greek philosophy, and that about four hundred years afterward, when P. Cornelius and M. Baebius were consuls, in a time of heavy rains, a violent torrent washed away the earth, and dislodged the chests of stone; and, their covers falling off, one of them was found wholly empty, without the least relic of any human body; in the other were the books before mentioned, which the praetor Petilius having read and perused, made oath in the Senate, that, in his opinion, it was not fit for their contents to be made public to the people; whereupon the volumes were all carried to the Comitium, and there burnt. (Plutarch, translated by John Dryden, at http://classics.mit.edu/Plutarch/numa_pom.html)

Between Augustine's invocation of Cicero's praise of Varro's account of Rome's institutions and their origins and his retelling of Varro's commentary on the retrieval of Numa's religious institutions, Augustine invokes Seneca to raise afresh this problem of the knowledge of ancestral civic-religious customs and their origins, comparing Rome with Israel. "The Jews," opined Seneca, "understand the origin of their rites, whereas the greater part of the Roman people do not know why they perform theirs" (quoted in CG VI.12, 264). Seneca wrote this more than two generations after Varro's encyclopedic work of recovery that Cicero lauded. Why was there still such ignorance?

Recall that part of Varro's civil-religious project, as Augustine reads it, was to ennoble public rites, even some recalling and/or requiring acts not befitting the *honestas* (uprightness, or character) of a good human being and Roman citizen, and to encourage their continued observance. Varro did this in the wake of the legendary loss of documentation concerning Rome's religious origins (Numa's story and its aftermath), by offering philosophic, natural-theological interpretations of these beliefs and practices. As Augustine reads Varro, were the latter free to speak his mind plainly, he might have written something along these lines:

We Romans are already much attached to these rituals and the stories of allegedly great deeds of the gods and heroes that undergird them. These stories glorify Rome and so justify civic devotion, encouraging public service. The people cannot bear the truth that they are a pack of lies and so come to worship the true divinity. What can a philosophic scholar and devoted Roman patriot do in these circumstances? No more than reinterpret those same stories and rituals in accord with the order of the cosmos, of nature and its rhythms. In this way, the many may at least be brought closer to true opinion, and public religion become somewhat less superstitious and offensive through its assimilation to nature. I will endeavor, moreover, to write in such a way that discerning readers will grasp the disjuncture, even the conflict between my natural theology and our civil theology and rituals, and so be led to philosophic inquiry. This is all I can hope to achieve in my intellectual public service. To attack the rites directly would be perilous for me and my *patria*.

Varro's naturalistic or philosophic account of Rome's ancient rites, moreover, may have received indirect support from the version of the tale of the rediscovery of Numa's books recorded by Plutarch, according to which this king studied philosophy assiduously and buried books of "Greek Philosophy" together with those on Rome's civil religion (see note 24, in this chapter).

After Augustine has elaborated at some length, in book VI, on his sympathetic critique of Varro's project of civil-religious revival, he revisits it at even greater length in book VII.[25] Augustine explains that some of his readers may yet be unconvinced of his argument, because book VI treated mainly run-of-the-mill gods and goddesses, leaving unscathed the so-called select divinities, namely the Olympians (by Latinized names) and others near them in grandeur around whom Rome's public rituals revolved (CG VII.1, 267–68). At the close of book VI, and again in the preface of book VII, Augustine identifies the most difficult obstacle for such readers to overcome: not false conviction per se, but rather "the force of inveterate custom" (*veternosae consuetudinis vis*) and its "very deep roots" in the human and civic psyche (*CG* VI.12, 266; cf. VII, preface, 267). In order to uproot such deeply ingrained, false conventions, a sustained and repetitious engagement may be required. Augustine is willing and ready to make this effort, and launches into it in book VII of *The City of God*.

Augustine, following Varro's ordering of topics in *Antiquities*, moves from ordinary and more locally honored divinities, which Varro discussed under the classification "certain gods" and "uncertain gods," to treat the heart of the civic cult of Rome, the public worship of its "select and principal gods" (*CG* VII.1–2, 267–69). Varro wrote of these in the last book of his *Antiquities*. Moreover, Varro prefaced his discussion of Rome's select divinities with a brief discourse on natural theology, suggesting a special convergence there of philosophy and civil religion (*CG* VII.1.6, 276; VII.17, 288).[26] This indicates further why Augustine

---

[25] Burns (2001) and Rousseau (2009) read Augustine's approach to Varro as one of appreciative critique, as do I, in contrast with other scholars who judge Augustine's response to Varro to be chiefly adversarial or polemical (Balot, 2019; O'Daly, 1999a, 101 and 105). Burns writes:

> Augustine's use of Varro differs from that of his [North African Christian] predecessors in a number of ways. He takes the text itself much more seriously by laying out its organization and by citing title and book quite frequently. In addition to these formal differences there is a basic respect for Varro's views, which enables Augustine to be sympathetic yet critical. (2001, 41; cf. 40, 42–43, and 64)

[26] Crosson (2005, 80–81) writes that "Augustine does not unfold, by commenting on it," any classical text containing both esoteric and exoteric teachings – both what the author thought prudent and safe to communicate to most readers, and what he thought true and wished the (comparatively few) readers capable of understanding to grasp. On my reading, Augustine's explication of book VII of Varro's *Antiquities* does seem to offer his readers an example of a classical work containing *both* what the author understands as the truth, if simplified or in short form, and indications that all that is argued is not simply true but rather useful for most readers, while hopefully moving their errant opinions closer to true opinion.

cannot omit rhetorical-dialectical engagement with Varro's rationalization of Rome's principal divinities and the rites performed in their honor, if these especially exemplify the god and/or gods of nature. Throughout the bulk of book VII, Augustine comments on Rome's "select" gods and goddesses, all together, one by one, or in small clusters (see *CG* VII.2–4, VII.7–16, and VII.19–27), indicating how and why Varro's identification of these mythical divinities with phenomena of nature fails to persuade.

Two features of *The City of God*, book VII, are especially noteworthy for this chapter's consideration of nature and convention in Rome's civil religion, and vis-à-vis our broader focus on humility and pride. The first is its introduction of a new facet of Varro's naturalizing project, namely Varro's claim, apparently also in his *Antiquities*, that the original intention of the founders of Roman religion included the representation and portrayal of nature and nature's God or gods, through Rome's public rites and religious art. The second special feature is seen in Augustine's clear break in the flow of his argument on the select gods and goddesses of Rome's civil cult, about midway through book VII, to pen two chapters highlighting Varro's skepticism about the true origins and meaning of these select divinities, and elaborating on an alternative, more compelling interpretation, intimated by learned pagans as well.[27]

Early in book VII, Augustine introduces a new account offered by Varro of Rome's civil-religious institutions' original intention and meaning:

Varro commends these naturalistic explanations so highly as to say that the men of old invented the images, attributes and adornments of the gods precisely so that, when those who had approached the mysteries of the doctrine had seen these visible things with their eyes, they might also see with their mind the soul of the world and its parts: that is, the true gods. He also says that those who made the images of the gods in human form seem to have believed that the mortal mind which exists in the human body is very similar to the immortal mind. (*CG* VII.5, 274)

On this account, Rome's political theology was founded as an expression and pedagogue of philosophic or natural theology. Indeed, one might say that there was only one theology of note for the ancient citizen-sages who first formulated the civil cult: the natural theology.

Augustine does not call this contrast to his readers' attention explicitly, but the reflective reader will recall that an earlier quote from or

---

[27] For an illuminating analysis of the ways in which the center of a text can be given an "axial" or "structuring" function, with regard to Augustine's *Confessions*, book V, see Crosson (2015, 32–55).

paraphrase of Varro indicated precisely the opposite, that Rome's civil religion was not founded on philosophic reason. Varro wrote that, had he been founding a new city and its religious institutions, he would have written "according to the rule of nature" (*formula naturae*). As it was, he found himself a citizen of an already ancient city and so was compelled to follow its customs (*CG* VI.4, 246; cf. IV.31, 182).[28] What is one to make of this apparent contradiction: In one formulation, the originators of Rome's civil religion in fact followed the rule of nature; in another formulation, Rome's religious institutions compelled Varro to write according to custom rather than nature?

We may surmise Augustine's reply to this query from what he says in response to another question arising from Varro's argument that the ancient Romans intended to worship the divine soul of the cosmos through their civil cult and its images. Augustine notes that, in a different work, Varro opined that the earliest Romans worshipped *without* images, and that the introduction of the images that Varro in *Antiquities* interprets according to the order of nature, in particular with regard to the intellect or rational soul, in fact led Roman civil religion away from truer worship according to nature. Augustine's remarks seem to indicate that, for Varro, the mystery shrouding Rome's beginnings, and so the origins and development of the civil cult, allowed him the freedom to ascribe multiple meanings to it, all plausible under the venerable protection of the "men of old" whom Augustine considers Varro's "authorities" in such matters (*CG* VII.5, 274–75).

The title of Varro's major work investigating Roman religion, *Antiquities*, thus appears well-chosen by its eminent author. Whether or to what extent the most ancient civil cult indeed followed nature, no one living in later eras can know. What Varro can and does know with solid certainty, according to Augustine, is that in Varro's own time Rome's

---

[28] See Rousseau (2009, 170–73), for a discussion of individual and community, nature and convention in Varro's *De lingua latina*, making evident the difficulty of interpreting Varro coherently on these questions. This passage, quoted by Rousseau, illuminates Varro's sense of *civitas* and civic compulsion, referenced regarding Varro's political works by Augustine:

The people [Varro writes] has power over itself, but the individuals are in its power [*populus enim in sua potestate, singuli in illius*]; therefore as each ought to correct his own usage [*suam ... consuetudinem*] if it is bad, so should the people correct its usage. I am not the master – so to speak – of the people's usage, but it is of mine. As a helmsman ought to obey reason ..., and each one in the ship ought to obey the helmsman, so the people ought to obey reason, and we individuals ought to obey the people. (Varro, *De lingua latina* 9.1 [6], quoted in Rousseau, 2009, 173)

public religion required considerable reformulation and revision to move beyond mere convention and toward nature, via philosophy. Varro seems to opine, moreover, that there was at least some error present in the civil theology from the beginning. Augustine construes this from a comment by Varro, that the introduction of images of the gods "increased error in cities" rather than introduced it. Augustine concludes from this choice of phrase that the learned Roman "wishes it to be understood that error already existed even when there were no images" (*CG* IV.31, 183).

Varro's Knowledge, Opinion, and Skepticism

In book VII, Augustine advances a second significant argument, suggesting that Varro intentionally cast doubt on his rationalized account of Rome's civil religion. The central section of Augustine's *City of God*, book VII, comprised of chapters 17 and 18, stands apart in its subject matter from the arguments that precede and follow it about Rome's "select" divinities. This pair of chapters argues for Varro's acknowledged skepticism about the origins and natures of Rome's gods, and ultimately, for Varro's disbelief in the naturalist explanations he himself offers concerning the Roman civic cult's original intention and meaning.

Augustine opens chapter 17 by recalling his previous analyses of Varro's discussions of the nature of the gods. He has just stressed anew, at the close of chapter 16, the many ways Varro's explanations contradict one another. The earth, for instance, is said at one time to be Juno; another time, the Great Mother; and yet another, Ceres. At the same time, Minerva is identified both with the highest heaven and with the moon, which dwells in the lowest heavenly sphere (*CG* VII.16, 287–88). At the outset of chapter 17, Augustine sums up the conclusion, as he understands it, to which Varro's contradictions intentionally point: "And as with those things which I have cited as examples, so with all the rest: *they complicate rather than explain* ... as errant opinion impels them; so that even Varro preferred to doubt everything rather than to affirm anything" (*CG* VII.17, 288; emphasis added). How can Augustine be sure of Varro's civil-theological doubts?

The penultimate pair of books in Varro's *Antiquities*, discoursing on Rome's "certain" and "uncertain gods," includes this disclaimer by Varro, at the start of his treatment of the uncertain divinities:

"I ought not to be reproached when, in this book, I set down doubtful opinions concerning the gods. For if anyone supposes that a firm judgment can or should be given, let him give one for himself when he has heard what I have to say. For my own part, *I can more easily be led to doubt what I have said in the first book* [concerning 'certain gods'] than to bring what I shall write in this one [on 'uncertain gods'] to any final conclusion." (*CG* VII.17, 288; emphasis added)

Augustine notes that Varro thereby quietly conveys his uncertainty about Rome's certain gods, as well as regarding the uncertain ones. Near the start of the third and final book of *Antiquities*, just after a brief discourse on natural theology, Varro issues a similar disclaimer: "I shall in this book write of *the public gods of the Roman people*, to whom they have dedicated temples, and whom they have signally honored by many adornments. But ... I shall give an account of my opinions, not of what I know; for, in these matters, man has opinions, but only God has knowledge" (*CG* VII.17, 288–89; emphasis added).[29] Thus Varro in his writings appears confident of the essentials of his natural theology, but utterly doubtful concerning his interpretation of the civil (*CG* VII.17, 289). He thereby once again indicates to thoughtful readers that his project of interpretive identification of these two theologies is most uncertain. This is the case, according to Augustine, not only because Varro's natural theology was itself incomplete and in some significant ways errant but also because Varro was "oppressed by the authority of tradition" (*maiorum premebat auctoritas*)[30] in "describ[ing] the institutions of men" (*CG* VII.17, 288–89). Convention's force in these matters was much stronger than the force of nature.

Augustine continues in chapter 18 to propose a more plausible alternative – or rather, to echo one offered by other Roman philosophers and statesmen – that the civic gods did not begin as analogs for heaven, earth, and stars, but rather originated as men and women whose exploits were sung by the poets and whose postmortem worship some ordinary citizens, civic elites, and even malicious spirits encouraged (*CG* VII.18, 289; cf. XVIII.18, 844–45). Augustine earlier references no less an authority than Cicero to support the hypothesis that these gods are really deceased human beings, deified by mortals due to public and/or elite admiration and civic pride (see *CG* III.15, 113–14). Augustine's analysis suggests that civic theology divinizing dead mortals may have preceded and inspired the mythic. First, "those who chose to worship [deceased eminent men]

---

[29] Cf. Socrates on human wisdom's limits vis-à-vis divine wisdom in Plato's *Apology* 23a. For Augustine's understanding of Socrates and his famed "turn" to human things, see *CG* VIII.3, 314–16, discussed in Chapter 4 of this book.
[30] On *mos maiorum* (ancestral custom and standards) and its import in Roman thought and civic life, see Earl (1966, 28, 30), and Hammer (2014, 15–17).

as gods" established "sacred rites and solemn festivals" in their honor, to each "according to his genius, character, actions and circumstances." Later "[t]hese rites, creeping little by little into the souls of men ... spread far and wide as the poets adorned them with lies and deceitful spirits seduced men to accept them" (*CG* VII.18, 289).

At the outset of book VII, Augustine's rhetorical dialectic continues by asking how Rome's "select divinities" were selected from the rest of the gods for public cult. He examines the stories of these divinities and concludes that they – and before them, the human beings whom they personify and purport to elevate to heaven – could not have been selected for nobility or goodness. They were most likely "selected" on account of luck, publicity, or even notoriety (*CG* VII.3–4, 269–74). In contrast with most of the "lesser" divinities, paradoxically including Felicity, Virtue, and Quiet, Augustine observes that "there is hardly one of the select gods who has not received upon himself the mark of some notable scandal. The [famous principal gods] have descended to the humble tasks (*humilia opera*) of the obscure gods; but the obscure gods have not risen to the sublime crimes (*sublimia crimina*) of the select ones" (*CG* VII.4, 273). Consider Saturn, who ate his offspring and castrated his father. Not surprisingly then, the people of Carthage were cowed into placating this terrible god by child sacrifice, though Rome to its credit rejected this practice (*CG* VII.26, 300). Saturn was overthrown by his son Jupiter and afterward was represented with a sickle, as Varro suggests, to symbolize agriculture. Augustine suggests that perhaps the origin of this portion of the tale was "a leisured king [who] became a toiling laborer under the rule of his son" (*CG* VII.19, 290). Augustine concludes that one should identify gods like Saturn not with elements of nature but rather with dead human beings or evil spirits if one wishes to achieve a measure of greater truth and certainty concerning the origins of such civil-religious matters (*CG* VII.28, 303–4).

Varro's naturalized explanation of civil theology, as already noted, extended to its origins. Wise men of yesteryear, Varro opined, crafted images, characters, and narratives of the pagan pantheon "so that, when those who had approached the mysteries ... had seen these visible things with their eyes, they might also see with their mind the soul of the world and its parts: that is, the true gods." He further notes, in Augustine's paraphrase, that the anthropomorphic representations of divinities indicated that Roman religious founders held a high opinion of "the mortal mind ... [as] very similar to the immortal mind" (*CG* VII.5, 274). After showing to his satisfaction that this charitable interpretation is not persuasive, as Varro himself seems to have recognized, Augustine, at last, leaves the civil theology behind to engage more directly with Varro's pantheistic philosophic theology.

Early in book VII, Augustine summarized Varro's natural theology in this way: Varro holds that the cosmos itself is the one divinity, by virtue of its soul. "Here," Augustine notes, "Varro seems after a fashion to confess that there is one God." Yet Varro further divides the cosmos into the spheres of heaven and earth, and each of these he divides and makes inhabited by lesser souls, though still greater than human souls. "All these four parts are full of souls," mortal and immortal. The "heavenly gods" inhabit the upper regions; lesser gods ("Heroes, and Lares and Genii") dwell between the moon and earth's atmosphere. In this way, Varro combines philosophic pantheism with polytheistic principles or interprets polytheism from within the prism of pantheism.[31] Augustine notes that this pantheistic natural theology must be discussed more carefully after the civil religion is examined regarding the so-called select gods. Augustine stresses that such pantheistic theology was not Varro's alone, but had "pleased … many other philosophers besides" (CG VII.6, 276).

Near the close of book VII, Augustine reaches the point at which he can treat pantheism more directly.[32] He rejects the world-soul doctrine of God on both philosophic and revealed principles. In book VII, as in book IV, he alludes to Platonic philosophic arguments concerning the kinds of souls and their origin with the transcendent God, "who is wholly everywhere … not divisible into parts; … filling heaven and earth with present power; and with a nature which lacks nothing. And so he directs all the

[31] Gillian Clark (2010) notes that this sort of monotheism-cum-polytheism has come to be known as "inclusive" or "soft" monotheism, taking many forms in late classical thought (184). She argues that Augustine's critique of Varro's version of inclusive monotheism "did less than justice" to this form of pagan monotheism, but that Augustine's analysis nonetheless raises some legitimate objections to it, particularly of a social and civic variety (186; 200–201). For a collection of related chapters, see Stephen Mitchell and van Nuffelen, eds. (2010).

[32] Clark recalls Augustine's own notes in *The City of God* VI and VII of his need to engage Varro's natural theology at greater length, on its own terms. She sees the natural place for this engagement to be in book VIII and observes how Augustine there passes over Varro's philosophy of divinity to engage instead with Platonic philosophic-theology (Clark, 2010, 196). I concur with Clark's judgment that more direct philosophic dialogue and less confrontational rhetoric would have strengthened Augustine's argument against Varro (Clark, 2010, 197). Still, given what I take to be the rhetorical-dialectical nature of his inquiry in *The City of God*, Augustine's allusion to Platonic philosophic arguments and Christian faith and his enumeration of divine works visible in the world near the end of book VII (chapters 29–31) might suffice for most philosophically inclined readers regarding pantheist, or Varronian inclusive monotheist, positions.

things which He has created in such a way that they may perform and exercise their own proper movements. For although they can be nothing without Him, they are not what He is" (*CG* VII.30, 306; cf. IV.31, 183). Augustine thus pleads once again with his fellow Romans not to worship anything less than the one true deity. To worship a false God entails exercising a defective or false form of humility in place of a true one, and so to act in ways unbefitting human dignity (cf. *CG* II.29, 91–93).

Chapter 31, perhaps the pinnacle of book VII, comprises a brief, beautiful hymn to God's goodness, beginning with the blessings the best of philosophers have ascribed to God as the author of our human nature and its goods, then moving to the even greater blessings bestowed through revelation, redemption, and grace. Augustine continues this line of thought through chapter 33, where he suggests why philosophy, when it had come closer even than had Varro to the truth of things, still proved insufficient to free people from fear-and-falsehood-induced civil religion. Philosophy left largely to its own devices lacked a divine mediator in truth who could counter the pride of domineering human heroes and daemons from the full depth of virtuous humility. "From their most cruel and ungodly dominion man is set free when he believes in *Him Who, to raise man up, offered an example of humility as great as the pride by which they fell*" (*CG* VII.33, 308, emphasis added; cf. I, preface, 3). For Augustine, only this divine condescension can empower people to break the chains forged for them by poetic and political leaders, especially when these chains have been reinforced by erudite, philosophic-cosmological interpretation, however well-intentioned, and padlocked by "inveterate custom" (*CG* VI.12, 266; cf. IV.31, 182 and IV.32, 184). Full freedom, a major theme and concern of Augustine's rhetorical dialectic, is only found through the gift of a humble God, offered to brilliant philosophers and uneducated people alike.

From Varro to the Platonists

As we have seen in this chapter, in books VI–VII Augustine dialogues with Varro and Seneca concerning the nature and value of Rome's civil religion, and through it the meaning and achievements of the philosophic or natural theology Varro expounds. This portion of Augustine's rhetorical dialectic aids in his task of persuading noble Roman pagans that Christianity is not inimical to good citizenship on account of its refusal of Rome's civil theology. Augustine is in this respect primarily concerned with Varro as a "political man" or statesman (*politicus*; *CG* VII.23, 295;

cf. IV.31, 182, and IV.32, 184), not as a natural theologian.[33] Similarly, Augustine highlights Seneca's civic role as "a distinguished senator of the Roman people" in explaining his practical acquiescence in public rites he blamed in his writings (CG VI.10, 264). In this regard, books VI and VII continue and complete Augustine's political-historical study of books I–V.

At the same time, this lengthy rhetorical-dialectical engagement with Seneca and Varro is meaningful, and perhaps essential, for Augustine's upcoming dialogue with the philosophic theology of the Platonists and its rationale for upholding forms of pagan cult for the common people. Varro's highest theoretical intention, for his ablest, most reflective readers, as Augustine understands it, was precisely to lead them from civil to natural theology, as from falsehood to truth.[34] Thus read, Varro's *Antiquities* appears as much more than a treatise on Roman religion, even one endeavoring to refound the piety (*pietas*) – religious and patriotic – of the citizens of its author's ancient *patria*. It also comprises a protreptic, or exhortation, to philosophize about the cause or causes of things, about the divine. Which educated, attentive reader, asks Augustine, will fail to grasp that Varro "is endeavoring to prepare a place in men's minds for natural theology, which, he says, belongs to the philosophers?" (CG VI.9, 260).

Varro had worked for and come close to truth, as Augustine emphasizes. He perhaps lacked only the fortuitous encounter with Platonic wisdom that Augustine experienced to approach more closely to what unassisted human reason could grasp about God. In this task of preparing able minds for philosophic theology, Augustine's rhetorical dialectic aims to collaborate with Varro. He seeks to help those living long after the learned Roman to go further on this philosophic quest and to reach, or at least recognize, a natural philosophy of the divine that makes room for human immortality, for a firm hope of life eternal in bliss. Augustine

---

[33] Augustine's rhetorical dialectic on Roman civil theology in CG VII.23 seems to distinguish between Varro and "philosophers," even while reinforcing Varro's philosophic interest and relevance: "These are points which are, perhaps, to be discussed with philosophers. For the time being, however, I wish to approach him as a political man. For, though he may seem to have wished to lift up his head for a moment, as it were, into the freedom of natural theology, it is possible that, while still occupied with this book [*Antiquities*], he nonetheless glanced aside" to shore up public confidence in the religious customs of ancient Rome (CG VII.23, 295).

[34] Note the disjunction, unbridgeable in full for Varro, between his highest theoretical intention and his highest practical intention (to vivify Rome with a renewed reverence for its gods, duly re-interpreted and naturalized), and the extent to which Varro attempts to bridge it with a naturalist interpretation of civil theology.

was himself helped by "certain books of the Platonists" (*Confessions* 7.9.13; cf. 7.9.14–17) years after Cicero's dialogue *Hortensius* had first kindled in his heart a passion for philosophy (*Confessions* 3.4.7–8). By clearly and, as it were, publicly, expounding for all what Varro quietly intimated for a select few, and suggesting that even simple pagans longed for a felicity that transcended this mortal life (*CG* IV.25, 173–74; cf. VI.12, 265–66), a felicity that Varro's god of nature could not give, Augustine encourages readers to continue journeying on with him, to examine in books VIII–X Socratic and Platonic philosophy concerning the divine, which might in turn prepare them to receive the Gospel and seek citizenship in the heavenly city (*CG* VII.29–33, 304–8).

In his study of Varro, Augustine offers a compelling account of why pantheistic philosophy marshaled in the service of convention and civil religion could not achieve full, universal freedom in truth, and why it did not even attempt to offer its adherents a fully happy life after death, an eternal life (cf. *CG* VI.9, 260). Augustine also intimates in this pair of books why even Platonic monotheism, for which he has high regard, was similarly impotent. This discussion awaits elaboration in books VII–X, and it is to these books that we now turn.

4

The City of God VIII–X

Natural Theology, Philosophic Pride, and Divine Humility

> Do you wish to grasp the exaltedness of God? Grasp first the humility of God.[1]
>
> Augustine, *Sermons* III/4, 220; PL 38.67

> [I]f God, by Whom all things were made, is wisdom … then the true philosopher is a lover of God. But the thing itself whose name this is does not reside in all who glory in that name; for it does not follow that those who are called philosophers are lovers of true wisdom.
>
> Augustine, *The City of God* VIII.1, 312

With this new segment of Augustine's rhetorical dialectic, comprising books VIII–X, we reach the first peak, as it were, of his prosecution of vicious pride (*superbia*) and defense of virtuous humility (*humilitas*). When we reach books XIII–XIV of *The City of God*, we will descend with the work's author into a low valley, dealing with the pride of the first human sin. A slow, inconstant, pilgrim ascent marks the subsequent books through Augustine's history of the heavenly city. In books XIX–XXII, we will climb with the author of *The City of God* to a second, still higher peak of the defense of humility, again in the context of Augustine's debate with philosophers who do not accept Christ as Mediator.

Back in our current landscape, however, we find that book VIII's opening chapters offer readers a condensed history of philosophy, including a

---

Portions of this chapter were included in "Elitism and Secularism, Old and New: Augustine on Humility, Pride, and Philosophy in *The City of God* VIII–X," in Kabala, Menchaca-Bagnulo, and Pinkowski, eds. (2021, 227–46). See also the response by Paul Weithman (2021).

[1] *vis capere celsitudinem dei? cape prius humilitatem dei.* On God's humility, see also the Latin text of CG IX.20 and page 82, note 15 of this chapter.

reflection on the persons, wisdom, and impact of Socrates, Plato, and his latter-day disciples the Platonists.[2] This history continues in a less evident way throughout the remainder of book VIII and in books IX and X, in which Augustine's Platonic dialogue partners are introduced in chronological order: Apuleius, Plotinus, and Porphyry. What Nietzsche much later would term "the problem of Socrates" frames book VIII, highlighting a certain philosophic modesty, perhaps even humility, on the part of the contentious old Athenian.

When we consider books VIII–X as a whole segment in Augustine's rhetorical dialectic, though, it is the trope of the philosophic and biblical *peregrinus* – the pilgrim, traveler, or stranger in search of wisdom, God, and right worship – that forms the bookends of this trio of books. Augustine's philosophic *peregrinus* par excellence, evincing the humility of one who cannot find the fulfillment of philosophy on his own or only in his city, is none other than Plato, who left Athens for a time and traveled far in search of deeper and broader wisdom. To a lesser but still significant extent, this philosophic *peregrinus* is Porphyry of Tyre, who traveled to Plotinus's Platonic philosophic school and beyond, and who rejected the gods of his native Chaldea in his (esoteric) philosophic writings, in keeping with the faith and deeds of the patriarch Abraham. Augustine evokes Abraham and his pilgrimage near the close of book X, as we will see. This pilgrim framework in books VIII–X prepares us for the history of *The City of God* "on pilgrimage in this world" toward its heavenly rest (CG XV.26, 68; 7cf. *inter al. CG* I, preface, 3; XVIII.2, 824), whose pilgrimage Augustine will soon chronicle for his readers in the remaining books.

Within this framework, Augustine's dialogue with the Platonists, and particularly Apuleius and Porphyry, crystallizes in lengthy debates on natural theology. In his response to Apuleius, Augustine emphasizes the excessive or false humility that the philosopher promoted by endorsing the worship of daemons (*daemones*). In his rhetorical-dialectical debate

---

[2] Compare Augustine's other brief history of philosophy in *Against the Academics* III.17–19, written decades earlier during his stay in Cassiciacum. See also Crosson (2015) on Cicero's (and Aristotle's) understanding of dialectical reasoning and consequent "*incorporation of the history of philosophy into the ongoing process of philosophical inquiry*. The critical examination [via dialectic] of *endoxa* [widely shared opinions] that have been held by the *sophoi* is thus both for Aristotle and Cicero not a separate historical discipline (as the 'history of philosophy' is often thought of today) but an integral part of philosophical inquiry" (102; emphasis added). Augustine's presentation of philosophy and its history throughout *The City of God* reflects this Ciceronian influence.

with Porphyry, Augustine criticizes the philosophic pride that may have underlaid his interlocutor's ruthless critique of Christianity, even as Augustine more humbly makes excuses for Porphyry and lauds his intellectual achievements in book X's concluding chapters.

This chapter of our study of humility and pride in *The City of God* aims to elucidate the significance of Augustine's choice of framework for book VIII on its own and for books VIII–X read together, and to develop the roles played by humility, false or vicious and true or virtuous, and those parts played by vicious pride, throughout this crucial segment of Augustine's rhetorical dialectic. An alternative title for this chapter might be "Augustine's Philosophers,"[3] as our exploration will follow our author's discussion of his chief five – Socrates, Plato, Apuleius, Plotinus, and Porphyry – in the historical order in which they first take the stage in this pivotal portion of *The City of God*.

BOOK VIII: SOCRATES, PLATO, AND APULEIUS

Socrates

Augustine considers the history of the ascent of ancient philosophy to culminate in Plato and the later Platonists (and thinkers of any nation or era who have reached similar truths about the nature of divinity), as his short history of philosophy in book VIII reflects. Still, it is striking that it is what we might term, taking a cue from Nietzsche, "the problem of Socrates," rather than "the problem of Plato," that forms the bookends of Augustine's mini-history of philosophy and initial dialogue with Platonic natural theology in book VIII. What is this Socratic problem, according to Augustine, and why does it matter to his inquiry?

The first aspect is the famous "Socratic turn." When leading philosophers previously pursued questions concerning speculative truth and the intelligibility of the cosmos, why did Socrates direct his attention toward human things, that is, to questions of justice, virtue, and happiness? Augustine thinks that it is impossible to answer this query with certainty because of the old Athenian's penchant for "confessing [his] ignorance, or concealing his own knowledge" (*CG* VIII.3, 315). Socrates has come down to us chiefly as a character in the dialogues of Plato, and these dialogues often appear to have inconclusive resolutions (cf. *CG* VIII.4,

---

[3] Here I paraphrase Catherine Zuckert's title, *Plato's Philosophers* (2009). For a study of *Augustine's Leaders*, see Kaufman (2017).

316–17). Socrates led others toward truths about human well-being and virtue by asking them questions, usually uncomfortable questions meant to show the ignorance of those who think themselves wise concerning a good life. In this way, though Augustine does not say so explicitly, Socrates's philosophizing offers a lesson in the reasonable moderation of one's self-estimate regarding wisdom, and so can help counter vicious pride and prepare the ground for humility. Socrates's characteristic ironic stance, Augustine's dialectic implies, could even imply a form of virtuous humility that is expressed in "assum[ing] the character of an enquirer and the humility of one desiring to learn" for the sake of guiding another to discover the truth (*CG* X.11, 410).

Augustine's rhetorical dialectic engages two accounts of why Socrates applied his astute intellect to consider human things (see *CG* VIII.3, 315). The first account approximates Socrates to the early modern philosophers' famous "lowering" of their sights in the hopes of learning something "clear and certain" to help people lead better lives. The second account Augustine considers more "benevolent" but perhaps somewhat less believable. It comprises a Platonic reading of the thought of Plato's master. On this interpretation, Socrates realized that "minds sullied" by unruly desires for transitory goods were not worthy of reaching the source and summit of being and truth. Socrates, therefore, applied all his attention to the discovery of true goods and virtues, the love of which would purify the philosophic soul and enable it to rise unhindered toward heavenly contemplation. Only through virtuous and wise living can human beings reach the pinnacle of philosophic wisdom. In this way, Socrates the teacher of Plato is presented as a proto-Platonist.

At the close of his main discussion on Socrates (*CG* VIII.3, 314–16), Augustine invokes the hermeneutic with which he began: Socrates's "discussions" (*disputationes*; referring to those among Plato's dialogues in which Socrates plays a leading role; see also Aristotle's *Politics*, 1265a10–12) show that the philosopher "advances and maintains and demolishes all manner of propositions, [and so] what he himself understands the supreme good to be does not clearly appear" (*CG* VIII.3, 315). Just as the real reasons for Socrates's turn to the human things remain shrouded in mystery, so also his final word, if there were such, on the problems that were his life's pursuit can never be known with certainty. Socrates is therefore chiefly and rightly renowned for his way of life and the questions he doggedly posed more than for his teachings. He was the gadfly to a number of young residents of Athens, who took the lesson of their teacher's way of life so seriously as to make it their own, pursuing wisdom about the good to the death. Were it not for Socrates, Augustine's dialectic emphasizes, we would not have had Plato – at least the Plato we know and admire. Socrates's eschewing of fame through refraining from "publishing" and focusing instead on shared, lived inquiry may be another indicator for Augustine, if not of humility, at least of fitting philosophic modesty on the part of the "first to call philosophy down from the heavens and set her in the cities of men and bring her also into their homes" (Cicero, *Tusculan Disputations* V.4).

A second aspect of the problem of Socrates, as Augustine presents it, is the famed philosopher's relationship to his polis Athens. The cause of this at least is certain:

> It is at any rate well known that, with a wonderful grace [*lepore*] of argument and the most acute wit, he would hound and pursue the folly of ignorant men who thought they possessed some knowledge. He would do this precisely in relation to those moral questions to which he seemed to have devoted his whole mind. ... It was in this way that he stirred up the hostility as a result of which he was falsely accused, condemned and sentenced to death. (CG VIII.3, 315)

Augustine's analysis here concurs in broad strokes with Plato's *Apology*. Socrates's accusers seem motivated more by personal animus than by concern for justice or piety. The gadfly trying to awaken slumbering Athens, or at least some of its citizens, was crushed as an inconvenience to public peace. Even so, as Augustine reminds his readers, shortly afterward the Athenians resented the execution and repented of his condemnation, mourning Socrates in a pubic gesture of shared sorrow, stoked perhaps by belated gratitude. Augustine's Socrates, striving to speak and to live according to his sense of the truth about the best human life, and so unavoidably in tension with his beloved Athens, comes closer to embodying the integrity of truth and life that Augustine so values yet found wanting in the Roman sage Seneca (see *CG* VI.10, 261–64).

The final aspect of the problem of Socrates that book VIII's rhetorical dialectic explores is the question of Socrates's famous *daimon* (Latin *daemon*), the spirit which warned the philosopher whenever he was about to act unwisely or to bad effect (see Plato, *Apology of Socrates* 40 a–c). This dimension of the Socratic dilemma is raised by Augustine at the midpoint of book VIII (*CG* VIII.14, 332–33) and guides the rest of the book's analysis. Against arguments that worshipping *daemones* is futile, the Platonist Apuleius, on Augustine's account, brought out powerful ammunition, that the greatest teacher in the history of philosophy acknowledged and at times seems to have relied on advice from a *daemon*. Thus the title of one of Apuleius's works was *De deo Socrates*. We will return later in this chapter to consider Augustine's critique of Apuleius's argument apparently supporting the worship of *daemones*. Suffice it for now that Socrates re-enters Augustine's narrative at the close of book VIII, and that the problem of Socrates frames and comprises an important theme of book VIII, Augustine's first sustained rhetorical-dialectical encounter with the Platonists and their esteemed predecessors in *The City of God*.[4]

Plato

Augustine's Plato is both Athenian citizen and philosophic pilgrim (*peregrinus*).[5] Thanks to his fortunate birth into a leisured, honorable family in the city of philosophers, Plato encountered and spent his formative years with Socrates, who launched Plato on his life's course.[6] Augustine stresses Plato's grateful acknowledgment of his debt to Socrates and his tremendous admiration for his greatest teacher: "He singularly loved his master Socrates" and so "made him the principal speaker in virtually all his dialogues" (*CG* VIII.4, 316). From Socrates, Plato learned to pursue and to excel in "the active part of philosophy" regarding "the conduct of life, that is, ... the regulation of morals" (*ad agendam vitam, id est ad mores instituendos*), and also to write his dialogues with a good measure of Socrates's famed wit and grace (*CG* VIII.4, 316).[7]

Still, Augustine surmises, following a traditional biographic narrative, Plato the Socratic could not rest content with the wisdom that Socratic inquiry provides. Plato yearned to bring philosophy to perfection, or at least closer to perfection, and for this cause he left his homeland and "travelled (*peregrinatus est*) as far and widely as he could" (*CG* VIII.4,

---

[4] Socrates also figures in *The City of God* XIV.8, 596 (on Socrates's education of Alcibiades), XVIII.37, 875 and XVIII.41, 881 (on Socrates as teacher of other eminent philosophers holding diverse views as to the highest good and its bearing on the choiceworthiness of a life active in politics). Socrates plays a lesser role in Augustine's mini-history of philosophy in *Against the Academics* (Augustine 2019, III.17; cf. II.6); see also *On True Religion* (*De vera religione*) 1,1–2, 2, in Augustine (2005, 29–30).

[5] For scholarly commentary on the reception of Plato and his philosophy in late antiquity, including essays on Plotinus, Porphyry, and Augustine, see Herold Tarrant et al., eds. (2018).

[6] Augustine's discussion of Plato in *CG* VIII.4 commences: "But among the pupils of Socrates the one who shone with a glory so illustrious that he entirely eclipsed all the others, and not, indeed, unworthily, was Plato. He was an Athenian by birth, of honorable standing among his countrymen" (316).

[7] Augustine uses the same word, *lepore* (from *lepos, leporis*), in his description of Socrates's way of discourse and examining others in the preceding chapter (*CG* VIII.3). Dyson (*CG* VIII.3–4, 315 and 316) translates *lepore* in both instances as "with grace."

316). The Athenian philosopher thus became a pilgrim, a denizen of the
world, a wanderer in search of wisdom from whomever and wherever he
might find it. In book X, as we will see, the dialogue between Augustine
and the Platonists concludes with an evocation of Abraham, the wanderer who left his country at God's command and worshipped the true
God in truth (*CG* X.32, 444). While Augustine in book X explicitly
develops a parallel between Porphyry and Abraham, it does not seem
accidental that at the opening of this segment Augustine highlights the
pilgrim and the universal or cosmopolitan nature of Plato the philosopher, more so than the Athenian citizenship that Augustine's descriptions of Socrates stress. Plato's philosophic journeys led him to Egypt and
thence into Italy, where Pythagorean philosophy flourished. Under the
Pythagorean influence, Augustine surmises, Plato returned to speculative
or "contemplative" matters, "the investigation of natural causes and the
purest form of truth" (*CG* VIII.4, 316). Plato thus reunited the active and
contemplative branches of philosophy, in which together "the pursuit of
all wisdom is understood to consist" (*CG* VIII.4, 317).

Augustine's rhetorical dialectic in book VIII also underscores the
difficulty of ascribing any theory or teaching with certainty to Plato.
He explicitly rejects a piecemeal or proof-text approach to discovering
the eminent philosopher's positions. Plato, Augustine notes, followed
Socrates in "concealing his own knowledge or opinions" (*CG* VIII.4,
317); and Augustine the theologian and busy bishop is at any rate not
in a position to interpret the whole Platonic corpus, to discern whether
it contains a coherent teaching.[8] *The City of God*'s author thus com-
municates clearly to his readers that when he appears to ascribe a teaching to Plato, he does so in a loose sense. It may be that Socrates utters
this teaching at a significant juncture in a Platonic dialogue, or that the
philosophic heirs of the Academy most devoted to the memory of Plato
interpret the teaching as Plato's, or that it is a development of an argument from one of the Plato's works. Augustine thus takes a humble
or modest approach to interpreting the great philosophic master, who
himself exhibited modesty by not placing himself front and center in his
justly renowned dialogues.

For Augustine, the most noteworthy philosophical insights of
Plato's eminent disciples – the late classical neo-Platonists – involve the
nature of God and his relation to creatures, especially human beings:
"[These philosophers] find in Him the cause of existence, the ground

---

[8] For a contemporary work undertaking this task, see Zuckert (2009).

of understanding, and the pattern according to which we are to live" (*CG* VIII.4, 317; cf. VIII.5–11, 318–29). The theocentrism of Platonism reflects a deep truth for Augustine, one that is in principle able to ground a truly virtuous humility, a true way of humility. We human beings are not our own cause, nor our own wisdom, nor our own happiness; rather, we participate in these great goods as gifts from another. To use the highest gift with which we are by nature endowed – our intellect – to seek and deepen this realization is a free choice requiring fortitude. In this noble philosophic endeavor, among those following in Plato's footsteps, Augustine not only considers "[t]he Greeks Plotinus, Iamblichus, and Porphyry ... the most eminent," but also finds worthy of note "the African Apuleius, who was learned in both ... Greek and Latin" (*CG* VIII.12, 330).

Apuleius

Augustine begins his critical engagement with the Platonists, who for all their achievements still supported forms of polytheistic worship, from Apuleius (c. 123–c. 170 AD). Read within the broader context of Augustine's argument about pride and humility in *The City of God*, the significance of his dialogue on religion with his fellow African (see *CG* VIII.12, 330) becomes clearer. Many scholars have noted Augustine's appraisal that Apuleius erred in permitting or recommending the worship of daemons with a view to purifying the soul to some degree.[9] Less noted about Augustine's critique is its focus on the ignoble, false *humbling* of human beings, which our author finds in Apuleius's religious counsels for the mass of humanity.[10] This section of our chapter recaps Augustine's critical dialogue with Apuleius, with special attention to the diverse forms of humility Apuleius's religious philosophy encourages for philosophers on the one hand, and nonphilosophers on the other.

---

[9] I render the Latin *daemon, daemones*, with an older English form "daemon," plural "daemons," rather than "demon," plural "demons," to preserve the classical spectrum of meanings for this term. See the entry for "demon" and its various forms and meanings in the *Oxford English Dictionary*. Augustine argues that even in his time, the term was acquiring a pejorative meaning among pagans, as well as Christians, but he does not deny that in earlier classical culture it was used more broadly, even positively (*CG* IX.19, 384).

[10] O'Daly, for instance, notes that "Augustine stresses that the human capacity for goodness makes humans potentially superior to demons," but does not seem to develop the implications of this point or connect it directly with Augustine's trope of humility (O'Daly, 1999a, 117).

Unlike Plato's Socrates in book II of *The Republic*, Apuleius allowed for the worship of lower divinities (*daemones*, from the Greek *daimonia*) subject to the flux of passions, as fitting in itself and as the only way available to most people for happiness in the afterlife. Apuleius writes of this practice in his book *De deo Socrates* (*On the god of Socrates*). With other Platonists, Apuleius considers the One to have created three classes of souls: the immortal and all-good gods; the immortal but impassioned and unpredictable daemons; and the souls of mortal human beings. The daemons mediate between needy humans and the great gods, concerned for human affairs, but are so high above them as to be ignorant concerning them. Humans placate daemons, their fickle but powerful mediators, with prayers and sacrifices, seeking the purification of their souls from evil and the gift of immortal felicity after death. The wrath of daemons when sacrifices are omitted indicates that they desire these divine honors, and so it appears unwise for their supplicants to omit them. That even Socrates seems to have honored such a being, moreover, adds seriousness to their demands (*CG* VIII.14–16, 332–37).

Augustine's critique of Apuleius's account of daemonic mediation centers on the concept of false, demeaning humility (*CG* VIII.17, 337–38; see also VIII.18–22, 338–45). Why, asks Apuleius's fellow African, should we humans worship beings whom, if we are wise at any rate, we do not want to imitate? Is not the imitation of the divinity, so far as we are able, the highest form of worship? Why, given what Apuleius himself acknowledges as the anger of the daemons, their inconsistency and untrustworthiness, their *vices*, should we consider them superior to us in the most significant sense? Do we not also possess immortal souls? Are we not then their equals, and if we are virtuous, their betters? Addressing Apuleius directly, Augustine asks: Why do you, a learned philosopher, counsel others less learned to engage in such unjust, humiliating practices? Why do you engage in them yourself?

Augustine's argument here harkens back to his preface: true, virtuous humility, far from compelling persons to poor self-esteem, raises human beings, elevating human dignity to a point high "above all the earthly pinnacles which sway in this inconstant age" (*CG*, I, preface, 3). False humility is found where we are bound by it to inconstancy, and where we are lowered by it to honor or engage in vice. Augustine's endeavor in book VIII thus comes to light as an unmasking of excessive or vicious humility where it is endorsed by exalted philosophy, and so opens a path to retrieve human dignity. On Augustine's account, the cult of the daemons involves not only false humility but also vicious pride or *superbia*.

If the daemons are real, then their desire for higher excellence than is theirs by nature and right and their usurpation of worship due only to God show "detestable pride" (*CG* VIII.19, 341; cf. also VIII.22, 344). So also does their refusal, so far as the poets and the philosophers tell us, to acknowledge their errors and injustice, repent of their vices, and request pardon out of a true "humility deserving of mercy" (*CG* VIII.19, 341; cf. V.26, 235 and *CG* XVII.20, 812).

Also of concern to Augustine is the human pride involved in daemon worship. This he finds expressed in Apuleius's work *Asclepius*, in which the Platonist has the Egyptian sage Hermes discourse on what it means for humans to be made in the divine image. Just as the one God, Father and Creator, created the lesser gods, so also human beings, endowed with reason and crafted in the divine image, invent the art of making divinities *in their own image*.[11] They do this by fashioning bodies out of wood, stone, and the like and by inviting spirits who are willing to come and inhabit them. In this manner, humans may be said to be "maker[s] of those gods who are content to dwell in their temples as the neighbors of mankind" (*CG* VIII.23, 346). Apuleius does not seem to share Hermes's view on the origin of the gods, and even Apuleius's Hermes admits that this art stems from error and turning away from right worship (*CG* VIII.24, 349). Yet Apuleius, as Augustine reads him, appears to lament with Hermes what he foresees as the future undoing of this great "art" at the hands of the Christian religion. The temples of magnificent divinities will be replaced with the tombs of dead men – perhaps signifying shrines honoring the Christian martyrs (*CG* VIII.26, 356).[12] In reply, Augustine

---

[11] For a modern, political-theoretical parallel, see chapter 2 of Cooper's *Secular Powers*: "Modesty: Hobbes on How Mere Mortals Can Create a Mortal God" (2013, 44–69). Cooper argues that "Hobbes' claims for the power of human artifice, and the possibilities of human mastery, are more modest than scholars have realized" (Cooper, 2013, 67).

[12] For studies of Apuleius on Christianity and Christians, see Baldwin (1984), Hunink (2000), Schmidt (2003), and Warren Smith (2012). For Augustine's interpretation of Apuleius's critique of Christianity's displacement of paganism and its cult of the martyrs, through Apuleius's character Hermes the Egyptian, see especially *CG* VIII.26, 354–56. Augustine notes, in letter 138.19, written the year before he began writing *The City of God*, that Apuleius performed the duties of provincial priest (*sacerdos*), which function, translator and editor of Apuleius Christopher P. Jones observes, "implied a considerable degree of wealth and status," and reflected the high social and political rank of Apuleius's father and family (Apuleius, 2017, viii). Augustine, in this passage in letter 138, interprets Apuleius's performing of the civil religion's priestly function, together with other honor-seeking activities attributed to Apuleius, to comprise a sign of great political ambition on the part of the philosopher.

explains to pagan readers that Christians do not worship martyrs; rather, in honoring martyrs they praise God for his gifts to them of grace and courage. At their shrines, as in all churches, Christians offer worship to God alone (*CG* VIII.27, 356–58). As many pagan sages including Apuleius's character Egyptian Hermes observe, moreover, all or most pagan gods originally *were* human beings who after their deaths received divine honors from peoples. The pagan world, Augustine observes, was already filled with temples honoring dead human beings long before the coming of Christ (*CG* VIII.26, 354–56).

For humans to create gods in their own image and likeness, whether by opinions and myths regarding the passions and sins of the daemons, or by divinizing dead men, or by sculpting images for wayward spirits to inhabit if they will, for Augustine seems reflective of a form of hubris or *superbia*. Speaking of Apuleius's Hermes, Augustine quotes Paul's critique of those who

"knowing God, glorified him not as God ..., but became vain in their imaginations, professing themselves to be wise" (Romans 1:21ff.). ... Hermes, indeed, says many things concerning the Maker of this world which have the appearance of truth. I do not know how he has been brought so low ... as *to desire men to be always in subjection* to gods who, as he himself confesses, are made by men, and whose future abolition he laments: as if there could be anything more wretched than for a man to be in thrall to what he himself made. (VIII.23, 347; emphasis added)

Yet this human pride *cum* excessive humility may have a deeper, more troubling root than Augustine's strong critique in this chapter acknowledges: Perhaps it stems from the hopelessness of those who think they are "without God in the world" (Ephesians 2:12).[13] Perhaps it is in an effort to combat eschatological despair that humans so readily craft divinities for themselves, in a last spirited resistance to loneliness, insignificance, and death. If this is so, then despite Augustine's principled dissent from the philosophies that foment or condone the cult of such gods, their makers and worshippers may merit from Augustine the considerable comprehension and compassion he accords those who commit suicide to escape the cruelty of their fellow human beings (cf. *CG* I.17, 26–27). Augustine will treat this problem of human mortality, being, and nonbeing vis-à-vis pride and humility especially in books XIII and XIV, as we will consider in Chapter 6 of this study.

---

[13] See Benedict XVI's Augustinian reflections on Ephesians 2:12 in *Spe Salvi* (2007), §2.

BOOK IX: APULEIUS AND PLOTINUS

Book IX continues Augustine's dialogue with "[t]he Platonist Apuleius" and his work *De deo Socrates* (*CG* IX.1, 360).[14] As in book VIII, Augustine opens book IX by reminding his readers of the "excellence" of Platonic philosophy and the great achievements of its leading lights, "the most distinguished and noble of the philosophers" (*CG* IX.1, 359; cf. VIII.1, 312–13). Just as Augustine brought to light in book VIII the false, degrading humility fostered by certain Platonists' support for the worship of daemons, so in book IX he argues that even good daemons, if such exist, ought not to be worshipped, since they are not God, nor are they capable of mediating between God and men in a truly salvific manner. Their cult thus appears as another form of misguided humility that cannot exalt its practitioners. Its antidote is to be found not in the self-sufficiency of human reason – in the pride of philosophy – but via the powerful, virtuous humility lived and taught by a humble and most wise Mediator (*CG* IX.15, 378; IX.20, 384–85).

In pointing to Christ as the humble and true Mediator, near both the center and the end of this book, Augustine underscores an important argument made throughout *The City of God* and evoked early in book IX: that excellence and wisdom are rightly sought in order to share them with and to serve others. In this right love and use of high human goods, human beings can benefit from passions, especially *compassion*, rightly moderated and directed, and from the lowly human body (see *CG* IX.5, 365–66). We learn this lesson from looking aright at our own humanity, even philosophic humanity. We may grasp this truth of wisdom as common good especially, Augustine proposes, from looking at the action of God in Jesus Christ (*CG* IX.15, 377–79). Self-giving – even self-emptying for others – free and loving, leads to exaltation and fulfillment, while self-inflating – even on account of and through great knowledge – leads not to wisdom but to tyranny, slavery, and misery (*CG* I, preface, 3), and ultimately, as we will see in books XII and XIII, toward the void. To escape the pathos of pride, political and philosophic, humanity must look not only to what is highest in itself but also to the enlightenment and healing

---

[14] On Apuleius's Platonic theology, see Mortley (1972). The first word of Apuleius's *De Deo Socrates* is "Plato" (Apuleius, 2017, 346). Although he is now known chiefly for his literary genius, Apuleius seems to have been known in his own time and in Augustine's mainly as *"philosophus Platonicus"*: "Apuleius … talks of himself only as a philosopher in the 'school' of Plato, and all his extant works to different degrees reflect his allegiance to Platonism" (Apuleius, 2017, general introduction, viii–ix).

offered from another and infinitely higher source, who as Augustine's rhetorical dialectic repeatedly emphasizes, came humbly to humanity in its lowly flesh (*CG* IX.20, 384–85).[15]

As a prelude to arguing that the daemons described by Apuleius cannot be good and virtuous given their unruly, tempestuous passions, Augustine reviews for his readers some Platonic, Peripatetic, and Stoic teachings on the passions and their objects as experienced in a good and wise human soul. Despite the Stoic tendency to deny that most objects of disturbances of the passions are true goods, Augustine suggests that Stoic theory here differs only (or mainly) semantically from that of the schools of Plato and Aristotle. Even a wise man will experience fear in the face of death, for example, despite the fact that the threat to his bodily being does not bear directly on his soul's state. The real question is, will this fear over-power his tranquility of spirit or lead the philosopher to unjust desires or actions? If not, wisdom and virtue remain unscathed. And these are the chief goods of humankind, as all these philosophic schools agree.

What Augustine adds to these arguments is an enhanced emphasis on the other-directedness or sociability of true human virtue. Virtuous persons will be inclined to fear more for the possible losses of others than for their own. When a ship is dangerously tossed at sea, for exam-ple, they will weep more readily for the sorrow or loneliness of others than for their own. And they will be rightly roused by anger, especially when another human being is unjustly harmed and requires defense. Compassion is a critical root of human virtue, Augustine underscores once again. A philosopher slow or loath to experience this "disturbance" of soul has not yet come into the fullness of wisdom or virtue (*CG* IX.5, 365–66). Perhaps philosophic pride is blocking the way.[16]

Apuleius, as we have seen in his literary dialogue with Hermes the Egyptian in *Asclepius*, considered the ways in which human beings reflect God's image in their being and craftsmanship. By contrast, in a poignant passage in *De deo Socrates*, the African Platonist highlights the ways humans differ from divinities. Augustine recaps Apuleius's description of binaries or opposite traits in this regard. The gods are exalted, entirely immortal, and perfect in nature – blessed. Humans, by contrast, dwell on lowly earth, are mortal in body, and are subject to misery and want (*CG* IX.12, 373–74; cf.

---

[15] Dyson's translation reads, "Against this pride of the demons ... there stands the great vir-tue of God made manifest in Christ" (*CG* IX.20, 385). The *CAG* Latin emphasizes more specifically the "humility of God" and its "great virtue" or power, *dei humilitas quae in christo apparuit, quantam virtutem habeat*, which Dyson seems to omit in his rendition.

[16] On this subject, see Byers (2012b, 130–48); cf. also Ogle (2019, 38–39).

IX.8–11, 368–72). Apuleius's description of the pathos of human beings merits lengthy quotation in Augustine's *City of God*, and also here:

Men who dwell upon the earth ... rejoice in reason. They are gifted with speech, immortal in soul, mortal in members, weak and anxious in mind, brutish and obnoxious in body, dissimilar in their characters, alike in their errors, obstinate in their audacity, pertinacious in their hope. Their labor is vain, their fortune precarious. Each of them is mortal, even though their whole race is eternal, with each generation replaced by another. Their time flies swiftly away, but their wisdom is slow. Their death comes quickly, and their life is lamentation. (*CG* IX.8, 369, quoting from *De deo Socrates*)

Apuleius here articulates grounds for a theory of philosophic humility, a perspective with which Augustine can agree in part. The greatness and lowliness, joy and misery, mortality and immortality that together express human life as we know it reminds the human being that he or she is not God, that he or she is not his or her own source of life and fulfillment. Yet other aspects of the humility Apuleius seems to endorse here appear false, or at least flawed, to Augustine. Of special note is Apuleius's depreciation of the human body as "brutish and obnoxious" (human beings are *brutis et obnoxiis corporibus*, *CG* IX.8, 369). Augustine concurs that the soul is the more divine aspect of our nature, but he sees our bodies too as good and as reflecting the divine goodness (*CG* X.28–30, 433–39; XI.22–23, 476–80; XIV.3, 584–86). Also misleading for Augustine is the ascription by Apuleius and others of eternity to the human race as a species (see *CG* XII.10, 511–12; XII.14–15, 516–19).

Augustine seems to agree with Apuleius that an effective intermediary between God (or the gods) and humans must really be *in the middle* – not in the sense of hovering in a sort of limbo between heaven and earth, for if that were all, then the "mediator" could reach neither, but by sharing somehow in the being of both God (and, for Apuleius, also the gods) and humanity. The daemons of the Platonic cosmos seem good candidates to mediate, for according to Apuleius and others, they share immortality of body and soul with the gods, and they partake of unruly passions in common with humanity (see *De deo Socrates* §13, in Apuleius, 2017, 373).[17] Augustine's rhetorical dialectic, however, presses Apuleius about

---

[17] As Zhuoyue You observes (2021), Augustine's interpretation has a good basis in passages from *De deo Socrates*, yet seems to pass over or to miss the playful dimensions of the philosopher's discussion of *daemones*, as well as the chief aim of Apuleius's discourse in *De deo Socrates*. A full reading of this short work suggests that Apuleius intended it as a protreptic to philosophy and an exhortation to a philosophical life, as exemplified by Socrates and Plato. For an account of what Augustine's philosophy may itself have gleaned from Apuleius's *De deo Socrates* on the existence and nature of the *daemones*, see Byers (2012a, 184–86).

this apparent conclusion: If the daemons are not stable, trustworthy, or completely good – and on notable classical accounts seemingly never can become such – how can they present our good desires before the gods in any dependable manner? Would it not be better for us to seek out a mediator who shares permanently in divine blessedness (and so virtue and wisdom) and transitorily in human mortality, rather than the daemons who share divine immortality together with human vices and misery (*CG* IX.13, 374–76)?

In chapter 14, as Augustine continues his rhetorical dialectic, he raises a "great question," whether perfect happiness or "blessedness" is possible to mortals. He contrasts the understanding of those who, like himself, "take a humbler view" of human prospects for happiness here below (*quidam enim condicionem [hominis] humilius inspexerunt*), with that of others who consider that "the achievement of wisdom" can make humans truly happy in this mortal life. If this were so, Augustine argues, it would have been wiser for the philosophers to teach the people to turn to themselves for mediation rather than to direct them to daemons (*CG* IX.14, 376–77).

Apuleius himself, in Augustine's estimation, approximates a better answer concerning the possibility of humans' attainment of happiness when the Platonist speaks in *De deo Socrates* 3 of the highest happiness possible for philosophers in this life. "Regarding the one supreme God, the Creator of all things, Whom we call the true God," the only intellectual vision even the greatest philosopher can have of him is brief and occasional. "Apuleius also says that the knowledge of this God which wise men have, when by the power of their mind they have removed themselves as far as they can from the body, is like the briefest flicker of lightning illuminating the deepest darkness" (*CG* IX.16, 379–80; Apuleius, 2017, 353). Moreover, the philosophers so enlightened cannot communicate this experience to others due to the poverty of human speech (*CG* IX.16, 380–81; Apuleius, 2017, 353). As far as partial blessedness in this life is concerned, then, the Platonic philosopher can only hope for his own and other philosophers' happiness – humbly, to be sure, recognizing it as a divine gift, yet also one he hopes to merit by his own diligent effort to live by intellect and transcend his corporality.

Augustine alludes to philosophy itself as the way to happiness that the Platonists tried to follow, to fit their minds for divine illumination even in this life, paraphrasing a beautiful passage from Plotinus's *Enneads*: "We must fly, therefore, to our beloved fatherland, where dwells both our Father and all else. Where is the ship, then, and how are we to fly? We must become like God" (*CG* IX.17, 382; see Plotinus's *Enneads* I, 6, 8, and I, 2, 3).[18] God would be contaminated by contact with bodily beings, the great Platonists argue or at least imply, and so the body must be left behind on the way to God. To this Augustine wonders, are the sun's rays contaminated when they enlighten and heal our material world (cf. *CG* IX.16, 382)? How could true divinity suffer a loss of dignity by contact with the human body? Moreover, how could the Creator be incapable of contact with the creation that depends on him for existence? Augustine's conclusion is that to posit, as the Platonists do, the separation of the soul and its life from the body, as an essential prerequisite to vision of and union with God, is not persuasive even on purely philosophic grounds.[19]

Augustine's rhetorical dialectic now pleads once again with philosophic readers, to consider that God incarnate in Christ Jesus, made mortal for a time and now dwelling with a glorified, perfected corporality united to his human soul, and with body and soul united to his divinity, offers humanity a much better mediator than any daemon. "We need a Mediator Who is united with us in our lowest estate by bodily mortality, yet Who, by virtue of the immortal righteousness of His spirit, always remains on high. ... Such a one can afford us aid which is truly divine in cleansing and redeeming us" (*CG* IX.17, 382). Only faith can convince humans that this marvel of God's magnanimous condescension and healing love is real. Reason may yet open the way to this realization, however, by considering that there is no impossibility or indignity – though there is certainly a great, mysterious humility – involved in the Incarnation of God in his Word. Through the Incarnation, the divine word that could not be communicated to the human mind becomes visible, touchable, and hearable. Through his Resurrection, the fear of Christ's bodily mortality and our own can be overcome, and the true way to the Father and lasting blessedness embarked upon (*CG* IX.17, 382–83). But, notes

---

[18] On "The Metaphysical Monotheism of Plotinus," see Kenney (1991, 91–149). Kenney considers both Plotinus and Augustine as significant "earlier figures in philosophic theology" whose works merit consideration in philosophy today (Kenney, 1991, xv). On contemplation in classical-Platonic and Christian monotheism, see Kenney (2013). On Plotinus and his philosophy, see also Rist (1967).

[19] Howard Rachlin (2014), focusing on Augustine's early dialogue *On Free Choice of the Will*, argues that "Saint Augustine's main philosophical problem was the reconciliation of Plato's intellectual elitism with the inclusiveness of Christianity" (25). Rachlin's observation here dovetails with this chapter's argument, yet relative to *The City of God* at least, Rachlin seems to overemphasize the role of introspection and "The Division of Mind and Body," as Rachlin's chapter is titled, in describing this reconciliation as effected in Augustine's thought.

Augustine, "this is not the place to speak as fully as I could" of the true and humble Mediator (*CG* IX.17, 383); that will come soon, in book X of *The City of God*.

In the final chapters of book IX, Augustine follows his usual method of bringing his arguments full circle, highlighting themes from the beginning of the book enriched with insights gained in the interim. Here the tropes his rhetorical dialectic reclaims and elaborates are two: the special excellence of virtuous orderings of the passions, mind, and will when they seek the good of others (cf. *CG* IX.4–5, 361–66), and virtuous human nature's great dignity, which any true and virtuous form of humility must acknowledge and support.

In chapter 20, Augustine compares the knowledge of the false mediators, the *daemones*, noting that their very name in Greek relates to knowledge, with that of the true Mediator. The chief difference resides in charity, in love of God, and so of all others, impelling one to procure the good of others, as well as one's own. Knowledge directed by charity toward what is perfectly good, desiring it to be shared by each and all of one's fellows, "'builds up,'" as St. Paul writes. By contrast, knowledge without charity "'puffs up'" (*CG* IX.20, 385, quoting 1 Corinthians 8:1). Augustine offers his readers a preview of the metaphysical study of pride and humility that is to come in books XI–XIV, with this gloss: "[K]nowledge is without profit if it lacks charity. Without charity, it puffs up: that is, it lifts us up with *a pride which is only an inflated emptiness*" (*CG* IX.20, 385; emphasis added). To combat this pride and free those bound by its tyranny, the divine Word takes lowly human flesh, humbling himself in visible form, and so revealing to humans "the humility of God, which has such great power" (*CG* IX.20, my translation; cf. note 115). Pride and loveless knowledge, daemonic as well as human, shackle and tyrannize, while humility and loving knowledge open a path toward wisdom and freedom. Humility and charity alone have the power truly to heal and liberate humanity (see *CG* IX.21, 385–86).

This is why, Augustine indicates, Jesus succeeds where the daemons and even the greatest philosophers have failed, because "it is through humility that the path of godliness (*viam pietatis*) ascends on high" (*CG* II.7, 58; cf. I, preface, 3). Augustine expresses this connection beautifully in another work: "There is no more exalted road than the way of charity, and no one travels it except the humble" (*Ennarationes in psalmos* 141.7).[20]

---

[20] *nihil excelsius uia caritatis, et non in illa ambulant nisi humiles.*

BOOK X: PLOTINUS AND PORPHYRY

Book X is pivotal to and a pinnacle of Augustine's rhetorical dialectic in *The City of God*, forming the culmination and conclusion of Augustine's dialogue in books VIII–X with some of the great Platonists on the subject of natural theology. Book X is pivotal also as the culmination and conclusion of what we might term the second part (books VI–X) of the first part (books I–X) of *The City of God*, in which Augustine debates with philosophers from Varro and Seneca onwards about the reasonableness of polytheistic worship for happiness after death. Book X is the summit too of the entire first half of Augustine's great work, books I–X, in its defense of God's city and virtuous humility against a myriad of historical, mythical, civic, and philosophic opponents. We may therefore expect Augustine's defense speech on behalf of lowly humility to reach a new height with the rhetorical dialectic of book X.

Recall that Augustine observed at this long work's outset how hard it is to convince the proud of the excellence of humility (*CG* I, preface, 3). If the great harm pride can cause in human affairs is most apparent in politics and history, it may be much less obvious in philosophy, especially truly brilliant philosophy. Philosophic achievement in the classical tradition typically lessens social envy for lesser goods such as wealth and prestige and eschews violent means to its own eminence. It enhances self-sufficiency and counsels and habituates its practitioners to civic and moral moderation. Philosophic discoveries, moreover, are far more excellent achievements than forceful political dominance or mastery. As superior to the mere opinions held by others, philosophic truths seem in justice to afford those possessing them a greater claim to exaltation or elation. What could be so bad about philosophic pride?

Augustine in book X will both vindicate and refute this line of argument, considered under different aspects and in diverse circumstances. He will refute it by showing that, in elevating the intellect over the body so as to denigrate or seek to escape corporality, Platonic philosophy, perhaps especially as seen in Porphyry's writings, errs and blocks the path toward its own *telos*. Such philosophy limits the divinity's power unreasonably, even as it elevates philosophic minds excessively in the search for happiness, either on account of philosophers' own sense of superiority, or by catering to the "vain" opinions of the many (*CG* X.1, 390; cf. IV.3, 147; XII.1, 498; XIV.9, 602). In counseling or permitting the masses of human beings to perform polytheistic sacrifices, Platonic philosophy too quickly despairs of their prospects for blessedness, especially after the coming of Jesus and the spread of his Gospel.

In book X, readers encounter with the author of *The City of God* his most challenging interlocutors in the realm of philosophy about divinity, those whose wisdom makes his "great and arduous" task most daunting on a theoretical level. Like Augustine, the Platonists lift up the human soul, but far more than Augustine they lower the body and its passions. Like Augustine, they understand blessedness as union with God, a gift of God, and like him they seek a "mediator" and a "universal way" to this blessedness. Yet they cannot accept the humility or the corporeal humanity of that way, Augustine will argue in this crucial segment of *The City of God*.

Augustine's rhetorical dialectic in book X is often read as a critique of certain aspects of, or conclusions prominent in, the tradition of Platonic philosophy to his day, despite Augustine's patent admiration of and indebtedness to Platonic thought.[21] So, for instance, Robert Russell emphasizes the "major turning-point" comprised by book VIII (and continued in books IX and X) with its critical appraisal of Platonic philosophy in Augustine's defense speech for the heavenly city (Russell, 1995, 403; quoting J. H. S. Burleigh, 1949, 81). Russell attributes the emphasis on refutation in these books to Augustine's aims as an apologist, upon whom "it was incumbent to show ..., not where Platonism had *succeeded*, but where it had *failed*" (Russell, 1995, 410; emphasis in original).

The author of *The City of God* certainly takes issue with apparent manifestations of philosophic pride, especially in his debate with Porphyry and his followers and in his defense of the lowly human body. In book X, however, Augustine also stresses repeatedly the great Platonic achievements in ethics, logic, and metaphysics, and indicates ways in which these give rise to true, if imperfect, forms of philosophic humility: the humility of enquirers into truth, willing on occasion even to lower themselves before others in order to lead them to truth (*CG* X.11, 407–10) and to accept that true happiness is only possible as a gift of the One (*CG* X.29, 435–36). Along these lines, Peter Brown observes that "[i]n the hands of Augustine, [Porphyry, 'the bug-bear of the average Christian'] achieves heroic stature ...; and so the demolition of paganism can close with the generous evocation of a magnificent failure" (2000, 306).[22] In passages

---

[21] On Augustine's Platonism, see Byers (2013), Cary (2000), Crouse (2000), and Dodaro (1995).

[22] Brown's commentary continues, "Augustine's treatment of the Platonists throughout *The City of God*, shows the extent to which a part of the pagan past was still alive in Augustine, stimulating his finest thought, and challenging him to a continuous inner dialogue that would last up to his death" (2000, 306).

praising the eminent achievements of Platonic philosophy, culminating in the conclusion of book X, moreover, Augustine himself sounds humbler in his appraisal of the philosophers' *grandeur* and their *misère*. In the end, he seems full of hope for them, perhaps even for Porphyry the great philosophic-political opponent of Christianity, just as he was for the plain popular pagans, who, groping for a god or goddess able to give felicity to mortals, showed themselves closer to finding felicity than even they might have known (*CG* IV.25, 173–74). In this light, Platonic philosophy was not *essentially* a failure, even a "magnificent" one, as it is understood and appraised in Augustine's rhetorical-dialectical inquiry.

Humility and Religious Worship: Chapters 1–10

Augustine's rhetorical dialectic in book X begins by continuing the trope of true greatness and its surprising link with true or virtuous humility. In the opening chapters of this book, Augustine considers right worship and sacrifice, rooted in virtuous *humilitas* capable of raising its practitioners to great heights.[23] Such worship cleanses and elevates and even divinizes, while worship that is wrongly directed in terms of its object and/or mode denigrates and demoralizes. True worship unites elites and commoners, learned and unlearned in genuine community, whereas false or wrongly directed worship divides, humiliates, and antagonizes. As Gerard O'Daly observes on this book of *The City of God*, "the themes of renovation of the heart, of mercy, and of worship are powerfully linked" (1999a, 124).

Against the forms of humility correlating with false worship, Augustine enlists the support of the philosopher Plotinus: "This great Platonist therefore says that the rational ... [or] intellectual soul has no nature superior to it except God, Who made the world, and by Whom the soul itself was made" (*CG* X.2, 393). Augustine asks then whether it makes sense to worship gods who did not make human beings and cannot constitute happiness for them, when as no less an authority than Plotinus concurs, the intellectual soul of humans has no superior in the order of nature other than God the Creator and *telos* of souls? Where is the justice and goodness in this sort of humility? And yet, as Augustine notes, many Platonists advise or forebear the popular worship of good gods – perhaps not daemons, but not the one God either. "Even these

---

[23] For reflections on worship, sacrifice, mercy, and their connection to social, economic, and political life in Augustine's thought, see Menchaca-Bagnulo (2019), Nunziato (2020), and O'Daly (1999a, 123–24).

philosophers, however – whether as a concession to the vanity and error of the people, or, as the apostle says, 'becoming vain in their imaginations' – have supposed or allowed others to suppose that many gods are to be worshipped" (*CG* X.1, 390, quoting Romans 1:21).

Worship involving sacrifice "due to divinity, or … more expressly, to the Deity" alone, is called *latreia* in Greek and *servitus* in Latin. It is chiefly with this absolute, radical worship, rather than honor or ordinary piety, that Augustine deals in book X. Augustine argues that, strictly speaking, it is improper to call this worship cult (*cultus*) because "we say that we 'cultivate' not only *those things to which we subject ourselves in religious humility* but also certain things which are *subject to ourselves* [e.g., fields and crops]" (*CG* X.1, 391; emphasis added). Anything to which humanity is by nature equal or higher is not a right object of our humility, complete devotion, or worship. To worship such things is beneath us in truth, while to worship the true God is right by nature and opens us to the grace by which He elevates, even divinizes, our nature via participation in God's own existence and life. If more powerful beings, whether we call them gods or angels, instruct humans to worship rightly, they will direct that *latreia/servitus* be given to God alone, not to themselves. Angelic beings too must offer "the sacrifice of humility and praise" to the deity, loving humans as their fellow citizens and leading them to true good and blessedness (*CG* X.3, 395). "If any immortal power … no matter how great the virtue with which it is endowed, loves us as itself, it must desire that we find our blessedness by submitting ourselves to Him, in submission to Whom it finds its own blessedness" (*CG* X.3, 396).

For their part, human beings should avoid addressing each other with words of reverence or praise properly pertaining to divine worship, though Augustine knows that this is too often the common practice. "Many terms belonging to divine worship," Augustine observes, "are, indeed, wrongly used in showing honor to human beings, whether out of an excessive humility (*humilitate nimia*) or because of the pestilential practice of flattery" (*CG* X.4, 396). What befits humanity is humility *before God* – not before the idol, the angel, the philosopher, or the prince. Right religious humility is shown by seeking to walk with God in true repentance of heart, justice, and mercy (cf. Micah 6:6–8, quoted in *CG* X.5, 398). Here, in the prophet's summons to journey with God, Augustine gestures again to what he has argued, that the Platonists err when they contend God, or even the lesser gods, cannot associate directly with human beings. This is another mistaken, misleading humility, perhaps masking in some cases a form of pride. Jewish and Christian humility, enlightened by revelation, acknowledges that God's greatness can bridge the gulf between infinity and immortality on the one hand, and finitude and mortality on the other. It recognizes that human weakness is not so great that it could lessen God's strength or grandeur, and conversely that God's providential agency is not in competition with human activity or responsibility.

A related error common to Platonic philosophers, especially prominent in Porphyry's philosophy and its wake, one which will take center stage before the end of book X, is in Augustine's view their understanding of felicity as obtained through abstracting from the body, fleeing from corporality to the greatest extent possible, even in this life.[24] Only thus, the great Platonists maintained, is the soul set free for wisdom and made fit to receive rays of divine light, here and especially hereafter. The true worship and imitation of God by the philosopher entail striving to become, to the greatest extent possible, immaterial as is the deity, in the quest to participate more fully in the being, light, and goodness of that deity. Against this view, Augustine argues that the body has a necessary role in our humanity, and so also plays its part in virtuous humility, right worship, and complete happiness. As he wrote in book V, God created human beings as "rational animal[s] composed of soul and body" (*CG* V.11, 206).[25] The body assists and serves the soul, and so when "used rightly and with reference to God," it is taken up into the "reasonable service" (*rationabile obsequium*; quoting Romans 12:1) offered to God by the whole human person and community (*CG* X.6, 399). For human beings, reasonable spiritual worship must go hand in hand with physical forms of honoring God. This in turn, for Augustine, highlights the importance of mercy in genuine worship. If both our soul and our body need the merciful healing of God, perfected through Christ's self-sacrifice on the cross, then humans' reverent imitation of and participation in God's goodness require extending a compassionate heart and hand to others in every way possible (cf. *CG* IX.5, 365–66; cf. Byers, 2012b, and Menchaca-Bagnulo, 2019). In this way, human beings may make of their

---

[24] See Chase (2004) and TeSelle (1974, 134–41). On the body-soul relationship in Plotinus's Platonism and its relationship to Porphyry's views, see Rist (1996, 391–93).

[25] On this point, see Byers (2012a, 176–80). Byers concludes this section, "Augustine the Aristotelian? Soul and Body," by observing, "Thus, while Augustine's account is not identical to Aristotle's, it is more similar to it than it is to Platonic and Cartesian dualism" (179). Byers also explores Plotinus's impact on Augustine's understanding, in Plotinus's incorporating Aristotelian thought into his Platonism and in his own statements concerning body and soul in human nature.

very existence and activity a sacrifice or holy service to God, personally and in fellowship with one another, as members of "the whole of the redeemed City" united to Christ (*CG* X.6, 400).

The body enters more powerfully still into Augustine's theology of virtue and humility, in his appropriation of the scriptural teaching that the people of God together comprise Christ's body. Christ "the great High Priest" gave himself as "a universal sacrifice ... offer[ing] even Himself for us in the form of a servant, so that we might be the body of so great a Head."[26] Augustine offers support from St. Paul for this conclusion, in this passage which constitutes a call to humility in humans' social relations: "'I say ... to every man that is among you, not to think of himself more highly than he ought to think. ... [S]o we, being many, are one body in Christ, and every one members of one another, having gifts differing according to the grace that is given to us'" (Romans 12:3–6; *CG* X.6, 400).[27] Right humility recognizes that God is the principal agent of our justification and divinization, though our free correspondence is also required.[28] True religious humility further understands that we are brought to righteousness and salvation, not as elite individuals, whether philosophers or kings, but as members of a single body who need one another, the greatest as much so as the least. Significantly, this body is neither in a strict sense natural or conventional for humans. It is neither "the king's body" of the renaissance/early modern European polity, nor the humanly constructed, artificial body of Hobbes's commonwealth. The whole body of Christ the Redeemer – *Christus totus*, the whole Christ, as Augustine describes the church united to Christ its head – exists due to divine grace and the nature of Christ as the incarnate word – divine and human. As such, the body of which each of us is called to be a humble member, dependent on Christ the Head and on the other members as well, transcends the political communities of this world. It can unite humans on a universal level and in a more holistic way than even the cosmopolis of the philosophers could achieve, while preserving the personality of each member of this body.

---

[26] In continuation, referring to what would become known as the Mass (the Eucharist or Divine Liturgy), Augustine observes that Christ's one sacrifice offered on the cross is also in its essence "the sacrifice of Christians ... and also, as the faithful know, the sacrifice which the Church continually celebrates in the sacrament of the altar" (*CG* X.6, 400; cf. *CG* X.20, 422).

[27] For a related reflection on human interdependency in the divine plan, see Catherine of Siena (1980, 37–38).

[28] As Augustine writes in a sermon, "God who created you without you, will not save you without you" (*Sermo* 169, 13; PL 38, 923).

Augustine's rhetorical dialectic next contrasts just humility and right worship with the pagan practice of seeking purification through theurgy: "[g]ood magic, for Porphyry ... closely linked with demonology" (O'Daly, 1999a, 124; see also Rist, 1994, 16). In Augustine's view, theurgy caters to the hubris of unsavory daemonic powers, if indeed it responds to anything real; and so it unjustly humiliates its practitioners. Moreover, according to pagan teaching, even a soul sincerely seeking cleansing through theurgic practices can be foiled by the stronger sacrifices of an evildoer. Justice, or at least the purification of the lower parts of the soul by theurgy, is indeed the "advantage of the stronger" in this view, *not* the common advantage or what is truly right according to reason.[29] Given the caprices of the spirits invoked in theurgy, one never knows just who the stronger one will be at any given time (see *CG* X.9, 405–X.10, 406). By contrast, truly good 'divinities,' called angels by Jews and Christians, "do not desire us to sacrifice to themselves, but to Him Whose sacrifice they know themselves to be in common with us" (*CG* X.7, 401). Augustine blames Porphyry in particular for endorsing theurgy's capability of giving "a certain kind" of cleansing to the soul, even while rightly "deny[ing] that this art can furnish anyone with a means of returning to God" (*CG* X.9, 404). Why Augustine thinks Porphyry selectively endorsed the theurgic practices that the philosopher also blamed will become clearer later, at the climax of book X.

Pride, Humility, and Right Pedagogy: Chapters 11–15

Augustine's defense of *humilitas* against *superbia* next takes up the theme of pedagogy – philosophical, political, and divine. This segment of his rhetorical dialectic begins from another writing of Porphyry, one in which Augustine thinks the philosopher reveals his greater wisdom and virtue regarding the art of theurgy, modeling a humble, effective approach that harkens back to Socrates's pedagogical practices (cf. *CG* VIII.3, 314–16). Augustine argues that, in writing to Anebo, a pagan Egyptian priest and sage, Porphyry "exposes and overturns these sacrilegious arts" by "acting the part of an enquirer seeking guidance" (*CG*

---

[29] Cf. Thrasymachus's definition of justice in book I of Plato's *Republic* (338c); cf. *Politics* III, 1279a15–21 and 1282b15–17, on justice as the political good and common advantage.

X.11, 407).[30] Porphyry did not here "proudly assume the authority of a teacher. ... Rather, in order to direct the Egyptian's mind to these things ... he assumed *the character of an enquirer and the humility of one desiring to learn*" (*quasi quaerentis et discere cupientis humilitate*) (*CG* X.11, 410; emphasis added).

One might raise the question here of whether such ironic, theatrical philosophic humility can be right and virtuous humility. Augustine seems to suggest that, while this humble approach cannot of itself comprise the full or highest form of the virtue he lauds, it does approach and reflect aspects of it. The ability to place oneself humbly before another, within the fundamental equality of the human condition, and seek his or her input, corresponds to the truth that humans are not individually self-sufficient for wisdom or goodness. Insofar as one reveals something of what one thinks one knows in the content of one's inquiry, only in a less strident or off-putting manner, perhaps simply in the form of a question, with the goal of leading one's interlocutor to a fuller grasp of truth, one cannot be said to lie or mislead. Rather, one seeks to draw in the interlocutor as an equal and perhaps a potential superior, one who can instruct as well as be instructed, though he or she may not now realize his or her neediness regarding wisdom; and thereby to prompt him or her to reconsider even long-held opinions, judgments, and practices. If Augustine is correct, well-intentioned and justly practiced Socratic irony constitutes an expression or form of virtuous humility (cf. *CG* VIII.3).

Augustine reads Porphyry's dialogue with Anebo as concluding that the "gods" to whom theurgic rituals are offered "have nothing of value or profit to say on the subject of blessedness. They cannot, therefore, be either gods or good demons. Either they are that spirit who is called the Tempter, or merely human inventions" (*CG* X.11, 410). The problem with the latter conclusion, as Augustine reasons, is that many marvels really do seem effected by these spirits through "theurgic arts" (*CG* X.12, 410), to the point where it is difficult to deny a real power behind them.

---

[30] Augustine indicates late in the chapter that Porphyry's questions to Anebo may have been sincere and expressions of ignorance, yet even if so, they prompt a discussion revealing the truth and so are praiseworthy. Still, given that this section of *The City of God* begins and ends with a description of Apuleius as "assum[ing]" or "act[ing] the part of an enquirer," and that Augustine writes that this interpretation involves "taking a better view of the philosopher" (*CG* X.11, 407, 409–10), this particular possibility seems to hold special significance in Augustine's dialogue with Platonic philosophy. Note also the parallel of this discussion with Augustine's earlier commentary on the Platonist Apuleius's literary dialogue with "the Egyptian Hermes" (*CG* VIII.22–26, 344–56), discussed earlier in this chapter, and the importance Augustine attributes to these philosophic-religious-cultural conversations.

Augustine, therefore, turns next to the subject of apparent miracles, on account of reports of which many turn to the occult and magical. Given the proliferation of palm-reading and similar "services" in our own times, Augustine's critique of Porphyry concerning theurgy may be more relevant to contemporary concerns than we might at first think.

The Platonic philosophers with whom Augustine dialogues deny that God or the good "gods" created under him work miracles in the human realm, seemingly for the same reasons they deny that God or the gods have direct dealings with humans. These judgments leave those human beings hoping for miracles at the mercy of unscrupulous human beings and daemons alike. Augustine begins by noting that the philosophers who deny that the deity works miracles, "believe that He made the world. ... [T]he wonders of the visible order of nature are held in low regard because they are always before us, yet, when we view them wisely, we see that they are greater than the least familiar and rarest of miracles. For man himself is a greater miracle than any miracle performed by man" (*CG* X.12, 411). Just as Augustine earlier suggested in dialogue with Cicero that the ways of justice and goodness may often be hidden in lowly persons and realities, where the glory-seeking statesmen or scholar would not deign to glance (cf. *CG* V.13–14, 213–14; discussed in Chapter 2), so he now admonishes the wise persons who fail to realize the miraculous character of finite existence, of all creation and nature, even the little, the lowly, and the commonplace among creatures. In support of this vision, Augustine can paraphrase a beautiful teaching of "the Platonist philosopher Plotinus" on providence, as reaching down to (though not directly, we may presume) or drawing up the beauty of even the smallest flower (*CG* X.14, 413). Augustine reads Plotinus here as close to Christ, who praises the beauty of wild lilies as greater than the splendor of King Solomon, and recalls that this beauty is given to the flowers of the field and to us who behold them by the Father himself (*CG* X.14, 413; cf. *Enneads* 3.2.13; Matthew 6:28, ff.).[31] Seek not the "miracles" of the theurgists, Augustine urges; rather, in humility, recall and recapture the miracles of yourself, our fellows, and your world – true wonders which

---

[31] In *CG* X.17, 419, Augustine reminds readers of this important argument:

The philosophers, and the Platonists especially, are more justly to be congratulated on their wisdom than other men, because, as I remarked a little while ago, they have taught that even lowly and terrestrial things are governed by divine providence. They infer this from the testimony of the innumerable kinds of beauty which are to be seen not only in the bodies of animals, but in plants and grasses also.

by nature are accessible to all at no material or moral cost. In this portion of book X, Augustine foreshadows for his readers the detailed account of miracles – ancient and contemporary – that he will offer in book XXI, and especially in book XXII, and the call to philosophic and religious wonder that this defense of the miraculous contains.

From reflection on God's action in nature, Augustine's rhetorical dialectic moves on to consider God's action in history. The divine presence and intervention in human affairs are attested to in scripture and sacred tradition; to acknowledge this divine activity, Augustine argues, is not contrary to reason. As a part of this discussion, and with special relevance for politics, Augustine contrasts the divine pedagogy of God in giving the law to Moses on Mount Sinai with the purportedly divine origin of the legal code Lycurgus laid down for the Spartans. The former did not cater to the pride of an elite leader or ruling clique, causing the people to cower in fear before a law whose true origins were kept secret from them. Augustine observes, "the people of Israel did not believe in Moses in the way that the Spartans believed in Lycurgus," who claimed private illumination and legislation from the gods. Rather, God gave the Sinai legislation, which directed the people to true worship, through angels to Moses in the accompaniment of miraculous prodigies of nature, visible to all the people.[32] "[I]t was fitting, therefore," writes Augustine, "that the Law of God should be given not to one man, or to a few wise men, but to a whole nation and a great people." Then "marvelous signs and portents appeared before the sight of the people ... as creation served its Creator in giving that same Law" (*CG* X.13, 412). Divine miracles continued to educate the people of God throughout history, recalling for them both their great dignity and the root of true humility in their closeness to and dependence upon God (*CG* X.14, 412–13). Together with quotidian and philosophic consideration of the flowers of the field, the experience and memory of miracles in history teach humanity a just humility and right worship of God, "that they have need of Him by Whom they were created, both for their existence and their well-being" (*CG* X.15, 414).

Reason, Nature, Mediation, and Mercy: Chapters 16–22

In the next, and central, segment of book X, Augustine brings his rhetorical dialectic back around to the question of what is right for human beings, according to their shared human nature and the light of human

---

[32] Cf. Seneca's observation that the Israelites, unlike most Romans, understood the origins and rationale of their religious law (*CG* VI.11, 264).

reason. Augustine argues that the vision of God is the only good capable of making a human being truly blessed and fulfilled, and that human reason is by nature capable of recognizing this. He refers once more to the wisdom of Plotinus, paraphrasing the *Enneads* in which the "great Platonist" observes that the "vision of God is ... of such great beauty, and is most worthy of a love so great ... that, without it, even he who enjoys all other good things in abundance is wholly unhappy" (*CG* X.16, 414–15). Which of the gods or angels, then, should be believed, Augustine inquires, returning to a now-familiar trope, those who humbly direct worship to God who alone can fulfill the hopes of angels and human beings alike, or those who desire humans to worship them with divine honors? Significantly, Augustine does not appeal to revelation here, but rather to nature and reason. "Let the Platonists answer; let philosophers in general answer; ... let all human beings answer, if there still endures in them any part of that natural perception which they possess as rational creatures" (*CG* X.16, 415; cf. *CG* II.25, 91). Even if lesser spirits, lusting for worship, were to perform miracles, while those gods or angels who lead us to worship God did not, we still should follow "*the reason of the mind*" [*ratione mentis*], and trust the counsels only of those "who proclaim not their own pride" (*CG* X.16, 415; emphasis added). Note also Augustine's preceding point: If no gods or angels, good or malicious, performed wondrous signs to testify to the truth of their messages, but simply gave humans precepts concerning worship, which should be believed, those directing sacrifices to be offered to themselves, or solely to "the one God"? Augustine surmises that "piety itself would be enough to discern which of these commandments comes from the stronghold of pride, and which from true religion" (*CG* X.16, 415).

Augustine continues on to enquire of his readers: Since great "wonders" are to be seen "from time to time [occurring] for hidden reasons having to do with the nature of this world," why should one hold that the author of that nature could not cause wonders to occur outside the ordinary workings of nature (*CG* X.16, 416; cf. X.17, 417–19)? What good reason is there not to be open in principle to the miracles recorded in scripture as wrought by the one true God (*CG* X.18, 420), especially when Platonists agree with Jews and Christians that "a divine nature exists and concerns itself with human affairs" (*CG* VIII.1, 312; cf. X.17, 419)?[33]

---

[33] Augustine will elaborate on this argument in much greater detail in books XX and XXI, near the culmination of his *City of God*, to be discussed in Chapter 8 of this book.

Throughout this segment of *The City of God*, Augustine's rhetorical dialectic stresses, repeatedly and with urgency, that nature itself in no way separates humanity from God. God is by nature far too great, and human nature itself is too good and too dependent upon participation in God for its being, for nature to divide them. What separates humanity from God is only human sin (*CG* X.22, 424), which culminates in the unjust arrogation of divine honors to mere creatures, whether angelic or human. The political implications of this argument are considerable, for if Augustine is correct, with prideful usurpation of God's exaltedness come deception and unjust domination (*CG* X.19, 420–22) and the violent compulsion and persecution of those unwilling to cooperate in iniquity (*CG* X.21, 422–24). The usurpation and perversion entailed in the denial of God's rightful place through proud lies and tyranny are resisted by the holy angels and just human beings, who likewise refuse to receive worship even when it is offered them by others (*CG* X.19, 420–22).[34] Ultimately, Augustine observes, sin is overcome only by the perfect (and indeed, far greater) antithesis of satanic pride: "the man Jesus Christ" (*CG* X.20, 422; cf. 1 Tim. 2:5). In a passage evoked by Augustine (*CG* X.20, 422), the apostle Paul describes Jesus's tremendous, redemptive humility thusly: "Though he was in the form of God, [he] did not count equality with God a thing to be grasped, but emptied himself, taking the form of a servant, being born in the likeness of men. And being found in human form he humbled himself, becoming obedient unto death. ... Therefore God has highly exalted him" (Philippians 2:5–9).

"Hence," concludes Augustine, "the true Mediator, the man Christ Jesus, became the Mediator between God and man *by taking the form of a servant*" (*CG* X.20, 422; emphasis added). The work of our justification itself constitutes a work of humble, "divine compassion" and "great mercy," through which "we are guided by faith in this life and, after this life, we shall be led onwards by it towards the greatest fullness of perfection by the Vision of immutable truth," which the greatest philosophers also identified as the human *telos* and sought with all their strength (*CG* X.22, 424; cf. X.2, 393–94; X.5–6, 396–400; X.16, 414–17).

---

[34] "[T]he holy angels have in this respect been imitated by holy men of God. For Paul and Barnabas were thought to be gods when they performed a miracle of healing in Lycaonia, and the Lycaonians wished to sacrifice victims to them; but they in humble piety (*humili pietate remouentes*) declined such an honor and preached to them the God in whom they should believe" (*CG* X.19, 421).

Philosophic Pride against Love of Wisdom: Chapters 24–29

Porphyry of Tyre, the great Platonist historically nearest Augustine, takes center stage in the next segment of book X, the climax of Augustine's debate with the Platonists on natural theology. What is most striking in this section is the vigor of Augustine's critical rhetoric regarding what he presents as Porphyry's vicious pride (*superbia*) in his philosophic way of life and subsequent social and civic status, coupled with the gentle and conciliatory – one is tempted to say, humble – tone of Augustine's concluding reflections on Porphyry and his legacy. While Augustine's critique of Porphyry and thus of philosophic pride has been justly stressed in scholarly commentary, the olive branch Augustine extends to his opponent, a writer of tracts against Christianity and counselor of nontolerance of the new religion in Rome's empire, has received less notice and seems no less significant. This portion in *The City of God* may lend support to scholarly hypotheses that Porphyry's philosophical works were personally and positively impactful for Augustine on the eve of his conversion to Christianity; that they may have paradoxically (given their anti-Christian aspect) assisted Augustine to overcome his previous philosophical materialism (see Beatrice, 1989, and J. O'Meara, 1959).[35] Augustine's humble, hopeful stance at the conclusion of book X also underscores his effort throughout *The City of God* to mediate between "elite" philosophic perspectives and common, civic, and religious thought and sentiment. In this regard, he has hope to offer our contemporary age as well, whose rifts between elites and "ordinary" persons seem to be widening. As Augustine clarifies in chapter 29, his dialogue's primary addressee in these passages is not Porphyry himself, long deceased, but rather Augustine's philosophic contemporaries (as well as philosophers of future times, perhaps) who are influenced by Porphyry against acknowledging Christ, the humble Mediator (see *CG* X.29, 436–37).

Augustine's argument in chapters 23–29 of book X revolves around the two signs of *superbia* that he finds present in Porphyry's teachings: the philosophic rejection of the "lowly" body – and therefore also of Christ as Mediator – and an unjust elitism endorsing or permitting theurgic rites of purification to the nonphilosophic majority of mankind,

---

[35] Alternatively, in Milan it may have been texts from Plotinus's *Enneads* that Augustine encountered so powerfully, edited first by Porphyry and translated into Latin by Victorinus. See Rist (1996, 404–9) and Rist (1994, 16–17, 19).

when Porphyry knew such rites to be useless. Harking back to his preface to *The City of God*, Augustine implies here that this sort of philosophic pride may perhaps be the hardest to heal in humility's name (*CG*
X.29, 436; cf. I, preface, 3). This is so precisely because Platonists like
Porphyry *are* so much closer to the truth about humanity, happiness,
and the path leading to blessedness than are the proud tyrants of politics, and so seem to have stronger grounding for their sense of superiority over others.

We have seen how Augustine's treatment of political pride in *The City
of God* I–III stresses the close connection of vicious pride (*superbia*) to
the disparagement of women, the rejection in word, deed, and law of
their full humanity and just dignity. *The City of God*'s author now makes
a parallel point, with reference to Porphyry's philosophic rejection of
Jesus as the Mediator between humanity and God.

You say, indeed, that ignorance and ... vices ... cannot be cleansed by any mysteries, but only by *patrikos nous*, that is, the mind or intellect of the Father. ...
But you do not believe that this mind is Christ; for you despise Him because of
the body that He received from a woman, and because of the shame of the Cross.
Your exalted wisdom rejects such lowly and abject things, and looks to higher
regions. (*CG* X.28, 434)[36]

This last sentence in turn recalls another critical theme introduced earlier in *The City of God* by Augustine, in dialogue with Cicero, concerning
things that are right and good yet lowly. They, therefore, are easily over-
looked or despised, more readily grasped and appreciated by the humble
than by the proud (*CG* V.13–14, 213–14). The Platonist Porphyry rightly
judges the soul to be higher than the flesh. He nonetheless prescinds too
quickly from the truth concerning the unity of body and soul in our common humanity, and the potential for human goodness and true worship
in and through the body.

Porphyry held [Christ] in contempt because of the flesh He took in order to
become a sacrifice for our cleansing. It was because of his pride that Porphyry
did not understand this great mystery: the pride which our true and gracious
Redeemer brought low by His own humility. ... Thus, the good and true Mediator showed that it is sin which is evil, and not the substance or nature of flesh. ...

---

[36] For a reading of Porphyry's quest for a universal way of salvation as intended to provide
an alternative to Christianity, see Simmons (2015). For other studies on Porphyry, Plotinus, Augustine, and Christianity, see Berchmann (2005), Boer (1974), Catapano (2018),
Chase (2004), Clark (2007), Digeser (2012; 2006); Evangeliou (1989), O'Meara (2003),
Rist (1996), Schott (2008), TeSelle (1974), and Torchia (1987).

For we were men, but we were not righteous; ... He assumed human nature, but it was righteous. (*CG* X.24, 426–27; cf. X.29, 436–438)[37]

In a parallel mode, Augustine chides Porphyry for making the path to happiness much harder for the many by recommending theurgic arts to those incapable of leading a philosophic life. These latter are "incomparably the greater part of the multitude of mankind" (*CG* X.27, 432). The same pride that can separate a Platonist from Christ the true Mediator separates him from the majority of his fellow human beings: "You raise yourself above [theurgy] by the intellectual character of your life ... for these [cleansings] are not at all necessary to the philosopher ... who [is] capable of higher things" (*CG* X.27, 432; cf. X.29, 438). If the philosophers were fully wise, could they not guide their fellows more truly toward wisdom, following the true Mediator, or at least refrain from giving false counsel? If they do not, might it be because they enjoy the sense of their own superiority more than they truly love wisdom? "[Y]ou are not ashamed of doing so much harm, even though you profess to be a lover of virtue and wisdom ... because [you are] puffed up with the pride of empty knowledge" (*CG* X.28, 433–34; cf. VIII.1, 312–13). Humility unites humans among themselves and with the good angels in a real *res publica*.[38] Pride divides the weak from the powerful and the foolish from the wise, placating the less gifted or less leisured with false promises, and preserving the road to happiness as a proper good of the fortunate few (see *CG* X.26, 430–31 and X.28, 433–34).[39]

Porphyry, Truest Philosophy, and True Religion: Chapters 29–32

Even at the height of Augustine's critique of philosophic pride in his response to Porphyry, however, Augustine's tenor begins to alter and his rhetorical dialectic to follow a more modest, humble, and unitive approach.[40] Early in chapter 29, Augustine alludes to what he considers

---

[37] Cf. Augustine's rhetorical dialectic a few chapters later, maintaining that "we know from the testimony of our own nature that a man is whole and complete only when the body is united with the soul" (*CG* X.29, 426).

[38] On this key point, see Balot (2019), Keys (2013), and Markus (1990).

[39] On this point, see also *CG* X.32, 443: "What is this universal way if not a way that belongs not to one nation as its special property, but to all the nations together, as a divine gift?"

[40] On Augustine's rhetoric and the tension sometimes obtaining between its aspirations and effects, see Kabala (2019); see also Keys, "The Power and Peril of Names: Rhetoric, Politics, and Philosophy in Augustine's *City of God*" (forthcoming).

the greatest insights of Porphyry's ethical, metaphysical, and religious thought. These center around a late classical Platonic theology of God and God's word (*logos*), as the *principia*, or principles, by which human intellect must be cleansed to return to the One who made it. Porphyry's theology was not in general as excellent as Plotinus's, Augustine intimates at times, and neither Platonist understood the substantial union of God and the Word, one *principium* together with the Holy Spirit, as revealed by Christ. Despite this, Porphyry grasped a great measure of truth: "You see after a fashion, although at a distance, and with a clouded vision, the country in which we should abide" (*CG* X.29, 435). Moreover, despite his critique of Porphyry for having claimed the road to blessedness as the proper possession of philosophers (*CG* X.28, 433–34), Augustine indicates here that Porphyry and his fellow Platonists understood that perfect wisdom and beatitude through union with God could only be a gift of God, and not an autonomous achievement of even the greatest philosopher. The way to happiness had been opened up for them with the gift of great minds, Augustine's Platonists consider, but the end of that road could only be a gratuitous blessing after death (*CG* X.29, 435–436). Philosophy clears the road and strengthens the desire to advance along it, but to be forever one with the One still exceeds the unaided powers of any mortal mind. Following cues from his teacher Plato, Porphyry and his philosophic followers at times express the conclusion that no one can "achieve perfect wisdom in this life, but that those who live according to intellect will find all that they lack supplied for them after this life by God's providence and grace." Thus even Porphyry's teaching, it seems, falls short of endorsing the *full* "sufficiency of man," even of the philosopher (*CG* X.29, 435–436). In this way, it remains modest and, in principle at least, open to humility.

Augustine continues on to laud Porphyry for one important advance in truth over the teachings contained in Plato's and Plotinus's writings. While Porphyry's greatest masters appear to have endorsed an eternal cycle of bliss, forgetfulness, and misery for souls, with even those returning to the Father destined to descend again into mortality, Porphyry rejected this view, arguing rather that the cleansed soul remains with the Father forever (*CG* X.30, 439–40). For this insight, Augustine praises Porphyry from the heart: "[H]ere is a Platonist dissenting from Plato and taking a better view: here is one who saw what Plato did not see, and who, even though he came after so great and so distinguished a master, did not hesitate to correct him; for he preferred truth to Plato" (*CG* X.30, 440–41; cf. Aristotle, *Nicomachean Ethics*, 1096a11–17).

Porphyry, as Augustine interprets him, considered further that there must be a "universal way" for souls to be cleansed and return to the Father forever. Porphyry admitted that he had not been able to discover this way, not from philosophy, even "the truest philosophy" (*CG* X.32, 442), nor from any religion which he knew. But since the One is good, and since humans receive souls and participate in intellect (*nous*) from his goodness, there must be a way given by "the one true God" by which all can reach bliss. In this Porphyry again judged rightly, in Augustine's estimation (*CG* X.32, 443–44).

By chapters 30–32, the conclusion of book X and with it the first major part of *The City of God*, Augustine is much kinder to the great Platonist who wrote against the Christian religion and offered qualified support for theurgy. He emphasizes now not Porphyry's pride, or at least the apparent pride of his philosophic elitism, but rather an intellectual mistake, together with some plausible circumstantial reasons for what Augustine considers the philosopher's false appraisal of Christ and the Christian religion. A critical error of Porphyry's lay in considering material things to be by nature evil (*CG* X.30, 439; cf. X.24, 426). This conclusion precluded him from realizing philosophically the complete identity and goodness of the *whole* of human nature, body and soul, and so from acknowledging an incarnate, suffering, and resurrected Mediator who is the Word of God, one with the Father, and truly human. Without this openness to the bodily and material – to the obviously humble aspects of our humanity – Porphyry could not recognize the road for humanity to the One to whom this philosopher so longed to return: the universal way given by the Father to "all the nations together," the "royal road to a secure and eternal kingdom" (*CG* X.32, 442; cf. *CG* I, preface).

Given all this, one might expect book X's conclusion to read as Augustine's "Tragedy of Porphyry," the story of a great human being whose fatal flaw, his hubris or *superbia*, led him to reject a portion of his own humanity and with it the gift of God for which he longed and looked his whole life. It is striking that Augustine's rhetorical dialectic in books I–X does not end on this sort of tragic note, for Porphyry or for philosophy. Augustine's endeavor here emerges as a quest to understand Porphyry's real situation sympathetically, to evaluate it both justly and compassionately, and so to excuse him, even though his hostility may have exacerbated the persecution of Augustine's coreligionists. Porphyry's failure to recognize Jesus as the universal way "is not to be wondered at." Seeing the fierce persecution of Christians in his times, Augustine surmises, must have solidified Porphyry's sense that this could

not be the right way, as it appeared doomed to destruction in short order
(*CG* X.32, 443–44). The imperial persecution might also have aroused
fear of the consequences of inquiring into the new religion too closely
(*CG* X.32, 443–44). Porphyry's failure to come into the Christian fold
now seems due not chiefly to proud disdain, but to a human lack of
understanding (*CG* X.32, 444).

This more capacious, kinder appraisal of Porphyry's unbelief seems
reflective of the very mercy that Augustine himself hopes to receive as
a gift from the one God, who is in important respects both the God of
Platonic philosophers like Porphyry, and the God of Abraham, Isaac, and
Jacob (*CG* X.32, 444).[41] Recall Augustine's description near the opening of book VIII of Plato as a *peregrinus*, a wanderer far and wide in
search of the highest wisdom and happiness. Now, as his dialogue with
the Platonists in books VIII–X draws to a close, Augustine recalls how
Abraham's deeds concurred with Porphyry's words, showing that the
polytheistic religion of the Chaldeans did not contain the full truth about
God or "the universal way of the soul's deliverance." The one seeking
the truth must therefore go out from one's home. "So that there might
be propagated from him a seed ... through Whom this universal way of
the soul's deliverance might be given to all nations, [Abraham] was commanded to leave his country and his kindred and his father's house" (*CG*
X.32, 444; 442–43).

Augustine thus cannot conclude with certainty that pride had the last
word in Porphyry's life's story. Indeed, he seems to hope it did not:

[Porphyry] said that the gift of God [the universal way] was not yet received, and
that it had not yet come to his knowledge. For even though he had not yet received
it as part of his faith, or even though it had not yet come to his knowledge, he did
not on that account conclude that the gift does not exist. (*CG* X.32, 444)

This humbler approach also seems more just from a human standpoint.
As Augustine notes in several passages throughout *The City of God*, only
God and the person concerned can know the truth of conscience, unless
a person chooses to reveal it to another through truthful speech (see *CG*

---

[41] Cf. *CG* XIX.22, 952–53, and XIX.23, 957. For philosophical reflections on Pascal's
famous distinction between the God of Abraham and the God of the philosophers, from
within the Jewish tradition, and drawing also on Thomas Aquinas's thought, see Ward
(1999). Ward concludes that these "are, after all, two faces of the same God, and each
is impoverished without the other" (170). His essay also ends with a welcome reminder
of the fruitfulness of honest, friendly dialogue among scholars of the Abrahamic faiths
(170; cf. 157–58).

I.26, 39 and XIV.28, 632), and Porphyry is no longer on earth to befriend and enquire as to his reasoning and final stance. Augustine's last sentence in book X likewise notes that the "two cities" of which he discourses in this work are not neatly divided or discernible by time or place, or even in an absolute and identifiable sense to us by persons known to their fellow human beings without error. The two cities and their citizenries, he writes, are "as I have already said, ... implicated and mixed with one another in this world" (*perplexas diximus invicemque permixtas*; CG X.32, 448). Augustine thus holds out hope that he and Porphyry, and we readers with them, may yet be friends and fellow citizens in the next world, on account of great mercy gratefully received, much more than from any personal merits, moral or intellectual.[42]

---

[42] For a study of Augustine on hope and politics, see Lamb (2018). On mercy and politics, see Menchaca-Bagnulo (2019).

5

The City of God XI–XII

Creation and the Metaphysics of Pride and Humility

[D]ivine providence admonishes us not to condemn things thoughtlessly, but rather to inquire with diligence into the utility of things. ... [The] concealment of utility is a means of either exercising our humility or overcoming our pride. For there is nothing at all which is evil by nature, and "evil" is a name for nothing other than the absence of good.

Augustine, *The City of God* XI.22

[The fallen angels] are miserable because they have forsaken Him Who supremely is, and have turned to themselves, who have no such supreme existence. And what else is their fault called than pride? ... [B]y forsaking Him, their nature became not ... no nature at all, but a nature with a less perfect degree of being, and therefore miserable.

Augustine, *The City of God* XII.6

What are the origins and metaphysics of humility and pride, and how may we know them? In the opening chapter of book XI, Augustine introduces readers to the second half of his magnum opus and its rhetorical dialectic, and therewith to these and closely related questions, especially concerning the origins of the two cities that form the chief subject of *The City of God*. The city of God, or the heavenly city, gloriously attested to in the scriptures, is lauded chiefly for its founder, whom Augustine has defended against those who blame him for the decline and impending fall of Rome. Those who refuse to open their minds and hearts to the kingship and mediation of this founder, Augustine suggests, those who recognize his unique excellence and yet resist acknowledging it, out of excessive self-love in individual and/or collective forms, comprise the earthly city – the foil and foe of the heavenly *civitas* (CG XI.1, 449–50; cf. I, preface, 3).

This opposition of heavenly and earthly cities, as we have already noted, conduces easily to an impression of fixed and unbending "binaries" in human affairs and among human beings in the present age (cf. Cooper, inter al., 2, 4, and 23). Yet in framing the inquiry and aims of the second part of *The City of God*, Augustine once again underscores complicating factors that caution against a binary or dualistic interpretation of human communities and human affairs in this world. In so doing, Augustine's rhetorical dialectic echoes emphases from the first and last books of the first part of *The City of God*, books I and X.

The first of these factors is Augustine's caution, to Christian readers in particular, against numbering themselves definitively among the triumphant citizenry of God's *res publica*. It is not an anguished uncertainty that Augustine aims to elicit, but rather a hopeful humility, conducive to and flowing from recognition that one is not perfectly given to seeking God's glory, and that one's virtue is never flawless or complete in this *saeculum* (see inter alia *CG* I.35, 48–49, and V.13–14, 213–14).[1] Hence, in opening book XI, Augustine writes that the heavenly city is one "whose *citizens we long to be* because of the love with which its Founder has inspired us" (*CG* XI.1, 449; emphasis added). This in turn is closely connected with a second mitigating or complicating factor: that those who seem most obstinately *not* to long to be such citizens, as Augustine suggests both near the end of book X and at the outset of book XI, are largely "misguided" (*deceptis*), not malicious (*CG* XI.1, 449). In their ignorance of the true God and Mediator, who is exalted in his humility, they worship gods as proud as they are false (*CG* XI.1, 449; cf. X.32, 442–44, regarding the ignorance of Porphyry, discussed in Chapter 4). And these first two factors open to a third: that the current state of affairs "in this present world" finds the two cities not neatly and discretely juxtaposed, but "*mixed together* and, in a certain sense, *entangled* with one another"[2] (*CG* XI.1, 450, emphasis added; cf. X.32, 448). Augustine has already stressed this mixed nature of the regime of earthly affairs among people in every polity, and even within each human being, in critical parts of his first 10 books, including closing sections of books I and X (cf. I.35, 48–49, and X.32, 448). That Augustine the rhetorician chooses to reiterate this strong saying once again, at the outset of the second and final part of his *City of God*, cannot but underscore its importance to his argument and his endeavor.

---

[1] On this aspect of Augustine's argument, see Herdt (2008, 58–61).
[2] The Latin reads *quas in hoc interim saeculo perplexas quodam modo diximus inuicemque permixtas*.

If the chief aim of Augustine's rhetorical dialectic in the first part of his magnum opus was critique, disproving or at least casting doubt on claims of pagan citizens that Christianity was bad for Rome's politics and culture and the cause of Rome's ongoing decline, the second and final part aims at construction, chronicling the foundation, development, and end of the heavenly city. In the course of this narrative, and to elucidate this city's nature and development also by way of contrast, key moments in the earthly city's narrative and anticipated end must likewise be recounted. The books to be analyzed in our fifth and sixth chapters, books XI–XIV, treat the two cities' origins: books XV–XVIII chronicle their growth and development in history; and in books XIX–XXII, Augustine develops as best he can their proper *fines* – their respective fulfillments or ends.

Although Augustine's rhetorical dialectic moves fluidly among several themes throughout books XI–XIV, the order of topics treated in them may be summarized as follows: In books XI and XII, Augustine treats the creation of the world, and of angels and human beings in particular, as well as the fall of some angels. Along the way he explores the connection between the church's scriptures and Christ the Mediator; argues for the nature of time and history; and defends the goodness of nature, including physical nature and human bodies. Books XIII and XIV focus mainly on the sin of the first human couple and the personal and social effects of their fall from grace for themselves and for their progeny. Once again, in this pair of books, Augustine finds occasion to defend the human body against its philosophic detractors and its religious and political manipulators. Significantly for Augustine, the origin of the earthly city is not to be found either in the body or the soul, according to their nature, but in the perverse, freely chosen use of angelic and human wills. The name of the principal vice that Satan and the first human pair reflected in their respective falls is, unsurprisingly, *superbia*, or vicious pride.

BOOK XI: BEING, FORMS OF GOOD, AND EPISTEMIC HUMILITY

We noted in Chapter 2 that Augustine begins his rhetorical-dialectical defense of humility as natural right *indirectly*, elucidating for his readers what is likely to be self-evident to them and to us with just a little reflection: namely, the pathos produced by vicious pride in political life, culminating in the lust for domination exhibited in republican and imperial Rome. Now, at the outset of the second part of his work, Augustine might reasonably assume that the reader who is still with him after some 500 pages has been persuaded of – or at least perplexed by – the effects of pride in politics and philosophy. So now, in book XI, it would seem that Augustine could defend humility more directly, showing how it is supported by the created world and woven into a natural human response to God the Creator and provident governor of creation.

Yet in book XI, "humility" hardly ever appears – prima facie evidence against the thesis just articulated. How can this be? Allen Fitzgerald offers a Christological explanation, rooted in the second chapter of book XI, in which Augustine once again emphasizes Jesus Christ as the only way for humans to return to the Father (see CG XI.2, 450–51). Without referring to humility explicitly in book XI, recalling Christ is tantamount to recalling for his readers the way of humility (Fitzgerald, 2014, 253–54).[3] Fitzgerald's interpretation strikes me as true and quite helpful, and yet there may be additional reasons for humility's curious absence from book XI, tied to its specific theme of the origins of the two cities and the foundation of the heavenly city with the creation of angels and human beings. Within this metaphysical perspective, Augustine may neglect to name humility in book XI because of its humble position among the virtues. It is hidden in the foundations of human, creaturely existence, a concrete slab to be built upon or an empty vessel waiting to be filled with justice and honest love. Humility is perhaps naturally at home with namelessness, in the sense of passing unnoticed at the service of higher goods, so that it needs no notice until it is challenged. All, or almost all, that Augustine writes concerning creation moves the reader to conscious wonder and love, and yet the *humilitas* these responses depend upon becomes visible and assumes a proper name only when a false path to divinization, *superbia*, rises up to challenge humility's intelligibility and excellence.

---

3 Fitzgerald writes:

> Any discussion of true religion has to include as well an understanding of the attitude of those who practice the true religion. That is surely one reason why Augustine began [*The City of God*] by saying that his focus was honed by the Scriptures ... as well as by a concern to explain the great power of humility. Hence, at the beginning of Book XI, he returns to the Scriptural descriptions of the city of which he speaks. But there is no emphasis on humility at this significant moment in this book. Augustine, rather, delves into the importance of the mediator who is both God and man ... the way. That way is about the humanity of Christ, the humility of Christ. This book thus begins to explain and defend the Christian religion by returning the focus to the *via humilitatis*, that is, to Christ. (2014, 253–54)

Pride, by contrast, demands and receives a name almost immediately, and in Latin at least, a name that appears to accept its fundamental deception at face value. The beings who assent to this vice consider themselves above (*super*) their true stature and merits, and indeed above their fellow angels or humans in a quasi-divine stance (*superbia*). Given the name it takes, and the easy evidence of its existence and impact in human affairs (see Chapter 2), pride seems simple to understand, while humility remains a mystery. Augustine's rhetorical dialectic in these pivotal books of *De civitate* reveals that the reverse is closer to the truth: Humility conforms to being and reason, foundational to right human existence and justice according to nature. Pride, on the other hand, is rooted in a seemingly unintelligible turn toward nothingness, an irrational revolt against being and humanity that removes its possessor from the fulfillment he or she seeks. *Superbia* has no real existence of its own.[4] Augustine's analysis thus underscores a perplexing paradox at the core of the ancient *mysterium iniquitatis*: the mystery of evil's undeniable existence, as it were, set against reason, and without actual being. Augustine will note in book XII, as we will soon see, that seeking to understand evil is analogous to defining darkness or silence, which he considers characterized chiefly by the *absence* of light or sound (*CG* XII.7, 507–8).

So by the close of book XI, after pride has brazenly come on stage in the revolt of some of the angels, humility once again requires Augustine's labor of definition and defense. Whereas this occurred in books I–V in the context of political affairs and in books VI–X in philosophic matters, in books XI–XIV the stage is cosmic – the realm of the universe, its myriad beings, and its first and final cause. We encounter here what we might term Augustine's *refounding of right humility* – humility according to nature – as a hidden base for the heavenly city and the ground of right interpersonal relationships. And in this renewed metaphysical and cosmopolitan foundation, Augustine will attempt to explain for his readers the inexplicable: the proud refusal of participation in the fullness of being, coupled with the disturbing tendency humans find in themselves toward irrational revolt against their nature and the happiness it craves.

We thus find in this central section of *The City of God* Augustine's metaphysics, his epistemology, and his foundational history of the "two cities" of pride and humility. All three of these themes are essayed initially by our rhetorical dialectician in book XI.

---

[4] On possible Plotinian influences on the accounts of *superbia* in Augustine's early writings and *Confessions*, see Torchia (1987).

The Metaphysics of Humility and Pride: An Introduction

In book XI, Augustine introduces a refrain he will repeat throughout this segment of *The City of God*: that all beings and all natures in the world are *good*, created for good by an all-good God. Drawing from Genesis, Plato's *Timaeus*, and later Platonic writings, Augustine concludes that "there is nothing at all which is evil by nature, and 'evil' is a name for nothing other than the absence of good" (*CG* XI.22, 477). Evil is not natural. *Good* is natural, with created beings participating in a finite manner in the infinite goodness of the Creator-God. Referring to a passage from the *Timaeus* (29d–30a), Augustine writes that "the most righteous reason for the creation of the world was that good works might be made by a good God" (*CG* XI.21, 476). In this regard, Plato seems to echo Genesis 1:31 – that God beheld all he had made and found it good.

The happiness of created beings endowed with intelligence and free choice (angels and humans) depends upon their living in a response of love and gratitude toward their Creator, and through union with him to grow toward the fullness of being, light, and love (cf. *CG* XI.2, 450–51). To refuse to acknowledge one's dependence upon the good God for one's own good, and to refuse to be happy through participating together with one's fellows in God's happiness, is to reject one's own deepest longing and to shut oneself out voluntarily from fulfillment. Humility, as we have seen, is the expression of virtuous "acknowledged dependence."[5] It is the foundationally just acknowledgment that we are not self-creators, although we are responsible for responding rightly to the Creator and to other creatures. Humility reflects a rightly ordered love of one's being and excellence, for the glory of God and in communion with one's fellow creatures. Humility thus comprises an openness to love the fullness of being, the most common good, for its own sake and the sake of all one's fellows. Whoever seeks his or her own fulfillment as a purely private good, as the result of autonomous action independent of or against the Creator, is bound to be frustrated. To seek and cleave to being is happiness; to reject it is misery. For being is good, and nonbeing where there should be being is evil. About all this Augustine will have more to say in the books to come. Suffice it for now to suggest that humility – though not referenced in the first twenty-one chapters of book XI – is silently borne witness to all Augustine writes in this segment, analogous to the silent testimony the heavens and the earth offer to their Creator's glory (see Psalm 19:1–4).

---

[5] This term is borrowed from MacIntyre (1999).

Epistemology, Humility, and Pride

Perhaps the most striking development of Augustine's rhetorical dialectic on humility and pride in book XI concerns human ignorance and paths to knowledge. In this regard, Augustine seeks to reveal the reasons for what we might call epistemological humility, an aspect or element of the fully virtuous, just form of humility that Augustine is defending. Book XI also highlights the enticing yet ultimately irrational and unproductive alternative: epistemological pride.

Augustine's dialectical argument in book XI for epistemological humility takes three forms. First, it highlights the necessity of trust, which flows from the finitude of our experience and study, and intimates the reasonableness of supernatural faith, which a contemporary spiritual author has described as "the humility of the mind."[6] Second, and closely related, is an argument from the gulf between divine wisdom and created (angelic and/or human) wisdom, coupled with the connection between participation in God's wisdom and the attainment of profound creaturely self-knowledge. And third, Augustine highlights the uncertainty and obscurity of many philosophical, theological, and practical matters. Rather than rest content with the resultant lack of knowledge, he urges the sort of magnanimous humility that is energized, not off-put, by wonder, ignorance, and doubt to embark on various paths to learning, recognizing the possibility of many-faceted approaches to truth regarding ultimate questions and matters of utility. Such obscurities motivate Augustine to urge courageous investigation in the hope of helpful discoveries, all the more so fueled by faith in the provident Creator.

Augustine's Sociology of Knowledge: Interdependency, Trust, and Faith

Near the outset of book XI, Augustine recalls for his readers the greatness and the weakness of human intelligence. In chapter 2, he writes that "the mind itself, even though reason and intelligence dwell in it by nature, is by its dark and inveterate faults made unable not only to embrace and enjoy but even to bear [God's] immutable light until it has been renewed from day to day, and healed ... and so it had first to be imbued with faith, and so purified" (*CG* XI.2, 450–51). Of the myriad things by nature perceptible to us humans, knowledge begins in the senses. Yet, since we

---

[6] See Escrivá (1987), no. 259.

cannot see, hear, smell, touch, or taste all – or even most – of the world's sensible beings in the course of a lifetime, we must trust to the senses of others in order to achieve a broader base of knowledge (*CG* XI.3, 451–52). If this is the case with sensible realities, how much more is it likely to be so with divine things that transcend the senses, and which even the wisest philosopher can at best glimpse at intervals over the course of a lifetime? And so, writes Augustine, "in order *that the mind might walk more confidently towards the truth*, the Truth itself, God, God's son, assuming humanity without putting aside His Godhead, established and founded this faith, that man might find a way to man's God through God made man" (*CG* XI.2, 451; emphasis added).

It is on this ground that Augustine argues for the reasonableness of accepting the trustworthiness of the Jewish and Christian scriptures, the authority on which he bases much of his analysis of the heavenly city's nature and history, in this book and in the books to come. Christ, he has argued already, is Mediator par excellence between human beings and God. As both God and Mediator, he has revealed to humans "as much as He judged sufficient, first by the prophets, then in His own person, and later through the apostles" (*CG* XI.3, 451). It is for Augustine in this personal and ecclesial context that scripture's authority emerges and is justified. "This Mediator ... *also* established *the Scriptures which are called canonical* ... and *we trust them* in all matters of which it is not expedient for us to be ignorant but which we are not capable of knowing for ourselves" (*CG* XI.3, 451; emphasis added). While we can have a good measure of knowledge of visible things, of which Augustine opines that the greatest is "the world," the world's beginning was and is not visible to us (*CG* XI.4, 452). And so, while Augustine also has offered metaphysical arguments for creation and the distinction between the Creator and creatures, he recognizes the Creator's authoritative word as the most trustworthy regarding, the cause of, and indeed the only *witness* to this grand cosmic beginning. Augustine here harks back to Genesis, the opening of the biblical scriptures accepted by Jews and Christians alike: "In the beginning God created the heavens and the earth" (Genesis 1:1; *CG* XI.4, 452).

Augustine argues that refusal to trust the Creator regarding his own nature and the world he created is likely to stunt intellectual growth. Simply put, trusting in trustworthy others – God first and foremost – leads those humble enough to rely on them to greater wisdom, while pride precludes such progress. This in no way implies though that perplexity and obscurity do not and will not always accompany our efforts to follow both reason and faith, as Augustine will soon be at pains to persuade his readers. Obscurity and perplexity – potential stumbling blocks on our minds' journey – are in actuality key moments along the path to human and divine wisdom. In this regard, Augustine's rhetorical dialectic concurs with a crucial conclusion of Julie Cooper's study of humility in modern political thought: namely, that our very finitude can and should motivate our human agency – not merely, or even chiefly, chasten it – in the tasks of learning, making, and governing (see Cooper, 2013, inter al., 152–58). Yet, as we will see Augustine underscore later on, human agency is never independent of divine agency: as God's being and goodness create and sustain human being and goodness, so God's truth and providence support and guide human quests for wisdom and good governance.

Self-Sufficiency or Participation? Creaturely vis-à-vis Divine Knowledge

In Plato's *Apology of Socrates*, the philosophic protagonist Socrates defends his way of life before Athens's democratic jury that must decide his fate. In so doing, he refers to the famous – or infamous – pronouncement of the Delphic Oracle, that no one among his contemporaries is wiser than Socrates. The inscription over the Temple of Apollo at Delphi read "Know Thyself," and so Socrates describes his life as a quest to interpret the mysterious oracle concerning himself and his wisdom. At the end of this quest spent questioning others – and presumably himself as well – concerning the nature of wisdom and virtue, Socrates reaches this conclusion: "It is probable, men, that really the god is wise, and that in this oracle he is saying that human wisdom is worth little or nothing" (Plato, *Apology*, 23a). Human wisdom for Socrates seems to consist chiefly, although perhaps not exclusively, in the *knowledge of ignorance* concerning the most important things; and Socrates makes bold to proclaim: "Probably I really am wise in this" (*Apology*, 20d and 21d).

Augustine incorporates this Socratic theme into his case for humility and against pride in book XI, with arguments concerning the limits of created beings' knowledge, especially when possessors of this knowledge do not acknowledge and humbly seek fulfillment by participation in divine knowledge. Paradoxically, when creaturely knowledge seeks to be self-contained or self-sufficient, it remains in the shadows tending toward night. By contrast, when creaturely knowledge recognizes its roots in God and orients itself toward praise of God, self-knowledge and knowledge of the world alike are enlightened, and one is led out of the shadows to witness the dawn.

Augustine thus seeks to lead his readers – whether Christian or pagan – to desire to follow divine wisdom in humility. This is a major theme of Augustine's treatment of the creation of the angels, as narrated in Genesis (see CG XI.7, 457–58, and XI.9, 459–61). A perceptive student of the Bible might retort that this foundational scriptural narrative makes no explicit mention of the creation of the angels, as Augustine acknowledges. Still, he notes that God is said to create "light" first and later to separate the light from the darkness. This is before he is said to create the sun, the moon, and the stars. So then, in what could this primordial created light consist, and what could constitute the succession of "evening" and the following "morning" in creation, noted for two more "days" before the heavenly bodies are said to have been established? Another great physical light, later to be replaced by the sun, is one possibility the bishop from Hippo considers, and he finds this plausible. Yet he spends more time on another interpretive option, one to which he will refer repeatedly throughout book XI: that this primordial created "light" refers to the angelic intellect and its loving knowledge of God, and of creation and the angels themselves in God. Conversely, darkness refers to those angelic intellects that choose after their creation to seek happiness and wisdom in themselves rather than in God. In so doing, they fall from full wisdom. Others, by far the majority as Augustine opines, choose instead to seek their wisdom in and from God and to know themselves in God yet more perfectly. Augustine's beautiful passage is worth quoting here:

[I]n comparison with the Creator's knowledge, *the [natural] knowledge of the creature is like a kind of evening light*. But when our knowledge is directed to the praise and love of the Creator, *it dawns and is made morning*; and *night never falls while the Creator is not forsaken by the creature's love*. ... And, indeed, the knowledge which created things have of themselves is, so to speak, shadowy until they see themselves in the light of God's wisdom and, as it were, in relation to the art by which they were made. (CG XI.7, 457–58; emphasis added)

These are Augustine's thoughts concerning the evening that came and the morning that followed, on the first day of creation. What of the primordial separation of *darkness* from light? From where did this darkness come? It is in this context that Augustine introduces his notion of evil as nonbeing, one with philosophic roots in Plotinus's thought. He does so via the biblical account of the *mysterium iniquitatis*, the mystery of evil that is encapsulated in the unfathomable rejection of being and light in favor of diminished existence and darkness. Whereas those angels

who did not fall rejoiced to be "enlightened by the Light that created
them" and to "[share] in that immutable Light," those angels who willed
instead to "[turn] away from God" became "darkness in themselves
because deprived of their participation in the eternal Light. *For evil has
no nature of its own*. Rather, it is the *absence of good* which has received
the name 'evil'" (CG XI.9, 461; emphasis added). One who consciously
rejects God – He who most truly and immutably *is* – "deludes himself
in his pride" (CG XI.13, 468). Such a created spirit willfully mistakes
natural angelic knowledge for divine knowledge, while there is in reality
an infinite gap in excellence between the two. Such is the situation with
the human soul, which if it would be wise seeks its ultimate wisdom and
fulfillment from a source transcending itself. "[T]he soul itself, though it
will be forever wise when redeemed in eternity, will be so by participation in an immutable wisdom which is not itself" (CG XI.10, 463).

Augustine returns to this theme near the close of book XI. There he
reiterates that "in God," in the "wisdom of God," righteous angels and
humans know or will know "every created being not in itself, but in this
better way … as if in the design by which it was created. And … they
[will] know themselves better in God than in themselves" (CG XI.29,
489). Therefore, those human beings "who, as yet, live by faith, who
hope for, but do not yet enjoy, equality with [the holy angels], are already
called 'light' by the apostle" (CG XI.33, 494). But this can only be the
case with those who struggle aided by grace against the mysterious tendency we human beings experience to desire to be our own light – bright,
proud, self-sufficing, and fully wise by and from our own nature. Again,
and perhaps more deeply, Augustine reveals humility well-understood to
embody and express the core of what is just, according to human nature.
When Augustine speaks about human beings living by faith or participating in the light of God, he once again indicates that persevering in abiding
in God as the source of our being is foundational for what it means to
be a creature. If this is so, humility becomes the foundational virtue that
angels and humans alike need in order to live according to their natures.

Obscurity, Uncertainty, and Plurality on Human Paths toward Wisdom

In the central chapters of book XI, Augustine's dialectic of humility
against pride develops and unfolds in a striking, even surprising, manner.
While not doubting reason's capacity to reach a good measure of truth
concerning material nature, humanity, and even divinity, Augustine here

highlights several sorts of uncertainty and obscurity encountered along human paths toward knowledge and wisdom. Some things become clear to reason with little effort, but many do not, whether with regard to physical, human, or theological matters. Augustine's rhetorical dialectic in these chapters urges readers *not* to be daunted by such difficulties. He intimates, moreover, that these perplexing states of affairs can be good for us – ethically and epistemologically – in our quest to discover, to discern, and to make.

The first lack of clarity and certainty Augustine brings to his readers' attention is already noted at the outset of book XI: uncertainty regarding one's own, final perseverance in piety and virtue and subsequent attainment of perfect blessedness as God's gift. The dialectic proceeds here in a manner analogous to Aristotle's in the *Nicomachean Ethics* (1098a16–20), when the Stagirite observes that *eudaimonia* is dependent on a full lifetime, and that "one swallow does not make a spring, nor does one sunny day." Augustine similarly stresses that no living man or woman – even one who seems firmly set in faith, hope, and justice and "readily obtain[s] divine mercy for the sins which, in [his or her] infirmity, [he or she] commit[s]" – knows for sure that he or she will continue along these profitable paths until the end of his or her days (CG XI.12, 466). There may be new tests of one's virtue awaiting, stronger and more tragic than one can imagine today. In one's freedom, one may later choose to live for lesser goods and so become indifferent or adverse to greater goods and to more demanding and self-effacing virtues. One never knows. "For what man can know that he will persevere to the end in the practice and increase of righteousness, unless he has been made certain by some revelation from [God]?" (CG XI.12, 466). Augustine himself is conscious of no such revelation, so far as we can ascertain here, and he implies that the overwhelming majority of men and women also live without such unquestionable clarity.

Yet on Augustine's own grounds, this epistemological situation has its benefits, not least in conducing toward humility vis-à-vis God and in disposing one to charitably judge one's neighbors. In this world before the final judgment there are no two identifiable-for-us, firmly fixed "cities" among human beings, as we have already noted following Augustine's lead. Each human being's identity, for Augustine, is given to him or her with a good purpose and oriented toward the fullness of love and justice. But one is never, or virtually never, fully *there*, at the end-goal, during one's earthly sojourn; and one can never be sure of persevering to the end of the way. How then could any human being presume to identify and separate the saved from the damned, the citizens of God's city from those of the earthly city, in a final, infallible way? How can one rightly glory in one's own virtue and justice, even if acknowledging them to be gifts of God, as if one were certain one would never lose them and then condemn another as bereft of these goods for eternity? This would be hubris, not righteousness or godliness.[7] Our certainty of God's goodness and mercy leads to hope, but being convinced of our own free, continued correspondence to these gifts, relying on our own power and good will, would signify presumption and pride. Once again, Augustine's epistemology and his rhetorical dialectic cut against a simplistic, rigid, "binary" view of human affairs, and in so doing, sides with moderation, humility, and humanity.

Augustine's rhetorical dialectic next develops the theme of complexity and perplexity vis-à-vis the study of the sacred scriptures. While some biblical passages are clear and their meaning unmistakable, others are more obscure, making it difficult to ascertain the author's intent and meaning or levels of meaning. Augustine makes no attempt to deny or downplay this difficulty. Since, as we have seen, he has already argued that the scriptures are a tremendous help on the path toward the truth about God, world, and humanity (see *CG* XI.3, 451–52), Augustine wonders why the good God might have made understanding these same scriptures at times a most perplexing endeavor. He concludes that the experience of doubt and difficulty may actually aid human beings on the path toward truth in its unity and multiplicity:

The obscurity of the divine word is beneficial in this respect: that it causes many views of the truth (*plures sententias veritatis*) to appear and to be brought into the light of knowledge, as one reader understands a passage in one way and another in another. Any interpretation of an obscure passage should, however, be confirmed by the testimony of manifest facts or by other passages where the meaning is not in the least open to doubt. In this way we shall, by the investigation of several views, either arrive at the meaning intended by whoever wrote the passage, or, failing this, the examination of a profoundly obscure passage will lead to the statement of a number of other truths. (*CG* XI.19, 472–73)

---

[7] See also Augustine, *De correptione et gratia* 24:

"For those who love God, everything works together unto good" (Romans 8:28) – absolutely everything, even to this extent, that if some swerve and sway from the path, he makes their very wanderings contribute to their good, because they come back humbler (*humiliores*) and wiser (*doctiores*). They learn that their rejoicing on the right path ought to be with trembling, and that they should not arrogantly rely on their own strength to remain on the path, nor say in times of prosperity: now we will never fall.

Precious pedagogical moments would be lost, Augustine implies, if all scripture were univocal and easy to interpret; if the serious reader did not need to consider each passage carefully on its own and within the context of its biblical book and of revelation as a whole; and if one did not also need at times the help of secular historical or geographic facts or philosophy to elucidate understanding. Moreover, Augustine's rhetorical dialectic encourages the student searching the scriptures to recognize that he or she is not self-sufficient in this task, any more than one phrase or passage of scripture can stand alone in an absolute way. In addition to humble dependence on the spirit of God for enlightenment, we need a magnanimous determination to persevere in this study, together with a critical yet capacious openness to other readers' readings, if we are not to miss out on new visions of truth and goodness, simple in themselves per-haps, yet so rich that a single consideration, syllogism, or angle of vision cannot suffice. Scripture's complexities and lack of clarity, which at first sight seem stumbling blocks on the path toward understanding, are in fact meant to serve more meaningfully as ladders – difficult to climb and requiring strenuous agency, but permitting a panoramic view to those who persevere and reach the peak.

In the ensuing chapters of book XI, Augustine examines this theme of complexity and darkness in the quest for knowledge vis-à-vis a central theme of this segment of *The City of God*: the goodness of nature – of all natures. In chapter 22, Augustine engages directly with some who ques-tion or deny the universality of this goodness. For are not some beings clearly evil by nature? Consider, for instance, a fire blazing through an ancient forest or a viper biting an unsuspecting child. How can one call these aggressive, destructive beings good, any more than Augustine con-siders human lust for domination (*libido dominandi*) to be good and beneficial?

The key to perceiving the goodness in all beings and in their natures, Augustine argues, is once again humility, coupled with prudent discern-ment among diverse senses of good. Augustine here alludes to three spe-cific senses. First, one can speak of the goodness of a being per se, as good in itself – good ontologically. Just as a flower or an ocean wave has existence, order, and beauty in itself, such that we would not be speaking intelligibly if we did not call it good, so also a viper has these properties and is thus in itself good. Second, according to Augustine, we can speak of something as good in the context of a whole of which it comprises a part: he refers here especially to the grand, complex, mysterious whole of the cosmos (see *CG* XI.22, 476–77). If the planet Venus, for instance, is good in its own existence, it is also good that it exists as part of the universe, adding to its dynamism and its beauty.

Third, we can speak of something as good in the sense of "good for me" or "good for us human beings." Augustine terms this "useful good," and it is this sense that poses particular problems for ascribing goodness universally to all beings. We can refer to the examples given earlier of beings that seem to possess evil natures, the forest fire and the viper.[8] The genuine difficulty in calling them good is a function of the damage and destruction they cause other beings, especially human beings. But to harm humans is not an *essential* property or attribute of fire, a viper, or a "wild beast." Thus, Augustine concludes that it is incorrect to term them "evil nature[s]" or "evil by nature" (*CG* XI.22, 476–77). Why are we prone to make that mistake? Perhaps because we tend to conflate ontological and useful notions of good, or to privilege the good as "useful for us" over a being's "good in itself" or its good in the context of "the universe as a whole … [as] a commonwealth (*in communem rem publicam*)" (*CG* XI.22, 477).

Augustine is in no sense denying that useful good is also real and indeed critical for human and other forms of life, or that the interaction of certain other beings according to their natures, with us according to ours, is likely to cause grievous evil to us. *To be burned* by fire or *poisoned* by a viper is of course *bad* for us. That fact does not, however, render fire and viper per se evil, or even evil *qua* parts of our common cosmos. Our humanity as *homo sapiens* is impoverished if we cannot acknowledge their real goodness and value. Such ignorance or indifference likewise comprises a great evil for us as rational animals.[9]

Augustine's dialectic goes still further to suggest that in a meaningful sense each created nature has some utility for us humans as well, as citizens of the cosmic *res publica*. The wave that could wash us out to sea may also deliver a catch of shellfish to shore for our nourishment. The fire that could destroy our home warms it instead and delights us by its light from within the safe confines of the hearth. And even poisons such as the viper's, Augustine suggests, can "become wholesome and curative when proper use is made of them; whereas, on the other hand,

---

[8] On the example of the viper as a potential "natural evil" in the thought of Al-Farabi, see L'Arrivee (2015, 14–15, and 220 ff.).

[9] "These persons do not notice how splendid such things are in their own places and natures, and … how much they contribute, in proportion to their own share of beauty, to the universe as a whole, as to a commonwealth" (*CG* XI.22, 477).

those things which delight us, such as food and drink and the sun's light, are known to be harmful if used immoderately or inopportunely" (*CG* XI.22, 477). Utility and harm are not fully, readily disclosed by beings in each instance; their discernment and discovery often require hard work, intellectual, moral, and artistic or technological.

Here we come to a key point to consider, in this portion of our study of Augustine's rhetorical-dialectical defense of humility against hubris or pride: that the hiddenness of utility for us in many of the beings of the created world, and in the ecological ordering of the whole and its larger parts (planets, forests, marshlands), is a call to humble diligence, even to faithful endeavor.

In this way, then, divine providence admonishes us not to condemn things thoughtlessly, but rather to inquire with diligence into the utility of things. ... [W]here our own intellect or weakness is to blame for our lack of knowledge, we should believe (*credere*) that a utility exists even though it is hidden, as we have found to be true of other things that we have discovered only with difficulty. This concealment of utility is a means of either exercising our humility or overcoming our pride. For there is nothing at all which is evil by nature, and "evil" is a name for nothing other than the absence of good. (CG XI.22, 477; emphasis added)

So in sum, by the concluding chapters of book XI Augustine has elucidated aspects of useful good, or "good for us" human beings, to be discovered in three obscurities that could seem irredeemably bad from our immediate vantage point: (1) obscurity of self-knowledge, and specifically as to our future character and deeds, whether we will persevere unto salvation; (2) obscurity of meaning, of the proper interpretation of passages of sacred scripture; and (3) even the obscurity of cosmological goodness, and the useful goodness for us humans of other beings and their attributes. These obscurities and perplexities may drive us, in our pride, to despair or to rush to dominate and manipulate. But if we approach ourselves, scripture, and other entities in the world with the humility of a gifted yet limited student, of one blessed being in a vast cosmos of beings, and as beloved by God yet not ourselves God omniscient, we can find hope and strength to investigate further, spurring discoveries in philosophic, scientific, artistic, and technological realms. Many of these will be useful for us in our human weakness, though Augustine rightly reminds us that all finite beings and goods, when used or desired immoderately or unjustly, may cause harm to ourselves, others, our societies, or our environment.[10]

---

[10] For a study of "Humility and Environmental Law," see Nagle (2016).

Augustine's philosophy and theology of hiddenness and obscurity thus cautions against simplistic "binaries" in our understanding of and relationships with our fellow humans and with other denizens of our universe. There is no really reasonable ground in Augustine's thought for definitive pronouncements, such as, "I am good/saved; you are evil/ damned," or "human beings are naturally good; vipers are naturally evil," or even, "vipers are entirely evil for us humans." If creation is the work of a good God who freely desires to make other good things, then we believe that there are utilities out there to be found, and that it is possible to unearth them while endeavoring to respect other beings' created integrity and goodness. Augustine thus considers that the hiddenness of useful good, of utility for us, constitutes a call to humble and magnanimous human agency. It summons us "to inquire with diligence," even when this can only be done "with difficulty," buttressed by the knowledge from reason and from faith that "there is nothing at all which is evil by nature" (*CG* XI.22, 477).

Concluding Book XI: Back to the Beginning

Chapters 31–34 close book XI, and with it Augustine's consideration of God's great work of creation, the mystery of his Sabbath rest, and the origins of the two angelic "cities," which will in time also welcome human beings into their citizenry. Augustine the master-rhetorician weaves into his prose here themes from earlier chapters of this pivotal book. In chapter 31, Augustine reminds readers how "tribulations" may "conduce to humility," and no matter how wise we may become, our wisdom in this age will never be for us perfect rest or bliss. As pilgrims or wayfarers, like Plato and especially like Abraham of old (see Chapter 4), we may intimate and begin now to participate in this rest, but never do so fully in this life. "For rest is in the whole, that is, in perfect fullness, while in the part there is toil. That is why we toil for as long as we know only in part ... that we toil even when we search into the scriptures themselves" (*CG* XI.31, 492). And in chapter 32, Augustine reminds his readers of his interpretation of the "let there be light" of Genesis 1:3–5, as marking the creation of the angels (*CG* XI.32, 492–93; cf. XI.9, 459–61). In so doing, he again stresses that the often-obscure depths of sacred scripture are a call to humble openness to diverse faithful readings and to diligent, even daring, efforts of interpretation. "For [these words] are so profound that they can give rise to many different opinions which are not at odds with the rule of faith; and this is a challenge to the intellects of those who read them" (*CG* XI.32, 493).

Augustine continues on, recapping his reading of the passage, "God divided the light from the darkness" (Genesis 1:4), as referring to the two angelic "companies" or "cities." The origin of the division has nothing to do with God's creation, in which all the angels received good natures; it has everything to do with the humility or pride freely embraced by each angelic will. "[O]ne [company] is both good by nature and righteous in will, whereas the other, though naturally good, is perverse in will" (*CG* XI.33, 495). This second group, comprised of those who desire to be their own light, to be self-sufficient as only God can be, "in its pride, seethes with the desire to subdue and hurt" (*CG* XI.33, 494) – in other words, with *libido dominandi*. The metaphysical or ontological goodness of humility for humans is reflective of the created goodness of all being. Thus grounded, virtuous humility is rational, righteous, and reverent. But if Augustine is correct in so concluding, what could explain a willing, proud refusal of what is good and just by nature? What could explain the free choice of a creature for misery and diminution of being? Augustine will explore this perplexity at greater length in the following books of *The City of God*.

BOOK XII: CREATION *EX NIHILO*, THE ANGELIC FALL AND THE CREATION OF MAN

The rhetorical dialectic of book XXII takes up three major themes related to the metaphysics of good and evil and of humility and pride within the context of the by-now-familiar trope that being is per se good, and that nothing was made evil by the Creator. The first theme is the connection Augustine discerns between love of a common good and humility, and conversely, between love of one's own private good above all else and pride. The second considers creation *ex nihilo* and the possibility and causality of the angelic fall. The third explores the creation of man and woman as narrated in Genesis and considers human nature as both like and unlike angelic nature.

Common Good and Private Good

Augustine opens the first chapter of book XII as he will open each of the following four chapters, by recalling for his readers the goodness of all being and natures: good as conceived, willed, and brought into existence by the Creator. Especially endowed with goodness and the potential and desire for beatitude are angelic and human beings, whose longing for fulfillment can be quenched only by union with God (see *Conf.* I.1.1, 3). "[T]here is no other good apart from God by which the rational or intellectual creature is made blessed. ... Those creatures ... do not attain blessedness by themselves ... but receive it from him by whom they were created" (*CG* XII.1, 498–99). If angels are created with intellect and a longing for happiness that cannot be found except in God, what then could explain the existence of *two* cities among the angels? Why did all the angels not pledge their allegiance loyally to the city in which they were created and to its founder?

C. S. Lewis in his *Screwtape Letters* wittily conveys the core of Augustine's answer. Lewis's memorable character, "ravenously affectionate Uncle Screwtape," a senior demon instructing his nephew Wormwood in the art of tempting human beings, expresses it as follows: "The whole philosophy of Hell rests on recognition of the axiom ... [that] my good is my good, and your good is your good. What one gains another loses" (*Screwtape Letters*, letter 18, in Lewis, 2002, 161). Put in Augustine's language, the angels who fall do so because they choose to prefer their own private, finite good to the "common" (*qua* sharable without diminishment), infinite good which is God. The origin of the heavenly city is in God's creation of the angelic beings as good, united to God by nature and by grace, and so also living in fellowship with one another; and in the angelic will's firm desire to "[cleave] to that which is the common good of all" (*CG* XII.1, 498). The origin of the earthly city (or perhaps better termed, in its angelic origin, the infernal city), is not at all in created nature but in the choice of some angels who, "delighting in their own power, and supposing that they could be their own good, fell from that higher and blessed good [God] which was common to them all and embraced a private good of their own. They preferred the elation of pride to the loftiest dignity of eternity; the sharpness of vanity to the most certain truth; zeal for selfish ends to the uniting force of love. They became proud, false, and envious" (*CG* XII.1, 498).[11]

This proud rejection of fulfillment through sharing beatitude with their fellows and finding it in God, necessarily involves the diminution of angelic being, Augustine argues. Only God "supremely is." The fallen angels thus

---

[11] On this theme, see Markus's "*De ciuitate dei*: Pride and the Common Good" (1990), which begins: "Anyone who has dipped into Augustine's *De ciuitate dei* will recognize in my title some of the key words of that great and exhausting work. ... The spotlight falls on pride at the very start ... [while the common good] lurks in the background, very close to some of its central themes; and it is there from the start" (245). See also Lavere (1983).

are miserable because they have forsaken Him Who supremely is and have turned to themselves, who have no such supreme existence. And what else is their fault called than pride? For "pride is the beginning of sin" (Ecclesiasticus [Sirach] 10:13) ... and, since they could have a greater measure of being only by cleaving to Him Who supremely is, therefore, by preferring themselves, they preferred that which has a less perfect degree of being. ... [B]y forsaking Him, their nature became not ... no nature at all, but a nature with a less perfect degree of being, and therefore miserable. (*CG* XII.6, 504–5)

This humble love for the common good that is God, comprises the analogically *political* virtue par excellence of the citizens of the heavenly city (cf. *CG* XV.1, 634–35). That the Creator intends the sharing of rational or intellectual creatures in this just and common good seems alluded to again by Augustine near the close of this book XII. Here Augustine recalls his opening preface and critical book II argument, one which will be taken up again and completed in book XXII, the last book of *The City of God*: that the only real *res publica*, the only *civitas* with a sharing of full justice and truly common advantage, is the one founded by God in Christ. In chapter 26 of book XII, Augustine emphasizes that the Creator-God is the founder (*conditor*) of what we might term the *res publica universarum naturarum*, the republic or commonwealth of all natures. God's work as founder of all creation far exceeds in excellence the work of the most famous human founders, including Romulus and Alexander. These men, through their "will ... design and command," caused Rome and Alexandria to be built, by the external imposition of architectural and civic forms on the matter at their disposal. "How much more," Augustine concludes,

are we bound to call God the founder of natures (*conditorem ... naturarum*); for he does not create from any material which he himself did not make, nor does he employ any workmen, except those of his own creation. And if he were to withdraw what we may call his "constructive power" (*potentiam suam ... fabricatoriam*) from existing things, they would cease to exist, just as they did not exist before they were made. (*CG* XII.26, 537–38)[12]

God is the very founder of human founders and of human nature itself. As Augustine emphasizes repeatedly throughout his magnum opus, the founder and ruler of the universal, godly *res publica* greatly desired the concord and flourishing of those called to become its citizens. How then

---

[12] Here I follow the translation of *The City of God* by Bettenson (2003/1984), who in this passage consistently renders Augustine's *conditor* as "founder" in the examples of Romulus, Alexander, and God the Creator. Dyson alters his translation of *conditor* from "founder" regarding Romulus and Alexander, to "Author" regarding God.

could some of the most resplendent and intelligent of God's creatures, the angels, come to reject the *summum bonum* (highest good) qua *bonum commune* (common good)? How can one explain what Augustine, following scripture, takes to be the historical fact that some angels actualized this prideful potentiality? In the central chapters of book XII, Augustine locates the metaphysical possibility of the angelic fall into pride, in the mutability common to all finite creatures, and more mysteriously still, in their creation *ex nihilo*.

Humility's Metaphysics and Epistemology

As we have seen already, Augustine considers that the created natures of finite beings, recognition that no creature is its own or another's creator, and acknowledgment of the dependence on the divine Creator that these natures entail, provide the ontologically and epistemologically first and firmest grounding of virtuous humility. God's creative action is not that of an indifferent watchmaker, who crafts his goods once and for all and then often abandons them to their own devices with no harm to their being or excellence. Rather, if God were to withdraw his "creative power" [*potentiam suam … fabricatoriam*] and his free and loving will that creatures should be, Augustine indicates, they would fall back into nothingness immediately (*CG* XII.26, 538). Finite being is utterly dependent on infinite being.

This radical dependence is in Augustine's view a caution against presumption, yet not a cause for fear or anxiety. God's will *is* that beings should be, and that human beings and angels should continue in being, united to him eternally. The Creator, Augustine suggests yet again near the opening of book XII, in light of scripture and Platonic philosophy, creates good things that they might be (cf. *CG* XI.21, 474–76). Everything that is, is good ontologically: "There can exist things which are wholly good; but … never … wholly evil" (*CG* XII.3, 502). "All natures, then, simply because they exist and therefore have a species … and a certain peace of their own, are certainly good. … [God] is to be praised when we contemplate all the natures which He has made" (*CG*, XII.5, 504). One is here reminded of a definition of love offered by twentieth-century philosopher Josef Pieper, that to love someone is, at its core, to mean and to say "it is *good* that you exist; how wonderful that you are!" (Pieper, 1974, 27).

Augustine's rhetorical dialectic alludes to another metaphysical motive for humility: the contemplative recognition of the great goodness and beauty of even the lowest living and inanimate beings, which like humans, "have God as [their] Author (*auctor*) and Founder (*conditor*)" (*CG* XII.4, 503). The chief obstacle to this humble recognition and praise of goodness appears again to be the domination of utility-based judgments. Augustine's example here is the locusts of the book of Exodus, "whose swarms smote the pride of the Egyptians" (*CG* XII.4, 503). Considered only in their fearful collective capacity to wipe out crops, we all too easily judge these lowly creatures to be bad. Viewed in their nature and existence, however, one sees a real beauty, a primordial goodness, a wonderfulness that they *are*.

Pride's Metaphysics and Epistemology, or Knowing by Not Knowing

If pride is the primordial vice, and if all vice sets one against God and one's own nature (see *CG* XII.3, 501), how can one explain the falling into evil of *good* beings created by an all-good God? What are the metaphysical presuppositions of pride and other forms of vice in angels and human beings?

As the rhetorical dialectic in book XII proceeds, Augustine offers two explanations of the possibility of pride, understood as the preference of oneself over God, and of other sins that similarly involve loving what is less perfect in being more than one loves the supreme being, the founder and cause of our being. Augustine's first account hinges on the mutability inherent in finite being. As we have seen, the angelic will is the cause of the angelic fall – not in its nature, which is good, but in its freely chosen use to prefer what is less perfect and fulfilling to what is more and indeed fully so. Augustine now elaborates that "[a]n evil will ... could not exist in an evil nature," since there is no such thing, "but in a nature good but nonetheless mutable" (*CG* XII.6, 505). Finite being, on its own, can change for better or for worse; and free finite beings can choose in such a way that they do become worse. Augustine is at pains to argue here that the created, finite being, which is loved and chosen no matter how lowly it may be, is never itself the source of evil, in and for the ill-chooser.

Yet Augustine cannot, it seems, rest content with this rendering of the metaphysical possibility of evil as rooted in mutability. Why would intellectual creatures, "good even though mutable," not always choose to embrace the fullness of goodness and being, upon which their happiness depends? Mutability most obviously grounds metaphysically the transition from good to better, from being toward its completion, not its fall into evil. Augustine's rhetorical dialectic asks, "[H]ow can it be that a natural creature ... should produce ... before his will has become evil ... the evil will itself?" Augustine's reply is profound and disturbing: the potency to fall, to sin, is rooted in "the fact that [an angel or human being] is a natural creature *made out of nothing*" (*CG* XII.6, 507; emphasis added).

Pride, and with it all sin, comprises a falling away from full being, a defect rather than an actuality. There is, according to Augustine, no properly efficient cause of the turning back toward nothingness. The causality of evil here, he considers, can only be described as "deficient": as a "voluntary," "not necessary" *lack* of will-to-being, a refusal of being's fullness as gift and common good, dependent on the Creator and his grace. "[T]he evil will is not an effect of something" (*CG* XII.7, 507); rather, "it is the defection of the will itself which is evil, because against the order of nature" (*CG* XII.8, 508). Greed is not caused by gold or its beauty, but rather "is ... the fault ... of the man who loves gold perversely, and who therefore neglects righteousness, which ought to be held in incomparably higher esteem than gold. ... Again, boastfulness is not the fault of human praise" (*CG* XII.8, 509).

Pride, too, can be understood only as a defection, a turning away from "that which supremely is" (*ab eo, quod summe est*) toward oneself and one's own power, and so toward lesser being (*ad id, quod minus est*). This prideful defection is the beginning of evil will, Augustine argues. Yet, as the action of defection or falling away has no *being* in itself, it cannot be directly comprehended in the way that the fuller being assented to and actualized by humility can. In attempting to explain pride, the original diabolic sin, the primordial vice, one is describing a void, a gap only partially intelligible through the lack of what we can know to be intelligible. Thus, analogously, we know darkness through knowing light and perceiving it to be absent; we know silence through first knowing sound and then perceiving it not to be (*CG* XII.7, 507–8). The implication of this portion of Augustine's rhetorical dialectic seems to be that we can *know* only humility, in a strict or precise sense of knowing, and then recognize its absence as pride. Humility, as elusive as it may seem in its virtuous senses, in its aversion to attention and praise, is less elusive per se than its nemesis pride. As Augustine wittily writes of the defection of evil generally and its "deficient" causality: "Let no one, then, seek to know from me what I know that I do not know; unless, perhaps, he wishes to learn how not to know that which we should know cannot be known" (*CG* XII.7, 508).

Continuing along these lines, Augustine next locates with greater precision what might be termed a plausible final cause of pride, a good the inordinate desiring of which results in the vice of pride: namely, power (*potestas*). Power is good in itself; it is only its coveting and ill-use that constitute evil. God cannot be faulted for making a world in which power exists and is essential in human affairs, for "pride [is not] the fault of Him who gives power, or of power itself." Rather, it is again "the perverse loving" of power that diminishes the goodness and being of a person who seeks or possesses it.[13] "Hence, he who perversely loves the good of any nature whatsoever is made evil through this very good even as he attains it, and is made wretched because deprived of a greater good" (*CG* XII.8, 509). Augustine's rhetorical dialectic here underscores the vanity of prideful and other vicious desires and actions, by asking readers: "What, in this case, do they [who are proud] achieve but *emptiness?*" (*CG* XII.8, 508; emphasis added).

Since all beings are created good by the good God, with angels and humans destined for eternal happiness and fullness of being, and because God is true to his word and hates nothing he has made, Augustine surmises that the possibility of falling back toward nothingness, which creation *ex nihilo* entails, is never fully actualized in angels or humans. What J. R. R. Tolkien (1999, 32) describes as "the ruinous path down into the Void," however, was commenced through pride and traveled far along by many angels, according to the biblical narrative. The angels were all created good by a good God, and they have the highest wisdom and power of any created beings: What could explain the choice of many of them, of less being over more, of themselves over God? Augustine seems unable to resist wrestling once again with this deeply problematic development, even as he doubts that any actual or positive knowledge is possible. Tentatively, hesitatingly, he will attempt again to explain the inexplicable, for his readers as well as himself.

Augustine is clear that the cause of evil is not in God or in nature. It is a "voluntary" cause, not a "natural" or divine one, "for if sin is natural, there is no such thing as sin" (*CG* XI.15, 469). As voluntary, the cause of sin, of pride, is in an action – not in the nature – of the will (*voluntas*). And as we have seen, Augustine argues that there is no efficient cause of an evil motion or choice of the will, only a deficient one, since strictly speaking evil embodies or effects no thing; it comprises or causes no increase of being. Pride's cause is a mysterious free defection from

---

[13] Cf. *CG* XI.13, 467: "[The devil] refused to be subject to his Creator; ... proudly rejoiced as if in a *power* peculiar to himself; and ... in this, he was both deceived and deceiving" (emphasis added).

the highest good and fullness of being, a tending to oneself and toward nothingness. Augustine glosses this argument early in book XII, opining that "even the vice which has come to seem natural because strengthened by habit or because it has taken an undue hold derives its origin from the will. For we are here speaking of the vices of a natural creature whose mind is capable of possessing the light of reason by which righteous is distinguished from unrighteous" (*CG* XII.3, 502).

How could it be, Augustine asks once again, that some of these most highly intellectually endowed beings willed to reject the source of their beings' fullness and blessedness, while others persevered in freely chosen union with that source? The Socratic question of whether and how one could knowingly reject one's own happiness is echoed by Augustine's doubts. His treatment of the problem here seems highly ambiguous. Augustine wonders aloud whether the angels who did not fall received "more grace of the divine love" from God to sustain their wills in goodness, compared with those who did fall into pride (*CG* XII.9, 510). Or again, Augustine muses, might the angels who would persevere in goodness have received the surety of the permanence of their eternal happiness prior to their free choice in favor of God, while the angels who would fall were not blessed with such assurance, together with the confidence and trust in the Creator that it entails (see *CG* XII.9, 510–11)?

An obvious, troubling difficulty here is that either option seems to trace the "voluntary," deficient cause of the angels' fall and the voluntary (though thoroughly grace-aided and sustained) perseverance in love of those angels who did not fall, back to a will of God to beatify only some angels and damn others, or at a minimum to make the path to holiness and justice much steeper for some angels (those less aided by grace, love, and/or knowledge) than for others. Either option seems to undercut the goodness of God, who creates good things for good ends, is the cause of nothing evil, and hates nothing he has made, according to scripture and Augustine. The perplexed reader has here, it seems, only this hope from Augustine in his concluding remark of this discussion: "But we have already treated of this point in the preceding book" (*CG* XII.9, 511). So it is back to book XI, chapter 13, that we now follow the author of *The City of God*, hoping for a more coherent analysis, and perhaps a more just conclusion.

In this critical chapter, Augustine argues for, or at least from, the proposition that *all angels were created equal* in terms of natural goodness, happiness, and knowledge: "It is hard to believe that they were not all created equal in felicity from the beginning, and remained so until those who are now evil fell away from the light of goodness by their own will" (*CG* XI.13, 467). Augustine glosses a passage from John's Gospel, in which Jesus teaches that "[Satan] was a murderer from the beginning, because he abode not in the truth" (John 8:44). Manicheans accept the Gospel's authority, and read this passage as supporting the existence of a primordial evil nature, or "adverse first cause," opposed to the essence of good and light, from whom "the devil has received an evil nature peculiar to himself" (*CG* XI.13, 468). We have seen that Augustine has already argued copiously, both from philosophy and from faith, against the possibility of naturally evil being, and now he will disprove it on the basis of careful interpretation of this passage from John:

[The Manicheans] fail to notice that the Lord did not say that the truth was absent from the devil's nature. Rather, He said that "he abode not in the truth." By this, He wished us to understand that the devil had fallen away from *the truth in which, had he remained steadfast, he would have been made a partaker*, and so would have remained in blessedness with the holy angels. (*CG* XI.13, 468; emphasis added)

Augustine favors this more reasonable interpretation of Satan's (and his fellows') fall, that from the first moment of his being, Satan used his freedom to rebel against the truth that his being was dependent upon God and its fulfillment to be found in humble union with and willing service to God, in equality of citizenship with angels and men. Therefore, Satan was never truly

blessed with the holy angels ... [because] he refused to be subject to his Creator; ... he proudly rejoiced as if in a power peculiar to himself; and ... in this, he was both deceived and deceiving. For ... he who refuses to hold fast in godliness to what truly is deludes himself in his pride and mocks himself with that which is not. ... [F]rom the time of his own creation he refused the righteousness that only a will subdued to God in piety can possess. (*CG* XI.13, 467–68)

Augustine's rhetorical dialectic continues along these lines through chapter 15 of book XI. Chapter 16 reviews orders of existence and goodness in created beings, concluding by emphasizing the high dignity and "great weight" of "a good will and rightly ordered love" (*CG* XI.16, 471).[14] In chapter 17, Augustine underscores once more that there was no flaw in the fallen angels' natures, that God created all angels to adhere to himself in love and so remain utterly fulfilled in being and in happiness.

---

[14] On goodness, unity, and order in Augustine's metaphysics, see Thompson (2012). On the contemporary relevance of Augustinian perspectives on the order of love and citizenship, see Gregory (2008).

Satan's angelic nature, as also rational human nature, is intended "to abide with God" its Creator (*CG* XI.17, 471). In light of these passages and Augustine's signal to revisit them in the most troubling portion of book XII dealing with the fall of some of the angels, we can conclude that, in his view, the opacity of angelic pride's causality is due to its voluntariness and its opposition to God's being, its falling away from the source of all being, and its movement toward nothingness. These are deficient causes, in Augustine's parlance, not efficient, and their possibility is rooted in finite beings' creation *ex nihilo*. We know deficient causes only by not knowing them. When we seek a firm grasp of their natural effects, we grasp in vain at emptiness.

Humility and Humanity: The Book of Genesis and the Creation of Man and Woman

The final chapters of book XII treat the creation of human beings as recounted in the book of Genesis. To prepare for this critical discussion, Augustine must disprove the necessity of, and question the reasonableness of, the cyclical view of history. On that view, closely linked to philosophic and mythic theses that the world is eternal, there was no initial moment of creation, hence properly speaking no *beginning* of humanity.

Augustine's criticism of this position is closely connected to his critique of human pride, whereby humans tend to make their minds and experience of the world into the measure of what is possible absolutely speaking, for other human beings and peoples, and even for God. While none of us may have achieved something radically new, created *ex nihilo*, if we were more rational and more humble, this should not put us off or surprise us, much less make us doubt the divine possibility of radical divine creativity, as described in Genesis. As Augustine writes:

With the help of the Lord God, manifest reason destroys these revolving circles which opinion constructs. For what especially leads our adversaries into error … is the fact that they use their own human, mutable, and limited mind to measure the divine mind, which is entirely immutable, infinite in its capacity, and capable of comprehending all things, however numerous, without alternating its thought from one to another. And so what the apostle says applies to them, for "comparing themselves with themselves, they do not understand" (2 Corinthians 10:12). (*CG* XII.18, 525)

Newness in history, Augustine's rhetorical dialectic stresses, need not and does not negate God's perfect unity and simplicity, nor vary his "eternal and immutable will" (*CG* XII.18, 525).

This metaphysical, natural-theological defense of the intelligibility and possibility of God's new actions in time continues through chapter 19 of book XII. In this chapter, Augustine again questions the reasonableness of us *homunculi*[15] – little men and women – setting limits to God's knowledge. Augustine's rhetorical turns of phrase embellish his summary of philosophy and theology.

> [God's] wisdom, which is simple in its multiplicity and uniform in its variety, comprehends all that is incomprehensible with a comprehension which is itself so incomprehensible that, though He has willed always to make subsequent events new and unlike all that went before them, He has not produced them without order and foresight; nor has He foreseen them only at the last moment, but by His eternal foreknowledge. (*CG* XII.19, 527)

Another, and perhaps especially compelling, argument Augustine develops against the cyclical view of history has roots in reason, as well as in Christian faith. It takes issue with the conviction, elaborated in classical myth and thought, that the souls of those humans purged from evil through philosophy and right conduct would be blessed a long while in heaven, but then would return to the material world to sin and suffer again. Eventually, their souls would find freedom anew in the vision of God (or of the gods of the myths), but not forever. The endless cycle of affliction and bliss was not thought to be escapable by most, or even by all, human beings' souls, to say nothing of their bodies.

Augustine questions whether this theory is compatible with the goodness and power of God, as understood by Platonists and Christians alike. He again notes with praise Porphyry's dissent from this standard Platonist doctrine, in favor of the soul being forever freed from evils once "it has returned to the Father" (*CG* XII.21, 530; cf. X.30, 438–41). Augustine exhorts his Christian readers, "How much more, then, ought we to detest and shun a falsehood so inimical to the Christian faith!" (*CG* XII.21, 530–31). For, as Cicero noted in *On Friendship* (*De amicitia*) and as Augustine asks, can one be a true friend, a loving one, to someone we know with certainty will betray or reject us later (*CG* XII.21, 529–30)? Christianity indeed holds as a central teaching that not only can the philosophic few be children and friends of God, but also each and every human being. Friendship is at the core of Augustine's view of happiness, as we will see Augustine argue in greater detail in book XIX – friendship with God, first and foremost, and with fellow human beings and good

---

[15] Both Dyson and Bettenson translate Augustine's *homunculi* here as "mere men," but the littleness implied by the Latin is lost in this translation.

angels. The theological certainty of the eternal bliss of the saints thus completes philosophy's quest for beatitude, in Augustine's view.

Philosophy well-followed further demonstrates, with help from Augustine's rhetorical grace, that "no necessity ... compels us to suppose that there was no point in time at which the human race began to exist" (*CG* XII.21, 531). Revealed Christian theology delivers the knockout blow to the nothing-new-in-nature-or-history theory: "For if," as Christian faith clearly teaches, "the soul, once redeemed, as it never was redeemed before, is never to return to misery, then *something is accomplished in it which was never accomplished before; and this something, indeed, is of very great magnitude [quidem valde magnum]*: namely, an eternal happiness which is never to end. But if there can occur in an immortal nature some new thing which never has been repeated in any cycle, nor ever will be, why should it be argued that such a thing cannot occur in mortal natures?" (*CG* XII.21, 531; emphasis added). And in order that this wonderful new reality might be, Augustine continues, "[i]n order that there might be this beginning ... a man was created before whom no man existed" (*CG* XII.21, 532).

Humility in the Creation of Humanity

"I must now speak, just as I did with respect to the angels, of how this [human] part [of the heavenly city's citizenry] arose from the same God's creation" (*CG* XII.9, 511). Augustine's study of human origins continues to follow the scriptures, especially Genesis. His rhetorical dialectic highlights two lessons motivating virtuous human humility, both of which he gleans from the account in Genesis of humanity's origins. In these chapters, as in most of book XI, Augustine makes no explicit mention of humility; it is woven into the very fabric of created being and human being, and so passes unnoted until challenged. Augustine's first observation, which he highlights already at the end of chapter 9, and which he will explicate and reiterate throughout the final chapters of book XII, is that God chose to create a unique first man; from him, to fashion the first woman; and from this first man and this primordial pair, God willed that the whole human race should descend (cf. inter alia *CG* XII.9, 511). A second point he stresses is that only God is the Creator of human beings, both in body and soul[16]; angels were not our creators. From these

---

[16] For example, "[r]ightly, therefore, does the true religion acknowledge and preach that the God Who created the whole world also created all living beings ... souls as well as bodies" (*CG* XII.28, 539).

premises, Augustine will craft arguments concerning the nature of human sociality and compare it with that of the angels. He will also distinguish human creativity and artisanship from the divine act of creation *ex nihilo*. And in all of these facets of properly human existence, Augustine finds motives for humility, as well as magnanimity, but never for hubris or *superbia*.

From Genesis, Augustine gleans that God formed the first man out of the dust of the earth. Echoing Aristotelian anthropology (probably acquired via Plotinus; see Byers [2012, 176–80]), Augustine's rhetorical dialectic emphasizes humans' natural sociability, possessed to a greater extent even than by other gregarious animal species. As if to underscore this natural tendency and the consequent human need of unity in plurality as well as plurality within social unity, Augustine observes that God did not create many first men and women simultaneously, as he did other animals, according to the sacred text of Genesis. Rather, "God … created only one single man: not, certainly, that he might be alone and bereft of human society, but that, by this means, the unity of society and the bond of concord might be commended to him more forcefully, mankind being bound together *not only by similarity of nature, but by the affection of kinship*" (CG XII.22, 533, emphasis added; cf. XII.23, 534). And Augustine reiterates these seminal points a few chapters later, at the conclusion of book XII:

Chief among the terrestrial animals, man was made by [God] in His own image. For the reason that I have already given, and perhaps for some other and greater reason, he was made one individual; but he was not left solitary. *For there is nothing so social by nature as this race, no matter how discordant it has become through its fault*; and human nature can call upon nothing more appropriate, either *to prevent discord from coming into existence, or to heal it where it already exists*, than the remembrance of that *first parent* of us all. (CG XII.28, 539; emphasis added)

In letter 155, written to Macedonius, Augustine commented that the bond of human beings' common rational nature is itself a powerful and moving reality, as evinced by the playwright Terrence's beloved lines *Homo sum: humani nihil a me alienum puto*: "I am a human being: I consider nothing human as foreign to me."[17] In this letter and elsewhere,

---

[17] For Christ, that is, the Truth, says that the whole law and the prophets depend on these two commandments, namely, that we love God with our whole heart, our whole soul, and our whole mind and that we love our neighbors as ourselves. *We should, of course, judge who our neighbor is in this passage not on the basis of blood relationship but on*

Augustine appears concerned about the particular claims of kinship over-riding the just needs of others and the rightful sharing of common goods. His point in this passage of *The City of God*, composed later than letter 155, seems to be that the advantage of Genesis's account of creation in its second chapter is that it unites and deepens our sense of community of nature among humans, rational animals made in the image and likeness of God, both male and female; and that the sacred text shows this shared nature to flow from a true common parentage, giving substance to the sense we are, quite literally, one big human family. The union of concord intended by the Creator is one of fraternal affection, care, and concern, as much as of reasoned reciprocity among those sharing the same nature. This concord is the result of interrelations among those who know they are needy, that they are dependent in an absolute sense on God, interde-pendent among themselves, social, and not naturally suited to isolation or autarchy. Why should they not be humble in this recognition?

Divine vis-à-vis Angelic and Human Artisanship

Near the close of book XII, Augustine devotes two chapters to distin-guishing divine from angelic and human modes of art, including the art of founding cities (CG XII.25–26, 535–38). Form may be given to a being from without or from within. An example of the latter is wood given the form of a chair by a skilled carpenter. The former, however, has to do with the *existence* of the tree from which the wood came, and

---

the basis of our sharing in the society of reason, in which all human beings are united. For if the bond of money unites people, how much more does *the bond of nature* unite them, which they share not by the law of exchange but by that of birth! For this reason that famous comic playwright – for the splendor of the truth is not lacking to brilliant minds – has one old man say to another:

Do you have so much leisure from your own affairs
that you busy yourself about the affairs of others
that are none of your concern?

And he added the response from the other:

I am a human being; I do not regard anything human
as of no concern to me.

They say that whole theaters, full of stupid and ignorant people, applauded that idea. The union of human minds naturally stirs the love of all human beings so that each human being in it feels that he is a neighbor of any other. (Augustine, letter 155, accessed online September 18, 2015, at www02.homepage.villanova.edu/allan.fitzgerald/Letter155.htm; emphasis added)

so of the coming into being of the wood *as wood*; it is an inner form that makes a thing to exist as what it is, and not as another, by nature. The most perfect form of artisanship, according to Augustine, is *creation* properly understood: to cause a nature to be where none has been before and to endow it with its dimensions and its potencies, which angels and human beings may then continue to shape and to bring forth. Only God can be in this absolute sense a creator, exercising the highest and most powerful form of making or founding. "Form in the first of these two senses can be attributed to every craftsman," runs Augustine's rhetorical dialectic, "but form in the second sense ... [can be attributed] to one Maker, Creator, and Founder[18] (*uni artifici, creatori et conditori*) only: to God, who made the world itself and the angels, when no world and no angels existed" (*CG* XII.26, 536).

Toward the end of chapter 26, Augustine compares two paradigmatic founders of great, ancient cities with God himself, as founder of what, again, we might term *res publica universarum naturarum*, the republic of all natures:

[A]s to that form which craftsmen impose on corporeal things from without, we do not say that Rome and Alexandria were founded by masons and architects, but by the kings whose will, intention and authority caused them to be built. Thus, the one has Romulus as its founder, and the other Alexander. We ought, then, to be all the more ready to say that God alone is the Founder [*conditorem*] of natures, since He neither uses in his work any material which has not itself been made by Him, nor any workmen who were not themselves created by Him. Moreover, if He were to withdraw His creative power, so to speak, from things, they would no more exist than they did before they were created. (*CG* XII.26, 537–38).

Platonists who regard angels as the creators of human bodies and other material beings therefore err, since such creative art is beyond the power of any being but the One, the "First Cause."

In this closing salvo of book XII, then, we see Augustine's rhetorical dialectic emphasize the real, rightful humility of all human foundations, even those that bring into being the greatest human cities, nations, kingdoms, and empires. Human foundations are radically derivative from, and should be ordered in service to, the natures and human beings whom *God* has founded and brought to be. True angelic foundations

---

[18] Here I render *conditor* as Founder, where Dyson has "Establisher." In other passages, where Dyson renders *conditor* as "author" or "creator," for instance, I use "founder" instead for consistency, if the sense of the text allows.

and makings are likewise at the service of God's foundations. If only the Platonists and the people they instruct, writes Augustine with anguish, "could ... be rid of the superstition which causes them to seek to justify the offering of rites and sacrifices to such gods as though they were their founders[19] [*quasi conditoribus*]," they could be free to understand themselves and human society, the angels and their *res publica*, and God their origin and end, in a much truer light (*CG* XII.25, 535).

We might add, following the logic of Augustine's rhetorical dialectic in books XI and XII, and its explicit and latent themes, that by this realization humans might be loosed from the shackles of angelic, daemonic, and human *superbia*, freed to exercise humbler and more truly magnanimous artisanry and agency in every facet of their personal and common lives.

---

[19] Here I modify Dyson, who translates *conditoribus* as "creators."

6

The City of God XIII–XIV

Being-toward-Life, Being-toward-Death

No life is evil as life, but only as it tends to death. Life knows no death save wickedness (*nequitia*) which derives its name from nothingness (*ne quidquam*).

Augustine, De vera religione XI.21

[T]o forsake God and to exist in oneself ... is not immediately to lose all being; but it is to come closer to nothingness. ... [I]t is good to lift up your hearts; not to oneself, however, which is pride, but to the Lord. This is obedience, which can belong only to the humble.

Augustine, The City of God XIV.13

Books XIII and XIV complete Augustine's inquiry into the origins of the two cities, an inquiry begun in books XI and XII. As Augustine writes: "Now that we have dealt with the most difficult questions (*dificillimis quaestionibus*) concerning the origin of our world and the beginning of the human race, the proper order of the discussion ... requires that we next discuss the fall of the first man – or, rather, of the first human beings – and the origin and propagation of human death" (*CG* XIII.1, 541). Augustine's reader therefore expects this segment of his rhetorical dialectic to begin with an explication of Genesis's story of the Fall of Adam and Eve, read within the context of sacred scripture as a whole and the tradition of the church. From there, the reader anticipates that Augustine will turn to human death, as a traumatic, tragic effect of this epic fall. Somewhat surprisingly, Augustine reverses the anticipated order, to focus first on death, the foil and cessation of life, and death's several senses and causes. As John Cavadini observes, "In book 13 of the *City of God* Augustine offers his reader what is in effect a short treatise on the subject of death" (1999, 232).

In order to understand death, it would seem, Augustine continues in book XIII to reflect on the meaning of life; for as evil is the absence of good, death is nothing other than the cessation of life, the absence of life where life once flourished. Only after this consideration of death, and with it of life, do we reach Augustine's detailed investigation in book XIV of the first human sin, its cause or causes, and its effects on human nature, human relationships, and the transmission of human life.

Augustine's *apologia* for humility (*humilitas*) against pride (*superbia*) in this pair of books aims to reveal humility as fertile soil for life, abundant life, while pride pollutes the ground and withers life at its root. Readers familiar with scripture may recall Moses's exhortation to the people of Israel: "I call heaven and earth to witness against you, that I have set before you life and death, blessing and curse; therefore choose life, that you and your descendants may live, loving the Lord your God, obeying his voice, and cleaving to him; for that means life to you" (Deuteronomy 30:19–20). As Augustine's rhetorical dialectic now considers Genesis and its account of the primordial human sin, addressing especially his Christian readers, he never neglects to recall pagan readers, especially those who, like Augustine himself and many others among their Christian peers, are influenced by or attracted to Platonic philosophy. For the sake of these audiences or sets of interlocutors, Augustine's dialectic intertwines experiential, philosophic, and theological lines of reasoning at key moments in his text. Humility, he emphasizes, undergirds what we might term being-toward-life, the Creator's benevolent intent for human existence. Pride perverts this orientation toward abundant life, spawning in its stead being-toward-death.

A second essential aspect of Augustine's rhetorical dialectic in books XIII and XIV is by now familiar to us, as a chief concern throughout *The City of God*: the defense of the humble human body and human emotions from their political, philosophic, and religious detractors. Those human beings who disdain the lowly animality of their condition, who wish to dwell free from flesh in the immutable world of forms, display a learned ignorance, a lack of hope, or perhaps, a prideful wish for superiority. On these grounds, Augustine debates with Platonic and other philosophers, arguing that the death that transpires when the soul departs the body is indeed an *evil* for human beings. Being-toward-death in this basic sense is not good for humans. Further, only those who can accept the body as good in itself, an indispensable part of our humanity, and who can perceive likewise the humanity of passions or emotions, can accept with ease and gratitude the humility of God in creating such humans in his image and likeness, and in taking on human flesh and human passions to redeem human beings from the pestilence of pride. To despise the body is to resist, albeit unknowingly, the summons to citizenship in the heavenly city. It is also to misunderstand the conditions needed for human being-toward-fullness-of-life, and unjustly to restrict the hope for such a fullness to an elite, philosophic few, as we saw also in Chapter 4.

LIFE AND DEATH IN BOOK XIII

After its brief introductory chapter, Augustine's rhetorical dialectic in book XIII explores three major themes; put another way, it engages in three debates, experiential, philosophical, and theological. The first follows from the biblical injunction that "the wages of sin is death" (Romans 6:23), and more specifically from God's prohibition against eating the forbidden fruit, "lest you die" (Genesis 3:3). With regard to what form of "death" does God admonish the first couple to obey his command? To answer this question, Augustine engages in a lengthy meditation on death and dying, along the way identifying and interrelating four distinct forms of death, and examining whether each is good or evil for human beings.

From this study, Augustine's rhetorical dialectic transitions into the central debate of book XIII, again in dialogue with the Platonists – as John Cavadini has shown (1999), philosophic Christians as well as pagans – who regard death as the separation of soul and body to be a good thing for the human being, freeing the human soul from the limitations and corruption of matter.[1] Augustine attempts to persuade readers of such philosophic persuasions that the death of the body is in fact an evil; and, therefore, that the Jewish and Christian hope in the resurrection of the body is one which all human beings implicitly share or are inclined by their very nature to share. In book XIII's final five chapters, Augustine studies what can be gleaned from scripture about the condition of humans' future, resurrected bodies, and why they merit our hope and desire, more so than eternal life as a human soul separated forever from its body should do. Throughout this portion of his rhetorical dialectic, Augustine employs arguments from widely shared human experiences; from nature or philosophy; and from revealed, ecclesial, and scriptural theology. He endeavors to lead his philosophic pagan readers

---

[1] On this theme, see also the chapters on Ambrose and Augustine in Jones (2007).

along, step by step, toward an embrace of, or at least openness to, the reasonableness and goodness of hope for the future reunification of soul and body. He likewise seeks to underscore the evil of bodily death for his fellow philosophic Christians, and so to lead them to realize more deeply the radical significance of the Incarnation, death, and Resurrection of Christ for humanity in its battle against sin and *superbia* (see Cavadini, 1999, 236–38, 244–46, 249).

With regard to humility and pride, as we will see, and as was the case also in book XII, book XIII's argument makes no explicit mention of humility (*humilitas*). Strikingly, it contains only one explicit mention of pride (*superbia*). As I will argue later in this chapter, the context of this lone instance is critical. Again in this chapter, humility is present though hidden, woven into the backdrop of created nature; in the just or right condition of human nature and human life; and in humans' relationship with and rightful stance toward their Creator. Pride is similarly lurking in the shadows, but in Augustine's discussion of death, rather than of life. Pride is at times alluded to by Augustine, using descriptions of or analogies to *superbia*, which he has also previously employed.

Augustine's rhetorical dialectic brings into the light of day pride's insidious workings in the Garden of Eden, in book XIV, where he confronts the original sin of Adam and Eve. Humility, too, will enter in a more obvious manner into Augustine's dialectic in book XIV. In this segment of the chapter, we will focus on book XIII and Augustine's endeavor therein to make an honest, humble study of our common mortality, and on the reasons for our author's hope that death will not have the last word in our lives, not even regarding the life of our bodies (cf. 1 Peter 3:15).

On Death and Dying: Chapters 2–15

Augustine's preoccupation with the problem of death comes to the fore in this thirteenth book, where over half of the chapters are devoted to its exploration. The first matter at hand is to identify various meanings or kinds of "death," and to ascertain to which of these God referred when he warned Adam and Eve of the perils of eating of the forbidden fruit.

In these chapters, Augustine's rhetorical dialectic concerning death is challenging to follow. He focuses on distinguishing between the "first death" and "the second death," following the book of Revelation (Revelation 2:11, 20:6, 20:14, 21:8). Yet in so doing, he identifies not two but four forms of death, and offers a rough sketch of their chronology and interrelation. Two of these are inevitable for human beings after the Fall, while the other two may be avoided by God's grace and free human correspondence.

The first form of death for Augustine is "the death of the soul" when it is separated from God, from whom it draws life in the fullest sense of the term. The death of the soul happens only through sin or as an effect of sin. The second form of death is the most obvious to us and is in some form universally acknowledged: "the death of the body" when it is separated from its soul (*CG* XIII.2, 541). The third form of death follows upon both of these, when the grace of conversion has not intervened or been accepted: the permanent separation of the departed soul from its God. Augustine poignantly describes this as "the *death ... of the whole man* [(*mors*) *totius hominis*] ... when the soul, forsaken by God, forsakes the body" (*CG* XIII.2, 541; emphasis added). The fourth form, to which Augustine also refers as "the second death," occurs with the reunification of the human body with its now "dead soul" [*anima mortua*], which unification is for the body a cause of torment and deeply diminished life for all eternity. This "final damnation," despite following the resurrection of the body and the reunification of human nature's key components, is "not unjustly called death rather than life" (*CG* XIII.2, 542).

Augustine at one time or another dubs each of the three first-mentioned forms of death, "the first death." This can be confusing for the reader, but on closer examination Augustine has a reasonably clear rationale for each appellation. He conceives of the "*first death*" as that which causes "the *separation of two united natures*, whether these be God and the soul [i.e., the death of the soul, through serious sin], or the soul and the body ['the first bodily death']" (*CG* XIII.2, 542; emphasis added). The unhappy succession of the soul and body's initial deaths yields the fullness of "the first death": "*the whole of the first death itself*, by which the soul is punished by *separation from both God and the body*" (*CG* XIII.12, 554; emphasis added). "The first death consists of two [deaths],[2] the one of the soul and the one of the body; and so *the first death is a death of the whole man (ut sit prima totius hominis mors)*" (*CG* XIII.12, 554; emphasis added).

As to the question of whether death is or may intelligibly be spoken of as a good thing for human beings, Augustine insists on discerning first of which kind of death one speaks. That the second death is an evil thing for

---

[2] Or, alternatively in the same passage, of two *parts*: "the first part of the first death" being the death of the soul; "the second part [of the first death], by which the body is deprived of the soul" (*CG* XIII.12, 554).

human beings Augustine takes to be self-evident on account of its pathos and eternal duration, and because by definition no good human being ever suffers it (*CG* XIII.2, 542). Analogously one can conclude that the first death of the soul, and even more so the "whole first death" of the whole human being, can in no sense be good for human beings, whose natures they wound and whose happiness they obstruct.

But what of the first death of the body? Is not that death at least "truly a good for good men," although evil for evil human beings (*CG* XIII.3, 543)? Augustine indicates that this is the most contentious of the questions he has raised regarding the goodness or evil of death, and that it is not easy to answer. To endeavor to do so in such a way as to engage his perplexed readers and those holding opinions different from his own, Augustine follows a rhetorical-dialectical path that includes reflection upon the experience, philosophy, and theology of death and dying. He addresses first of all believing Christians, elucidating for them scripture passages that might seem contradictory, with reference to the faith of the church. Nonetheless, Augustine is not solely interested in his fellow believers: Once again, he seems especially eager to debate also with those who are so near and yet so far, the pagan philosophers, especially pagan Platonists (cf. *CG* VIII.1, 312–13, and VIII.4–5, 316–20). Thus, Augustine's dialectical consideration of the body's death and its ontological implications for human beings begins from the *regula fidei*, the rule or guide of faith, moving on to engage in experiential and nature-based arguments that might resonate with more perplexed readers of all levels of education, and even with the greatest non-Christian philosophers of Augustine's era.

Augustine begins this portion of his rhetorical dialectic by conceding the prima facie reasonableness, from the vantage point of Jewish and Christian faith, of considering the first bodily death a good for good humans, even as it constitutes an evil for evil people: "Precious in the eyes of the Lord is the death of his faithful ones" (Psalm 116:15; see *CG* XIII.7, 548). Augustine's Christian readers might also recall Jesus's moving words to the good thief on Calvary: "Amen, I say to you, this day you will be with me in paradise" *(Luke 23:43)*. If the bodily death of those in God's good grace is precious to him, and if the departed soul may enter paradise at once in loving union with its God, how could this be termed an evil? Must it not be good?

Augustine appears to acknowledge that this conclusion is reasonable: "Of the first and bodily death, then, it may be said (*dici potest*) that it is a good for good men and an evil for evil men" (*CG* XIII.2, 542). In the ensuing chapters, however, his rhetorical dialectic calls this conclusion into question, as examining death and its status more closely. Augustine's first caveat comes from a reflection on Genesis and its narrative of the Fall. If Adam and Eve had persevered in goodness, there would have been no death for them, nor would their progeny have been born mortal. Death would have been "non-existent to them" (*CG* XIII.3, 543). If the truth is that there would have been no death for wholly good human beings, Augustine asks, how can death be good?[3] What can it be but a consequence of and punishment for sin? Augustine writes of our first parents that "[t]heir nature was changed for the worse in proportion to the condemnation attaching to the magnitude of their sin, so that what arose as a punishment in the first human beings who sinned also *follows as a natural consequence* (*naturaliter sequeretur*) in the rest who are born of them" (*CG* XIII.3, 543; emphasis added).

In this passage, it is not exactly that, as an old dictum puts it, "in Adam's fall we sinned all," but rather that because of Adam and Eve's fall, their progeny have all received a nature bereft of the special grace that had maintained its original integrity and union with God, and so by nature share in the punishment of the first couple.[4] But thanks to the grace of God given after sin – original and personal – humans have the possibility of making "good use" of the evil that is death, as when it is "embraced for the sake of truth" (*CG* XIII.5, 546; cf. XIII.8, 548). The martyrs are once again Augustine's paradigm case of such "[dying] well, even though death is an evil" (*CG* XIII.5, 547). He writes, "It was through the strength and struggle of faith, at least in times gone by, that the fear of death was mastered. This is especially true in the case of the holy martyrs" (*CG* XIII.4, 545).

So far, only believing Christians are likely to be convinced by Augustine's argument, coming as it does chiefly from sacred scripture and the tradition of the church. By the sixth chapter of this book, how-ever, Augustine begins to incorporate experiential and philosophical-anthropological reflections that he hopes may move a wider readership, pagans as well as Christians. He reflects on the universal experience of death qua "separation of soul from the body" (*CG* XIII.6, 547), and on

---

[3] Cavadini (1999) argues that *The City of God* XIII is constructed by Augustine to respond to and refute his mentor Ambrose's Platonic argument in *De bono mortis* (*On the Good of Death*), that death is a good for good people.

[4] See *CG* XIII.6, 547: "Death, generated in unbroken succession from the first man, is beyond doubt the punishment of all who are born of him (*procul dubio sit mors poena nascentis*). But, if undergone for the sake of godliness and righteousness (*pro pietate iusti-tiaque*), it becomes the glory of those who are born again."

the various meanings death can have even in this regard. One of these, the most evident to us in this saeculum, is the actual experience of dying, and so of the great suffering that ordinarily accompanies dying, and that we spontaneously experience and recognize *as evil*. Augustine describes this event of dying with poignancy, repeatedly in these chapters: "[A] sensation of anguish, *contrary to nature*, is produced by the force that tears apart the two things which had been conjoined and interwoven during life; and this sensation persists until there is a complete cessation of all that feeling which was present by reason of the union of soul and flesh" (*CG* XIII.6, 547; emphasis added). And again: "Death [is] an evil while it [is] in being: that is, while it [is] being suffered by the dying; for the dire and grievous sense of it ... [is] then present" (*CG* XIII.9, 549). And once again, a bit later: "Would that we had led such a good life in Paradise that there truly was no death! Now, however, not only does death indeed exist, but it is so vexatious that it cannot be explained by any kind of speech or evaded by any reasoning" (*CG* XIII.11, 552).

The suffering and sorrow that humans acknowledge to be associated with death point us back to Augustine's initial definition of "the first bodily death," as a sundering of a right and good fellowship: the intimate union between soul and body, the dual defining aspects of "the whole man" in humanity's specific (species) being and human beings' personal existence (see *CG* XIII.3, 543). This breaking of ontological communion, Augustine implies, is intrinsically evil, going against the good of human nature, which was created for good by the all-good God. After the Fall, due to the wounds inflicted by pride and other sinfulness on our souls and bodies, our very being is lessened and weakened. Where before human being was being toward life, fullness of life, it is also now being toward the death to which unchecked mutability inclines, and toward which indeed it races (*CG* XIII.10, 550–51). We will return later to this critical theme when considering the opening chapters of book XIV with Augustine's analysis there of the original sin itself, and with it of our key themes of pride and humility.

Augustine's rhetorical dialectic questions whether death is good or evil, if by "death" we mean the condition of a person after his or her soul has departed its body. Again, Augustine brings his argument back around to the Judeo-Christian common-sense position from which he began, one summed up in this passage from the book of Wisdom 3:1–4: "The souls of the just are in the hand of God, and no torment shall touch them. ... [T]hey are in peace." This condition cannot be evil for them. Augustine to a considerable extent appears to concur with this conclusion:

As to those of whom we say they are already dead, however, it is not absurd to say that, in their case, death is an evil to the wicked and a good to the good. For the souls which have been separated from the bodies of the godly are at rest, but those of the ungodly suffer punishment until their bodies rise again: those of the godly to eternal life, and those of the ungodly to the eternal death which is called the second death. (CG XIII.8, 549; cf. XIII.19, 564)

These considerations position us to follow Augustine into yet another amicable debate with certain Platonists, whom we can imagine replying to Augustine along these lines:

So you admit that the condition of the soul of the good and just man after death is a peaceful and happy one! In this you agree with us. We don't dispute that the pain and suffering of dying are not in themselves good. Rather, we argue that they are of little or no account compared with the condition of the virtuous soul after departing the body: the soul is what is best in humanity, as you also agree. Why can't you see with us that its return to the body is in no way beneficial for the wise and just soul, but rather comprises a new imprisonment for it?

In chapters 16 through 20 of book XIII, Augustine will confront and endeavor to refute these philosophic objections. It is to this critical segment of his rhetorical-dialectical engagement that we next turn.

Plato, the Platonists, and Pride: Chapters 16–24

Augustine next addresses two objections of Platonic philosophers against his view of the relationship of body and soul in human nature. The first is, as we have already seen, that the soul is truly in a better state when freed from the weakness and limitations the body imposes upon it. Therefore, death, understood as the condition of being dead, rather than as the process of suffering death, is no evil at all. It is by nature an improved condition, especially so for the soul of the wise and just person. The second Platonic objection Augustine raises is that the Christian belief in the resurrection of the body is an impossibility: The disintegrated matter from a lifeless human body cannot be reintegrated in a later era, not even by the divinity. Finite, mutable beings such as earthly human bodies cannot be made immutable and eternal.

Against the first objection, unsurprisingly, Augustine supports the conclusion that "[although] the souls of the righteous and godly dead live on in peaceful rest," as, *mutatis mutandis*, he and the late-classical Platonists generally agree, "*it would still be much better for them to be alive in healthy bodies*" (CG XIII.19, 564; emphasis added). Against the second, Augustine will urge that the power of the Creator-God, rightly understood, necessarily extends to the re-creation of beings such as bodies that have ceased to exist, and the reintegration of these bodies with their souls. Augustine's strategy in this regard is to identify passages in Plato's works that seem supportive of the Christian interpretation and to urge Plato's late-classical disciples to consider implications of these passages for their critiques of Christianity. Augustine will also, once again, incorporate experience-based considerations into his rhetorical dialectic, to indicate to readers of diverse religious and philosophic persuasions the reasonableness of this Christian belief.

At the outset of this discussion, Augustine indicates that there is a longer and more difficult path he could take but will not. In this case, the more arduous road-not-taken would be directly and "painstakingly to demonstrate that it is not the body, but the body's corruptibility, which is a burden to the soul" (*CG* XIII.16, 557). Augustine avoids this longer way because he judges that he has found one that is shorter yet no less effective for his pagan Platonic readers and for calming philosophic doubts for his Christian audience. This shorter path is to quote and comment on a passage from Cicero's translation of part of the *Timaeus*, and to show how accepting its truth, or even plausibility, entails openness to Augustine's Christian interpretation of body and soul, life, death, and resurrection.

As Augustine recalls a passage from Cicero's Latin *Timaeus*, the supreme God who fashioned the universe reassures the lesser gods, great souls joined to the bodies of heavenly beings such as stars, that although they are composite and so mortal by nature, by his good and trustworthy will, they will abide in being forever.[5] If God can give eternal life to these bodies, to the composite creatures of the heavens, and if his promise of their immortality is taken by Plato and his disciples to be a good thing, why should it be per se impossible, as many Platonists insist in response to Christian claims, that human souls too can become perfectly blessed in and with their bodies? To hold the possibility of full happiness for the soul together with its body to be impossible or absurd, Augustine argues, makes no sense to one who already accepts the premises and conclusions of this passage from the *Timaeus* (*CG* XIII.16, 557–59).

Augustine next considers a related position of Platonic philosophers: that earthly bodies, in contrast to heavenly ones, cannot be made eternal, because of the dust (Genesis) or earth (*Timeaus*) from which they have been fashioned. Here there is a strong Socratic-dialogic dimension

---

[5] As Gerard O'Daly observes, "*Tim.* 41a–b is meant: Augustine cites (inaccurately) Cicero's translation *Tim.* II. 40" (1999a, 151, note 31).

to Augustine's discourse, pointing out premises and conclusions from Platonic dialogues that his contemporary Platonists widely take to be true. Augustine asks in effect: If you disciples of Plato maintain that the earth itself is immortal because it comprises a part of the universe ensouled by a god lesser only than the Creator-God and that this composite world-divinity is not only blessed but eternal, how can you take it as given that God could not do the same for earthly bodies like our own? If God can maintain one form of matter incorruptible, when it is by nature composite and corruptible, why not another form as well (see CG XIII.17–18, 559–63)? As Gerard O'Daly (1999a, 151) sums up Augustine's rhetorical dialectic in these chapters, "Platonist objections to the Christian attitude to the body, especially in its resurrected form, are inconsistent with their own attitudes to embodiment."

Against this backdrop, Augustine asks why some pagan Platonists reject out of hand, as intrinsically irrational, Christian teachings on the resurrection of the body and its reunification in perpetuity with its soul. Might it not be because of vicious pride, *superbia*? Here Augustine stresses not the height (or depth) of *superbia*, by which one seeks one's own divinization in place of true divinity, or even the hubris of seeking to be self-sufficient in the quest for union with God. Rather it is *superbia* in the forms of vanity, vainglory, and arrogance that Augustine attributes to anti-Christian Platonists. Again, we see Augustine the rhetorician highly sensitive to the glory and honor accompanying certain *names*: titles that elevate oneself or one's group over others, implicitly or explicitly. In this way we may recall from Chapter 2 that Augustine cautions readers not to be taken in by the grandiosity of political and imperial terms such as kingdoms and empires, especially to the extent of being blinded by these names and the appearances they evoke to the realities at hand as just or unjust, good or evil. Now it is once again the honor and glory that accompany philosophic excellence and fame, together with the sense of exclusiveness and intellectual superiority they easily entail, that come to the fore in *The City of God* and its rhetorical dialectic. There are some philosophers (not all, Augustine implies) who rather than loving wisdom (see Chapter 4) with all their hearts as a common good, regard it as a private or quasi-private good and relish that ownership and its higher status. They

glory in being, or in being called, Platonists, and [their] pride in this name [*cuius superbia nominis*] makes them ashamed to be Christians. For they fear that if they share a name with the vulgar herd [*ne commune illis cum vulgo vocabulum vilem*], this will detract from the exclusiveness of the fraternity of those who wear the *pallium*, whose self-importance is in proportion to their fewness. (CG XIII.16, 559)

To keep their superior status, Augustine suggests, they seek something to criticize in Christian teaching. The body's status vis-à-vis the soul, and the hope of its future immortality, comprise their chief chosen target.

Here again it is important to grasp what Augustine does *not* understand himself to have proven, the truth of the Christian position on the resurrection of the body, although he implies that he might with great effort be able to demonstrate that the body's corruptibility, rather than its being, is a cause of unhappiness to the soul. What he endeavors to do, by his rhetorical dialectic, is open the hearts and minds of readers influenced against Christianity by late-classical Platonic philosophy. Augustine urges, if you believe, as many Platonists may, the teachings of the *Timaeus* as Plato's own, and therefore as likely to be true, why are you utterly closed to analogous and no more incredible teachings contained in Christian revelation (see inter alia *CG* XIII.17, 560)?[6] Is it reasonable to believe, Augustine prods further, that

> God has power to do nothing that Christians believe, but everything that Platonists wish? Are philosophers, then, able to know the purpose and power of God, whereas the prophets were not? On the contrary, the spirit of God taught His prophets to proclaim as much of His will as He thought fit to reveal, but when the philosophers sought to discover it, they were deceived by merely human conjecture. But they should still not have been so far deceived, by either ignorance or obstinacy, as to contradict themselves so blatantly. (*CG* XIII.17, 560; cf. II.7, 58)

Rather, the *Timaeus* of Plato should give them pause. Augustine endeavors to calm the passions of philosophic opposition, by promoting reflection on analogous premises that many Platonists in fact already accept, and so to open ears to the reasonable, hopeful words of the prophets, and to open minds to dialogue and frank, friendly discussion.

To speak in [Alasdair] MacIntyrean language, Augustine is himself versed in the tradition of Platonic philosophy and has learned its ways of thought, argument, and life from within. He endeavors in his rhetorical dialectic to uncover contradictions within the Platonists' thinking, especially where their own philosophy appears in tension with their philosophical critiques of Christianity. Augustine also seeks to show what in their teaching cannot be more than speculation or even myth and to suggest that the prophetic tradition of Judaism and Christianity is much

---

[6] Augustine argues this *a fortiori* in the case of philosophers who dissent from some late-Platonic teachings that are also rejected by Christianity, especially the re-incarnation of all souls, even those of perfect justice and virtue: see his assessment of Porphyry's views in *CG* XIII.19, 565–66.

more credible. His rhetorical dialectic once again seeks to clear a fresh path and to invite philosophic wanderers to travel along it with him for a while, as far as they wish and can go – to come along with him to see and to judge for themselves (cf. John 1:46).

As Augustine opens this path, moreover, he offers additional experiential evidence to buttress the credibility of Christian teaching on the body and its role in human happiness. What ordinary adult has not experienced that when his or her body is in good health, or at least better-than-usual health, when it is strong and robust, it is not felt to be a burden or is at least much less of a burden; that it is rather a source of energy and vitality, life-enhancing rather than life-negating for the soul? Why should a perfect body, as Adam and Eve possessed in Eden, be judged a burden to be shed on the path to happiness? And even if it were argued that humans would be still better off with the perfect agility of a pure spirit, without the limits of any human body as we know it, the new spiritual body promised for "our future immortality" would impose no such weights or limits (*CG* XIII.18, 563). Why could not the One Creator bestow this gift on human beings? And why should a true philosopher recoil from such a promise and prospect (*CG* XIII.18, 562–63)?

Augustine's argument in these chapters thus follows a now-familiar pattern: to endeavor to remove philosophic obstacles to the possibility of and reasons for faith; to offer evidence for his position from common human experience; and to describe the *City of God* and the final condition of its citizenry so as to elicit desire for membership in it. Philosophic pride comprises perhaps the most formidable of these obstacles. Hence, as we have noted already, Augustine's debate with the Platonists boasts the sole explicit mention of *superbia* in book XIII, together with a plea to the philosophers to lay it aside and so travel more lightly on their journey toward true wisdom and blessedness (*CG* XIII.16, 559).

In the concluding chapters of book XIII, Augustine offers a commentary on the Christian scriptures regarding the wonderful new condition we may hope for in our own bodies, in heaven when they are as immortal as the spiritual souls that vivify them. For in that happy *civitas* all will be vivified by God's own Spirit from whom both soul and body will derive their life and be "able to live wisely and blessedly"; and the immortal body, "entirely unable to die," will be "in this respect like the soul" (*CG* XIII.24, 579–80). We are thus brought back to book XIII's opening, highlighting how the soul even now draws its life from God and gives life in turn to the body (see *CG* XIII.2, 542). Augustine's readers are invited to marvel at the closeness of divinity to humanity, to *the whole human being*, soul and body, and so to hope for a future glory far surpassing fame, or even the truest wisdom of philosophy, apart from true faith.

Echoes of Humility: Life, Obedience, and Love in Book XIII

We have noted that the word *superbia* occurs only once in the whole of book XIII, and that *humilitas* does not occur at all, seemingly reflective of the book's thematic of the primeval fall and its consequences, none of which involves virtuous humility. Still, humility remains in the narrative's backdrop in many respects, both in itself and through virtues closely connected with it. As we have seen in earlier chapters, for Augustine, virtuous humility disposes one to love common goods, goods sharable with others and perfective of many, above purely private goods. In this way also, humility disposes humans to love justice and right. When Augustine reminds readers here in book XIII that the first human sin involved love of self and one's own will above love of God and his will, and so issued in disobedience, he harkens back to the struggle humans experience between humility and pride. "For if a man holds the will of God in contempt, he can indeed only do himself harm; and so he learns that there is a difference between cleaving to that Good which is common to all and delighting in his own good. For he who loves himself is abandoned to himself, so that, when he is thereby overwhelmed by fears and sorrows," he may repent and receive God's healing mercy (*CG* XIII.21, 568). Thus, God's remarkable humility is again made visible, in patiently leading the proud back to the right way to happiness.

In a related manner, in chapter 20 Augustine underscores the link between the right humility of rational creatures, as he has elaborated throughout the preceding twelve books of *The City of God*, and the obedience that God sought from Adam and Eve, which they rejected to their peril and ours. Before the Fall, our first parents refrained from eating "from the one tree that had been forbidden – not because it was in itself evil, but in order to commend the good of a pure and simple obedience, which is a great virtue of the rational creature established under the Lord its Creator" (*CG* XIII.20, 567).[7] Humility likewise is linked with, and present in the background of, Augustine's discussions in book XIII of life, love, and grace (see inter alia *CG* XIII.2, 542; 5, 546; and 24, 574–80).

---

[7] Here I modify Dyson's translation ("the great virtue") of Augustine's *magna virtus* regarding obedience. Cf. *CG* XIV.13, 609, indicating that for Augustine humility is an even greater, or more foundational, virtue: "[O]bedience … can belong only to the humble." Likewise, it is humility rather than obedience that Augustine presents *The City of God* as a whole as defending (see *CG* I, preface, 3).

Similarly, pride *qua superbia* is much more present in book XIII than its lone occurrence indicates. It is present in the backdrop of discourses on disobedience; on love solely of proper, private goods; and on death in all its senses. Thus Augustine writes regarding the genesis of concupiscence and lust following the first human sin:

> The soul, now taking delight in its own freedom to do wickedness, and disdaining to serve God, was itself deprived of the erstwhile subjection of the body to it. Because it had of its own free will forsaken its superior Lord, it no longer held its own inferior servant in obedience to its will ... as it would always have been able to do if it had itself remained subject to God. (*CG* XIII.13, 555)

The fall from humility into pride was the fault of the free will of the souls, not the bodies, of Adam and Eve, "[f]or God, Who is the author of nature, and certainly not of vices, created man righteous" (*CG* XIII.14, 555). And yet the fall of the soul had tragic consequences for the body as well, in its own mortality and in its relationship to the soul, its immediate principle of life. It is to these consequences that Augustine's rhetorical dialectic now turns, via a closer study of the biblical account of original sin, and therewith also of humility and pride, as he commences book XIV of his *City of God.*

BOOK XIV: SIN, *SUPERBIA,* AND THE SHARING OF LIFE AND DEATH

Book XIV is a book about original sin, constituting Augustine's deepest exploration in *The City of God* of the primordial fall's nature and causes. Together with book XIII, it also comprises his deepest probing of original sin's effects on humanity. Book XIV is therefore, as Augustine indicates throughout, a book about pride (*superbia*).[8] Of particular import to this portion of Augustine's rhetorical dialectic is the elucidation of the first sin's effects on the transmission of human life. Thus he emphasizes the impact of original sin and *superbia* on social bonds among human beings (*CG* XIV.14 and 15). In so doing, Augustine employs several political metaphors and alludes to sin's civic effects (*CG* XIV.11, 13, and 15).

Augustine's theological account of the aftermath of the Fall is, however, a hopeful one. So it should not surprise us to find at the summit of this book about sin and *superbia* in chapter 13 a strong discourse on and defense of *humilitas* (see *CG* XIV.13, 609–10). Book XIV thus harkens back to the preface of *The City of God,* in which Augustine

---

[8] In book XIII, there was just one explicit mention of *superbia*. In book XIV, there are approximately 20 references to *superbia* and its cognates.

casts his overarching purpose in terms of the *persuasion* of the proud concerning humility's great excellence (*CG* I, preface, 3). Given that not all the proud share his theological convictions, and that in book XIII he has underscored again, as in book X, the particular philosophic risk of a vain and complacent pride, it also comes as no surprise that chapter 13, treating humility and pride, is book XIV's most philosophical and metaphysical.

Throughout book XIV, Augustine engages his readers in a narrative leading to the recognition of pride, *superbia*, as the source, in themselves and in others, of an unnatural being-toward-death, in all of death's senses elaborated in book XIII. In illustrating the pathos of pride's impact on life and death, Augustine endeavors to elicit in his audience a desire for the graced humility that, he holds, alone can restore nature, heal humanity, and truly divinize human beings by participation in God's being and life. The turn to humility at the pinnacle of book XIV's rhetorical dialectic thus marks out for readers the road back to being-toward-life, indeed, to abundant life (cf. John 10:10).

The Earthly City, the Body, and its Emotions

Augustine opens book XIV with a return to his theme of "two cities," or "two orders of human society" (*CG* XIV.1, 581).[9] These are now described, following the apostle Paul in his epistles, as comprised by human beings "who live according to the flesh," and those who, by contrast, "live according to the spirit" (*CG* XIV.1, 581; cf. Ephesians 2:19; Philippians 3:20). In parsing out the meaning of this distinction, Augustine probes the scriptures and concludes that to live according to the flesh is not meant as only living for the benefit of the body and its flourishing. Rather, the sense of this phrase in scripture is living according to, and for the sake of, human beings alone, whether their goods are of body or soul or both, as if we humans were our own creators and *teloi*. "Flesh" in this scriptural sense refers to the whole human being, the whole of human nature (*CG* XIV.2, 582; cf. John 1:14), which in turn can be expressed as either or both of its chief component parts, body and soul. To live according to the spirit, by contrast, means to live according to God, seeking guidance from God and directing one's actions ultimately to God's glory.

---

9 *non tamen amplius quam duo quaedam genera humanae societatis existerent, quas ciuitates duas secundum scripturas nostras merito appellare possemus.*

Many themes familiar to readers of *The City of God* thus far re-enter Augustine's discussion in the first nine chapters of book XIV, not least the theme of pride. How can Christians in particular see the body as the source of their sins, when Satan, who was the first to rebel against God, has no body? The devil's chief offense was pride, *superbia,* leading to envy, *invidia*; and both of these begin in and from the spirit, from the soul or mind. Similarly, the deepest source of human sins is "pride, which [like-wise] reigns in the devil even though he is without flesh" (*CG* XIV.3, 586). Such pride constitutes and issues forth in an existential lie, a *lived lie.*

When [a man] lives according to self, however – that is, according to man and not according to God – he then certainly lives according to falsehood. This is not because man himself is falsehood; for his Author and Creator [*auctor et creator*] is God, who is by no means the Author and Creator of falsehood. Rather, it is because man was created righteous, to live according to his Maker and not according to himself, doing his Maker's will and not his own: *falsehood consists in not living in the way for which he was created.* (*CG* XIV.4, 586–87; emphasis added)

To live proudly, according to the flesh, is to live according to self, according to human nature unnaturally divorced from its Creator; to seek, albeit always unsuccessfully, to usurp God's place. It is moreover to live an emptier, more colorless existence, to fall away from the excellence and felicity for which we were made. To live humbly according to God is by contrast to live a life of fuller being in God, moving toward the fullness of being for us. It is to seek to be divinized in truth, not in falsehood, by participation in God's own life, knowledge, and love (see *CG* XIV.5, 588–89).

Here again, Augustine's rhetorical dialectic points to tensions between Platonic understandings of body and soul and his own philosophic and Christian interpretation of human being. Augustine finds in the "magnificent verse" of Virgil's *Aeneid* a poetic articulation of a Platonic teaching, in which "harmful bodies," though not evil in themselves as the Manicheans would have it, nonetheless weigh the soul down by "'desire, fear, joy and grief; [and these do not] look up to heaven, but are confined in a dark and sightless cave'" (*CG* XIV.3, 585; quoting *Aeneid* 6, 730ff.). As Augustine gratefully acknowledges, Virgil's vision is moving, even "magnificent" when expressed in his powerful poetry. Nevertheless, as Augustine also acknowledges without shame, "*Our faith ... is something very different.* For the corruption of the body, which presseth down the soul, was not the cause of the first sin, but its punishment; nor was it corruptible flesh that made the soul sinful, but *the sinful soul* that *made the flesh corruptible*" (*CG* XIV.3, 585; emphasis added).

As in book XIII, Augustine here again takes a shorter and easier road, not offering a philosophic demonstration of this conclusion but rather showing its plausibility even from a Virgilian-Platonic perspective, offering counterevidence to Platonic anthropology from Virgil's *Aeneid* itself (see *CG* XIV.5, 589). Augustine once again aims to remove a philosophic and literary obstacle to faith, seeking to persuade readers of the philosophic reasonableness (at the least, lack of demonstrated unreasonableness) of the Christian position, and so to help open minds to explore, embrace, and hold fast to it. As Augustine has written at the outset of this debate, so now he concludes, "There is no need, then, in the matter of our sins and vices, to do injustice to our Creator by accusing the nature of flesh, which, of its own kind and in its own due place, is good" (*CG* XIV.5, 588).

Augustine moves on to locate the good or ill of human passions in the goodness or evil of *wills* and in the *loves* that motivate them. In this segment, he circles back to his discussion in book IX with the philosophers, especially the Stoics, on the status of emotions, elaborating it here at greater length, for the first time in detailed dialogue with Christian faith and scripture (cf. *CG* IX.4, 361, ff.). Augustine argues now that it is the "quality" of the act of willing, and so of loving, that determines the quality of the emotions. "If the will is perverse, the emotions will be perverse; but if it is righteous, the emotions will be not only blameless, but praiseworthy" (*CG* XIV.6, 590). "A righteous will ... is a good love; and a perverted will is an evil love. Therefore ... [passions of desire, joy, grief, and fear] are bad if the love [motivating them] is bad, and good if it is good" (*CG* XIV.7, 592; cf. IX.5, 365–66). The mark of participation in citizenship of the heavenly city is not an absence of passions, nor an immunity of mind to their sway, but rather passions felt on behalf of the desire for true good, for God and his glory, and so for one's own real well-being together with that of others. Right passion or emotion involves being moved by *feeling for others*, including right grief or compassion for others as much as for oneself (*CG* XIV.9, 598; cf. IX.5, 365).[10]

It is in this context that Augustine depicts what he considers the apex of human pride, or a clear symptom of this vicious pinnacle, in a new way – as the very absence of emotion, the "insensitivity" of the mind to "any emotion whatsoever." Who could not recognize in this extreme of *apatheia*,

---

[10] See *CG* XIV.9, 601: "We must, then, lead a righteous life if we are to attain a life of blessedness; and such *a righteous life will exhibit all these emotions righteously.* ... Hence, it is now clear what kind of life the citizens of the City of God must lead during this pilgrimage" (emphasis added).

Augustine asks rhetorically, "the worst of all vices" (*CG* XIV.9, 600)? As Sarah Byers has shown (2013, 68), Augustine does not find this extreme *apatheia* in Stoicism but rather in cynical and skeptical philosophies.

In this discussion, Augustine seems to depict extreme *apatheia* as a vice worse even than *superbia*. The conclusion of chapter 9 and with it this critical segment of Augustine's rhetorical dialectic, however, shows extreme *apatheia* actually to express extreme *superbia*, self-exaltation, and "haughtiness" knowing no boundaries (*CG* XIV.9, 602). In his stirring conclusion critiquing such *apatheia*, Augustine refers back to a passage from Cicero (*Tusc. disp.,* 3, 6, 12, quoted in *CG* XIV.9, 600) which he has just quoted in defense of the presence of pain and sorrow in even the philosopher or statesman. Reflecting on the grief of Christ and the tears he shed, Augustine has just concluded that

[I]f we felt no such emotions at all while subject to the infirmity of this life, we should then certainly not be living righteously (*recte*). For the apostle [Paul] condemned and denounced certain persons who, he said, were "without natural affection." The holy psalm also blames those of whom it says, "I looked for some to take pity, but there was none." (*CG* XIV.9, 599–600; quoting Romans 1:31 and Psalm 69:20)

Here readers will recall Augustine's stirring praise much earlier in this great and arduous work of this sister of the Horatii for the affection she showed when she expressed her grief for her slain betrothed (*CG* III.14, 110, discussed in Chapter 2).

It is at this point in his rhetorical dialectic that Augustine notes the apparent concurrence of Cicero himself. "Indeed, if, while in this place of misery, we were to be entirely free from pain, this, as one of this world's scholars has understood and said, 'would not be attained without a great price: *savagery of mind, and stupor of body*'" (*CG* XIV.9, 600; emphasis added; quoting from Cicero's *Tusc. disp.* 3, 6, 12). Augustine clearly harkens back to Cicero's sound judgment in his own conclusion of this important chapter and segment of his argument. Those who seek perfect, absolute *apatheia* as an ideal, or evince it in their attitudes – perhaps including some among the politicians and philosophers of his era and other eras – evince a very great pride that turns against their own bodies and souls, as well as those of others.

Some of these, with a vanity as monstrous as it is rare, are so entranced by their own self-restraint that they are not stirred or excited or swayed or influenced by any emotions at all. But *these rather suffer an entire loss of their humanity* than achieve a true tranquility. For a thing is not right merely because it is harsh, nor is stolidity the same thing as health. (*CG* XIV.9, 602; emphasis added)

Again, the sister of the Horatii comes to mind as an exemplar, of whom Augustine wrote that by her affection and tears, she acted more humanely (*humanior*) than the victorious Romans did as a people (*CG* III.14, 110). By her acceptance of the pathos of humanity, hers and all of ours, this young woman anticipated the full humanity of Christ, with its humble acceptance of rightly ordered loves and passions (*CG* XIV.9, 599).

Pride's Fall and the Hope of Humility: Chapters 10–14

Augustine now returns to Eden before the Fall, inquiring of the emotions in the life of the first couple. They indeed felt all the passions with the exception of fear and sorrow, since there were no evils in their lives to trigger these. Yet the passions were experienced in a tranquil and happy way, subject to their free and godly reason and will.

The love of the pair for God and for one another was undisturbed, and they lived in a faithful and sincere fellowship which brought great gladness to them. ... There was a tranquil avoidance of sin; and, as long as this continued, no evil of any kind intruded, from any source, to bring them sadness. ... How happy, then, were the first human beings, neither troubled by any disturbance of the mind nor pained by any disorder of the body! And the whole universal fellowship of mankind (*universa societas ... humana*) would have been just as happy had our first parents not committed that evil deed. (*CG* XIV.10, 602–3)

Yet commit sin they did. Why would they choose to do so? We come here, with Augustine, back to the *mysterium iniquitatis*, the mystery of moral evil and injustice, now considered at its human, rather than angelic, origins. In probing this troubling question, beginning in chapter 11 of book XIV, Augustine reviews for his readers the metaphysics of good and evil, on which he previously elaborated, especially in books XI and XII. A good will, which Adam and Eve each possessed initially, was the "work of God" in them at their creation when God made them "upright." For as long as the first couple chose of their own free will to second this work of God in them, they persevered in righteousness. Their eventual fall by "the first evil act of the will," Augustine writes incisively, "preceded all other evil acts in man." This original sin, therefore, "consisted rather in its falling away from the work of God to its own, exclusive work, rather than in any one work," namely eating the forbidden fruit. Before the external fall in deed, there occurred a hidden internal fall in the will in each of our first parents, according to Augustine's interpretation of Genesis. Such an evil will contradicts nature. It can only exist in a nature as a vice or corruption and so affects that nature for the worse. The nature of God or of his eternally begotten, uncreated Word can be subject to no such defection into evil. Only created beings, created by the Creator *ex nihilo*, can fall back toward nothingness and death, as we have seen, via the evil workings of their own wills. Such are human beings and their origins, in body and in soul. "For, although God formed man of the dust of the earth, the earth itself and all earthly matter were derived from nothing at all; and when man was made, God gave to his body a soul which was made out of nothing" (*CG* XIV.11, 604).

And yet even in this critical, one might say tragic, context of the sin in Eden, Augustine's metaphysics of being remains a surprisingly hopeful one. He opines boldly:

[G]ood things prevail over bad. ... [Good things can exist without evil ones, while evil] things ... cannot exist without the good; for the natures in which evil exists are certainly good, insofar as they are natures. Moreover, an evil is eradicated not by the removal of the nature in which it has arisen, or of any part of it, but by the healing and correction of the nature which has become vitiated and depraved. (*CG* XIV.11, 605)

The Fall yields from the good God the promise and later the sending of such a healer, a savior and redeemer.

The human fall as presented in the biblical narrative was the result of the misuse of free will by Adam and Eve; yet this sin was not entirely autonomous or *sui generis* on the part of the first human couple. There was also the influence of the ancient serpent, of Satan working through the creature to converse with Eve. And in this context, pride re-enters Augustine's narrative with a vengeance – almost literally so. Into paradise, Augustine recounts,

came that proud angel, envious by reason of that same pride which had induced him to turn away from God and follow himself. With an ambition like that of a tyrant, he wished rather to gloat over subjects of his own than to be a subject himself; and so he fell from the spiritual Paradise ... and sought to insinuate himself, by crafty suggestion, into the heart of man, whose unfallen state he envied. (*CG* XIV.11, 605–6; emphasis added)

Vicious pride, Augustine again underscores, spawns envy, disordered ambition for domination, and tyrannical rule.

In succumbing to the proud tempter's promises and eating the forbidden fruit, what precise sin did Eve and Adam commit? In chapter 12, Augustine seems to identify this original sin easily enough as disobedience, "the unrighteousness of disobeying the command." In this discussion, Augustine argues that the virtue of obedience comprises "in a certain sense, *the mother and guardian of all other virtues in a rational creature.* For man has been so made that it is to his advantage to be subject to God, and harmful to him to act according to his own will *rather than* that of his Creator" (*CG* XIV.12, 607–8; emphasis added). So it seems here, perhaps, that disobedience expresses a worse vice even than pride, and conversely that obedience may embody a virtue greater and more foundational than humility. The following chapter of book XIV, however, will reveal that this apparent ordering of virtues and vices is not Augustine's own.

Chapter 13 comprises the high point, if one can speak so, of Augustine's investigation into the nature of the original sin. This chapter in book XIV also deals most deeply with humility and pride. All seven occurrences of *humilitas* and its cognates in book XIV are found in chapter 13, as well as seven out of approximately twenty occurrences in book XIV of *superbia* (including, as we will soon see, an important definition of pride offered by our author). Before sinning overtly, Augustine argues, the first humans' wills covertly turned toward evil. Before disobedience occurred, the sin of pride was committed.

[W]hat but pride can have been the beginning of their evil will? – for "pride is the beginning of sin" (Ecclus. 10:13; cf. *CG* XII.6, 505). And what is pride but an appetite for a perverse kind of elevation (*perversae celsitudinis appetitus*)? For it is a perverse kind of elevation indeed to forsake the foundation (*principio*) upon which the mind (*animus*) should rest, and to become and to remain, as it were, one's own foundation.[11]

This defection from true to false foundations for humanity occurred in Eden precisely as "an act of free will" (*CG* XIV.13, 608).

The mystery of this voluntary defection from reason, light, love, and happiness continues to perplex Augustine as his rhetorical dialectic in this segment develops. He returns afresh to the metaphysics of good and evil on which he has elaborated most recently in chapter 11, now linking this metaphysics explicitly with the sin of *superbia*. This act of betrayal by the free will of a creature constitutes a falling away from its own nature, from human nature as it was created; and this falling away from fuller being is only possible in a nature made "out of nothing" (*CG* XIV.13, 608). The original sin of pride is now identified as the starting point of the "ruinous path down into the Void,"[12] leading travelers astray in the direction of death and nothingness. Augustine stresses:

---

[11] *porro malae uoluntatis initium quae potuit esse nisi superbia? initium enim omnis peccati superbia est [Ecli 10,15]. quid est autem superbia nisi peruersae celsitudinis appetitus? Perversa enim est celsitudo deserto eo, cui debet animus inhaerere, principio sibi quodam modo fieri atque esse principium.*

[12] This phrase is from Tolkien (1999, 32).

[M]an did not fall away from his nature so completely as to lose all being. When he turned towards himself, however, his being became less complete than when he clung to Him Who exists supremely. Thus, *to forsake God and to exist in oneself –* that is, to be pleased with oneself – is not immediately to lose all being; but it *is to come closer to nothingness.* This is why, according to Holy Scripture, the proud are called by another name: they are called "self-willed." For it is good to lift up your hearts; not to yourself, however, which is pride, but to the Lord. This is obedience, which can belong only to the humble. (CG XIV.13, 609; emphasis added)

With this last remark, Augustine makes clear what the reader of *The City of God* may have already inferred, that although free, pious obedience to the Creator is a great virtue for the rational creature and constitutes "in a certain sense, the mother and guardian of all other virtues" (CG XIV.12, 607), humility comprises an even more foundational virtue. Without virtuous, pious humility, there can be no virtuous, pious obedience; such obedience "can belong only to the humble" (CG XIV.13, 609). And yet obedience also guards humility, as a natural extension as it were, safeguarding continuity in virtue from mind and heart into deed. These virtues together preempt the creature's potential desire for a disproportionate, unhealthy elation (*elatio*), for an unnatural self-exaltation over God; they defend their possessors against a perverse desire to usurp the place of God in small things as well as in large. Together these virtues of humility and obedience lead one to a rational and free subjection to and union with "Him who exists supremely" and so toward a fullness of being and life.

Augustine's rhetorical dialectic continues, at the pinnacle of this centrally important chapter, to offer readers an ode and exhortation to humility and an argument once again for its excellence.

In a remarkable way, therefore, there is in humility something which exalts the mind [*cor*], and something in [perverse] exaltation which abases it. It may indeed seem paradoxical to say that exaltation abases and humility exalts. Godly humility [*pia humilitas*], however, makes the mind subject to what is superior to it. But nothing is superior to God; and that is why humility exalts the mind by making it subject to God. (CG XIV.13, 609; cf. I, preface, 3)[13]

Back in Eden, Augustine surmises, because of their hidden, willful pride Adam and Eve were enticed, and even pleased by, the serpent's seductive promise: only eat the forbidden fruit, and "Ye shall be as gods" (Genesis 3:5). Instead of the anticipated exaltation came the most abject abasement, however, a greatly lessened, miserable existence. Augustine

---

[13] On the philosophic and biblical roots of *cor* as Augustine uses it and on the development of this usage, see Peza (1961, 1962); and Courcelle (1964).

comments, "Adam and Eve would have been better fitted to resemble gods if they had clung in obedience," and so in humility,

[T]o the highest and true ground of their being, and not, in their pride, made themselves their own ground (*principium*). For created gods are gods not in their own true nature, but by participation in the true God. By striving after more, man is diminished; when he takes delight in his own self-sufficiency, he falls away from the One who truly suffices for him. The first evil came, then, when man began to be pleased with himself, as if he were his own light; for he then turned away from that Light which, if only he had been pleased with It instead, would have made man himself a light. (CG XIV.13, 610)

Despite the human and cosmic disaster that was the Fall, Augustine's concluding reflections in chapter 13 are hopeful. Augustine previously noted that God performs all his works for good; that he foreknew Adam and Eve's Fall; that he permits evil only for the sake of mysteriously, miraculously bringing forth good from that evil (see *CG* XIV.11, 604); and that the divinely desired eradication of evil is not effected in the destruction of nature, but in its "healing and correction" (*CG* XIV.11, 605). Augustine suggests that Adam and Eve's external free fall into prideful disobedience was permitted by God, paradoxically *for the sake of mercy*, so that the first couple might recognize their sin and begin to turn away from their would-be self-sufficiency and back to their Creator for this healing and correction.

I venture to say that it is of benefit to the proud that they should fall into some open and manifest sin, which can cause them to be displeased with themselves even after they have already fallen through being pleased with themselves. Peter's condition [after thrice denying any connection with Jesus following His arrest] was more wholesome (*salubrius*) when he wept than when he was pleased with himself and presumptuous. (CG XIV.13, 610)

What seems a self-inflicted disaster can in this sense also be a great God-given mercy, the beginning of a return to humility and justice. It is on this note that Augustine brings this critical chapter to a close. "The holy psalm also says this: 'Fill their faces with shame; that they may seek Thy name, O Lord' [Psalm 83:16] – that is, let those who were pleased with themselves when they sought their own name be pleased with Thee as they seek Thine" (*CG* XIV.13, 610).

Before considering the consequences of the Fall for human life and death, Augustine brings out one more facet of the pride underlying original sin, the progress of this pride immediately thereafter in the hearts of Adam and Eve. There was an undeniable social dimension to the Fall as depicted in Genesis. First, when Eve has eaten of the forbidden fruit, she brings some to Adam, who also eats. Eve seeks to share her newfound "divinization" with her husband, at least so it seems. Then as Augustine interprets Adam's offense, the first man eats as well, not because of believing the serpent's word but because of a desire not to be separated from his companion and wife. Perhaps he was also in this prompted by a deep-seated fear of being alone in the world again (see *CG* XIV.11, 606–7).[14] With this dimension of the narrative, one might have expected the solidarity in sin of the first couple to be a unifying experience for them, an event that heightened their harmony and intensified their friendship and love.

An outcome of greater unity, however, emphatically did not obtain. Their prideful desire to exalt themselves led each, on Augustine's interpretation, to blame the other for their deed; to eschew personal responsibility, even at the cost of risking augmenting the other's punishment. In the case of Adam, ironically his sin for the sake of togetherness with Eve is followed by his attempt to foist full responsibility back upon her. "[E]ven worse and more damnable is the pride which seeks refuge in an excuse even when the sins are plain to see" (*CG* XIV.14, 611). This was the case with our first parents. "Nowhere here is there heard any petition for pardon, and nowhere any plea for healing. For though they did not deny what they had done, as Cain did [after murdering his brother Abel], *their pride nonetheless sought to blame their wrongful act upon another:* The woman's pride blames the serpent, *the man's pride blames the woman*" (*CG* XIV.14, 611, emphasis added). The divisive, disunifying impact of sin in society, especially in the original sin of the first man and woman, becomes frightfully clear here, and this is far from the last we will hear about it in *The City of God.*

Pride, Disunity, and Death: Chapters 15–27

The next major segment of book XIV's rhetorical dialectic focuses on the problem of lust (*libido*) as a fruit of pride and a force for division and death. Eve and Adam's attempt to take control of their own being, to be the source and summit as it were of their lives and actions, produced the

---

14 "They were alone together, two human beings, man and wife. ... [H]e complied with her wishes because of the closeness of the bond between them. ... Adam did not wish to be separated from his companion, even at the cost of sharing in her sin" (*CG* XIV.11, 606). On this aspect of Adam's sin, its rationale, and its implications, see chapter 5 of You (2021).

opposite effects. As Augustine emphasizes in chapter 15, pride in original sin resulted in a deep division within each of the first two human beings, a disunified being and existence that they were unable to repair on their own. And as Augustine emphasized earlier, in book XIII, the wages of this sin and division was death (cf. *Romans* 6:23) in all its instantiations. Pride's offspring includes diminished being, division, and death. In rational creatures created as social by nature, these effects obtained also in familial relations and in the transmission of human life. The original mutual self-giving and service of Adam and Eve were marred by lust in its many forms; and this vice had its effect on sex and procreation. Being-toward-life and social unity in affectionate, familial fellowship entered into battle against being-toward-death and division, a battle that being-toward-life could not win by nature alone.

In chapter 15, Augustine offers readers this summary of the anthropological effects of original sin:

> Man ... who, *in his pride*, had pleased himself, was now, by God's justice, handed over to himself. This was not done, however, in such a way that man was now placed entirely under his own control. Rather, he was *divided against himself*, and now, instead of enjoying the freedom for which he so longed, he lived in harsh and miserable bondage. ... [Then and now,] who can count the many things that a man wishes to do but cannot? For he is disobedient to himself: that is, his very mind [*animus*], and even his lower part, his flesh [*caro*], do not obey his will. Even against his will his mind is often troubled; and his flesh endures pain, grows old, and dies, and suffers all manner of things which we should not suffer against our will if our nature were in every way and in all its parts obedient to our will. (CG XIV.15, 611–13)

This disunity in each of the first humans, as Genesis recounts the tale and Augustine interprets it in his rhetorical dialectic, unleashes the force of lust (*libido*), which while it can be restrained to some extent by humans, can be defeated once and for all only by grace and redemption. Irrational, impure desire can have multiple objects and so multiple names. Unmodified, however, *libido* typically refers to an impure love, a desire to use or manipulate another human being for one's selfish enjoyment rather than to serve him or her and seek also his or her true good and common goods.

The spousal love of Eve and Adam, as the "nuptial blessing" given by God to the first couple before their fall expresses it, was intended to give rise to chaste, loving sexual union and so to "children to be loved" (*CG* XIV.23, 623). Sex and offspring are no "punishments of sin," but rather aspects of the very "glory of marriage" (*gloria conubii*; CG XIV.21, 620–21). The joy of mutual self-gift in sexual union, had there been no sin, would have been exercised is such a way that the passions would have been perfectly guided toward good by reason. Sexual union would have always expressed self-giving affection, seeking the good of the other spouse and the good of children to be born. It would have followed from and resulted in a fuller, united life, directing the couple toward the fullness of life. "What reason, then, is there for us not to believe that, before the sin of disobedience and its punishment of corruptibility, the members of the human body could have been the servants of the human will without any lust, for the procreation of offspring?" (CG XIV. 24, 627). As a consequence of sin's separating the first pair from God, who is the ultimate strength and support of their souls and bodies, they each experienced a struggle between their souls' higher potencies and their baser impulses. They felt the stirrings of lust and consequent confusion and sense of shame, a sign of their woundedness in being now tending toward death. In their pride they chose to turn toward themselves, and in so doing turned away not only from God but also from one another, no matter how motivated by social ties Adam's decision to eat the fruit Eve offered him may have been. Now they found, as would their off-spring after them, that virtue, modesty, and chastity are oftentimes dif-ficult in familial matters as well as in social and civic life, and that the love among family members itself lies beneath the shadow of death.

This then is the core of Augustine's narrative in book XIV of *The City of God* and his rhetorical-dialectical description of the ties between humility and life on the one hand, and between pride and death on the other. Where there is being-toward-life – fullness of life – there is happi-ness, more or less complete; where there is being-toward-death, misery and grief ensue. Only with righteousness, lost by original sin and the myriad of wrongdoings committed since that fateful day but attainable through God's grace, can a person be happy now in hope and hereafter blissful in glory. As Augustine observes:

Even the righteous man ... will not live as he wishes [viz., happily] unless he arrives at that state where he is wholly free from death, error and harm, and certain that he will always be free from these things in the future. For this is *what our nature desires*, and it will not be fully and perfectly happy unless it attains what it desires. What man is there at the present time who can live as he wishes, *when living itself is not within his power ... [when] he is compelled to die?* (CG XIV.25, 627–28; emphasis added)

Life in itself deserves in all justice to be loved, and to love life rightly entails "necessarily wish[ing] it to be eternal. Life, therefore, will only be truly happy when it is eternal" (*CG* XIV.25, 627–28).

In Adam and Eve's forfeiting their original gift of humility and succumbing to pride, humanity's very life became being-toward-death, struggling mightily with a just and natural love-toward-life – personal, social, and procreative. God did not desire, but permitted, this original sin, with a pedagogical intent.

[God] did not, by His foreknowledge, compel anyone to sin. By the experience which followed from that sin, however, he demonstrated to all rational creatures, angels and humans alike, how great is the difference between each creature's presumption and God's protection. ... God preferred not to remove the choice of whether to sin or not from [Adam and Eve's] power, and, in this way, He showed *how great is the power of their pride for evil, and of His grace for good.* (*CG* XIV.27, 631–32; emphasis added)

Humility and Pride in the Lives and Loves of the Two Cities

In concluding this chapter we recall that the chief theme Augustine treats throughout this book and the three books preceding it is none other than the famous "two cities" in their origins, and so also in their natures and characters. Augustine opens book XI with this thematic and returns to it at the beginning, middle, and end of the fourteenth book, as if to underscore his aim throughout this long rhetorical dialectic. Reading as a whole this argument concerning the beginnings or principles of the two cities once again helps us better ascertain Augustine's intent and approach. To this end, before summing up the discourse on humility, pride, love, life, and death in the two cities presented in book XIV, I will return briefly to the opening of book XI and the important reflection on this trope found there.

Recall that in chapter 1 of book XI Augustine announced to his readers that the Jewish and Christian scriptures teach of the existence of the city of God and elicit from their readers a longing to be citizens of this heavenly city "because of the love with which its Founder has inspired" them (*CG* XI.1, 449). Those who pledge allegiance instead to the earthly city do so largely out of ignorance, "prefer[ring] their own gods to the Founder of this holy city, *for they do not know* that he is the God of gods" (*CG* XI.1, 449; emphasis added; cf. I, preface, 3). In so doing, humans submit themselves to the tutelage and dominion of "impious and proud" divinities, who seek to be "worshipped in place of God" (*CG* XI.1, 449). Lest any readers conclude that they are already confirmed in their citizenship in the heavenly city, Augustine stresses once again that these two cities "in this present world" are "mixed together and, in a certain sense, entangled with one another" (*CG* XI.1, 450). If we long to become or to remain faithfully citizens of the heavenly city, it is because of the excellence of its founder – not our own – and because of the love he has inspired in us and can inspire in others, including those currently "ignorant" of his wisdom, goodness, and preeminence. If we long to be such citizens, it behooves us then not to take our citizenship for granted, nor to despair ever of others coming to share in it, but rather to be conscious of the mixing of the seeds of these conflicting cities in our own lives, as well as in those of others, and of the need all have for God's merciful grace.[15]

Between this description in book XI of the two cities and those Augustine offers in book XIV, as we have seen, the discourse of *The City of God* has run from the creation *ex nihilo* of heaven and earth, and of the angels and human beings especially, to the angelic and human falls; and thence, to the place of humility and pride, good and evil, being and nothingness, and life and death in these epic events and the two cities they established. At the outset of book XIV, Augustine reminds readers that God's desire was not only that "the human race should be united in a fellowship by a natural likeness" (*naturae similitudine sociandum*), but also that it be "bound together by kinship in the unity of concord, linked by the bond of peace" (*concordem pacis vinculo conlingamdum*; *CG* XIV.1, 581). God wished all human beings to be citizens of the heavenly city and members of his family. In refusing their free cooperation to this divine plan, Adam and Eve gave birth to the earthly city and transmitted slavery to sin and death to their offspring, the whole human family. In the final sense, with regard to these two eschatological *civitates*, no dual citizenship is possible, although in this life there remains a struggle for those who seek to follow the regime, so to speak, of the heavenly city and to emulate the example of its founder. The two cities differ in their ways

---

[15] On this topic, see also *CG* XIV.6, 590:

[T]he man who lives according to God and not according to man must be a lover of the good; and it follows from this that he must hate what is evil. Further, *since no one is evil by nature*, but whoever is evil is evil because of some fault, he who lives according to God has a duty of "perfect hatred" towards those who are evil. That is, he should not hate the man because of the fault, nor should he love the fault because of the man; rather, *he should hate the fault but love the man*. And *when the fault has been healed there will remain only what he ought to love, and nothing that he ought to hate.* (emphasis added)

of life: one living according to the spirit, a life according to and for God; the other according to the flesh, or life according to and for man himself. Instead of one unifying, true peace in a single fellowship, or "city," in this world comprised of humans and their human polities,[16] there are now two overarching forms of peace. "Each [citizenry] desires its own kind of peace, and, when they have found what they sought, each lives in its own kind of peace" (*CG* XIV.1, 581).

In the central chapter of book XIV, in which original sin emerges as hidden pride preceding and preparing the way for open disobedience, Augustine clarifies "the great difference (*magna differentia*) that distinguishes the two cities of which we are speaking," namely virtuous humility contrasted with vicious pride (*CG* XIV.13, 609). This all-important distinction is crystalized in the persons, characters, and lives of the two cities' respective founders and rulers. Christ "especially" exemplifies the fullness of *humilitas*, whereas *superbia* as "the vice of exaltation, the opposite of this virtue (*contrariumque huic virtuti*), holds complete sway over Christ's adversary, the devil" (*CG* XIV.13, 609). And as we have seen, humility and pride provide existential homes for and exemplify two loves. "In the one city, love of God has been given pride of place (*praecessit*), and, in the other, love of oneself (*amor sui*)" (*CG* XIV.13, 609).

Here it seems crucial to note that Augustine does not now, nor does he ever in *The City of God*, allege that humility is exemplified flawlessly and fully in the citizens of the city of God on pilgrimage here in this world, nor that the vice of pride "holds complete sway" in the lives and characters of the citizens of the earthly city in this present age. Humility is "most highly praised" by and is "commended" to the citizens of God's city on their pilgrimage – to those "long[ing] to be," completely and with no internal opposition or divided loyalties, citizens of this glorious *res publica* (*CG* XIV.13, 609; XI.1, 449). Humility is not now perfectly possessed by them, to say the least. Augustine's rhetorical dialectic in this book and throughout *The City of God* does not present the two groups of human beings, alive in this world, *qua* citizens of the two cities, as perfect opposites or binaries. Only their founders and rulers, Christ and Satan, are such in terms of opposing and (analogously, bearing in mind Christ's divinity and Satan's creaturehood) fully possessed virtue or vice.

---

[16] Recall this passage from much earlier in *The City of God*, noted in Chapter 2: "*[I]f men were always peaceful and just*, human affairs would be happier and all kingdoms (*omnia regna*) would be small, rejoicing in concord with their neighbors. *There would be as many kingdoms among the nations of the world as there are now houses of the citizens of a city*" (*CG* IV.15, 161, emphasis added).

Thus, at the conclusion of book XIV and with it of the third part of *The City of God*, when Augustine returns to describe the opposing loves that have founded opposing cities, the perceptive reader, whether pagan or Christian, understands well that these are not two perfectly fixed communities *in this world*. These two cities and their loves likely reflect aspects of the readers' own lives and characters, in tension with one another and requiring grace, freedom, and struggle for the heavenly city to win their final allegiance. When the reader finds himself or herself seeking superiority or human praise above all, for instance, he or she is tending toward the earthly city; when by contrast that same reader seeks to direct all the goods of this world, including political and philosophical goods and earthly honors, toward the glory of God and giving gratitude to God, content to dwell justly and moderately amongst ontological equals, then the heavenly city is gaining ascendency in his or her soul. When political leaders aim to offer their people – understood to be their equals – good counsel and public service, and other citizens aim to act in conformity with justice and right counsel, they reflect a degree at least of humility, the heavenly city's signature virtue. When by contrast they seek to rule over others, to exercise mastery over others as an end in itself, then they reveal pride and the earthly city's presence. For philosophers, those "able to know God," seeking wisdom and held by many to be wise, Augustine offers the same cautionary advice: to beware of "exalting themselves in their wisdom, under the dominion of pride" while failing to seek, honor, and serve the Creator of all earthly beings (CG XIV.28, 632). "[L]ove of oneself extending even to contempt of God," and conversely, the "love of God extending to contempt of oneself" correlate well with pride on the one hand, and humility on the other (CG XIV.28, 632).

This realization that the pitfalls of pride may be most present in the way of life and work deemed greatest among men – namely, in the government of peoples and the pursuit of philosophic wisdom – may prompt readers to seek and to cling to the one God who created and redeemed humanity. Such is the hope and aim of Augustine's rhetorical dialectic in book XIV and in this entire "great and arduous work" (CG I, preface, 3). Thus, Augustine's readers – great and small – may recommence with hope their pilgrimage along the path toward fullness of being and life, and reject roads that appear to enliven and aggrandize but instead lead them and their fellows toward nothingness and death.

7

The City of God XV–XVIII

Pride and Humility in History

In the penultimate segment of *The City of God*, books XV–XVIII, Augustine presents his readers once again with the pride of the earthly city and the humility characteristic – albeit imperfectly so during its time of pilgrimage – of *The City of God*. Now, he invites readers to see humility and pride in action throughout human history, after the Fall through to the Incarnation of God's Son and the redemption effected by Christ, the heavenly city's founder. In comparison with books I–V, books XV–XVIII give pride of place to the histories contained in sacred scripture and so to divinely inspired prophetic accounts of history. As Gerard O'Daly perceptively observes, "[T]he significance of historical events for Augustine is preeminently found in the course of scriptural history. ... [T]he special historical events of Scripture, prophetically mediated, are bearers of more than merely moral meaning" (O'Daly, 1999a, 194–95).[1]

In these four books, little new is offered readers regarding the meaning and character of humility and pride. Rather, key traits of this virtue and vice, introduced and highlighted throughout the previous fourteen books, are incorporated and referred to throughout this long historical narrative, which Augustine crafts from both secular and sacred histories. In their historical emphases and exemplars, books XV–XVIII harken back to the opening portion of *The City of God*, books I–V, with their critical appraisal of Roman history before Christ. Now, however, well into his masterwork, Augustine can hope that many readers will be better

---

[1] For a literature review regarding Augustine's writings on history and on "the question of whether he has a theory of history" properly speaking, see O'Daly (1999a, 194, note 63).

positioned to recognize pride (*superbia*) and humility (*humilitas*) in their brash and open as well as their more reticent and obscure manifestations, and so assess them religiously, humanely or morally, philosophically, and civically. The rhetorical dialectic of books XV–XVIII offers readers an extensive series of opportunities to identify and observe exemplars of *humilitas* and *superbia* and to reflect on their ramifications in individual lives and familial, social, and civic histories.[2] Augustine's rhetorical dialectic thus affords readers the opportunity to determine which quality of soul they will seek to cultivate and which they will strive to uproot – and ultimately, in which city they will seek their highest, lasting citizenship.

In this history, Augustine emphasizes again that the human return from evil to good depends in a radical way upon God's grace. At the same time, his narrative underscores the roles accorded by providence itself to human agency in preparing the way for and in cooperating with the gift of grace, for one's own welfare and also for the good of others. Human agency is part and parcel of the designs and workings of divine agency; men and women are in truth God's "co-workers" (3 John 1:8). Augustine's writing in this section continues, rhetorically and dialectically, to remove roadblocks for his readers and so to smooth their journeys through the perils of history on the pilgrim route toward the universal heavenly homeland. In much the same way that Varro's writings, as Augustine reads them, sought to prepare minds and hearts for the natural theology of the philosophers, these books of *The City of God* aim to assist in opening minds and hearts to receive God's gifts of faith, hope, and love, aided by the gift of humility and divine help to resist the pull of pride. While Augustine's ultimate goal is the increase and improvement of the heavenly city's citizenry in the long generations of earthly pilgrimage, he also underscores the limited but nonnegligible benefits such citizens can offer to social life and politics in this world.

BOOK XV: AFTER EDEN

Book XV chronicles key moments of the journeys through time of the two cities, from the years immediately after Adam and Eve's expulsion from Eden, through to the time of the famous flood and salvation of one

---

[2] Augustine's fascination with and pedagogy of exemplars seem to have long been a chief aspect of his teaching and learning: cf. his early dialogue *De Ordine, On Order*, at the conclusion of which his friend Alypius exclaims, "You have succeeded in imprinting in us the indelible memory of the most learned and great men (*memoriam doctissimorum ac magnorum virorum*)" (*De Ordine* 20.53, 121).

family (and numerous animals) aboard Noah's Ark. Book XV contains no explicit mention of *humilitas* and only two occurrences of *superbia* and its cognates, one near the book's beginning and the other approaching its end. The first, in chapter 4, reminds readers of the many wars begun and waged by pride. Here Augustine echoes his preface to book I, in tandem with his argument throughout books XIII and XIV, concerning *superbia* as a corrupting force tending to death. Augustine asserts that the victorious *patria* among such warring nations "is itself held captive by vices; and ... when it triumphs, it is lifted up in its pride, [though] such triumph brings only death" (*CG* XV.4, 638–39).

The second text, near the book's end, stresses the utility of scripture's anthropomorphic language, reflecting God's humility and loving condescension.

> [I]f Scripture did not use such terms [as "anger," e.g., in speaking of God], it would not communicate its meaning so clearly to all the race of men [*omni generi hominum*] for whom it has care [*quibus vult esse consultum*]. If it did not first bend down and, as it were, descend to the level of the fallen, it would not *terrify the proud*, arouse the negligent, exercise the inquirer and nourish the intelligent. (*CG* XV.25, 686; emphasis added)

Augustine here aims to persuade readers that God's humility, reflected in sacred scripture's language and rhetoric, helps effectively to meet diverse needs of peoples and persons, not least by jolting the proud from their complacency, and so contributing to free them from the double bonds of vice and death.[3]

As will become evident by the close of book XV, Augustine's history and the rhetoric with which he presents it have as their chief aim to enlighten and enkindle in readers humble hope in and love of God, who offers continuous healing and redemption to the repentant. The chief end of this text thus seems to be much the same one that Frederick Crosson has identified as Augustine's in his *Confessions*: "the disclosure of hidden providence" in the lives of persons as well as nations; and so also, Augustine hopes, in each open-minded reader's life (Crosson 2015, 32–55).

---

[3] On Augustine's initial struggle to accept the humble language and "simplicity" of scripture, see *Confessions* III.4.8:

> What I came upon was something not grasped by the proud ..., something utterly humble in the hearing but sublime in the doing. And I was not of the nature to enter into it or bend my neck to follow it. ... They were indeed of a nature to grow in Your little ones. But I could not bear to be a little one; I was only swollen with pride, but to myself I seemed a very big man. (41–42)

By offering exemplars of the citizenry of the two cities – of those who receive yet reject, and those who receive and accept, God's merciful help – Augustine's rhetorical dialectic in *The City of God* offers readers reasons for hope reaching beyond the contingencies of this world and its politics.[4] He himself hopes his readers, prompted by grace and aided in some real way by this text, may determine to "[hope] to call upon the name of the Lord" (Genesis 4:26; *CG* XV.18, 670–71) and not receive the gift of God's grace in vain (see 2 Corinthians 6:1). The end of book XV's narrative, then, is to enkindle in its readers a humbler, more just, and more perfect hope coupled with a more rightly ordered love.

Cain and the Primordial Politics of the Earthly City

From Adam and Eve come children who will populate both the heavenly and the earthly city, as Augustine reads their stories in scripture. Their first-born sons, Cain and Abel, exemplify this sad "civic" division. Cain's "devilish envy" of his younger brother – "of one who is good" and so whose sacrifices God receives with greater appreciation – reflects Satan's primordial, prideful envy of humanity. As Satan "was a murderer from the beginning" of his fall (*CG* XI.13, 467, quoting John 8:44), so Cain, ignoring God's admonition to quiet examination of conscience, contrition, and repentance, comes to murder his younger brother (Genesis 4:1–9). This sad story of fratricide will repeat itself in innumerable modes in the lives of persons and polities throughout the long years of history. While Abel is cut down before he can have children of his own, Cain lives to found a clan and eventually a city, one in which the self-seeking logic of the "earthly city" appears to predominate (*CG* XV.5, 640).

Augustine's rhetorical dialectic pauses here to note the parallels between this biblical narrative and the ancient story of Rome's founding by Romulus and Remus. These famous twins undertook the work of augmenting the citizenry and reordering the rough ways of the people who would comprise early Rome. Romulus reminds Augustine of Cain, not least for slaying his own brother, although Remus does not similarly mirror Abel. Each brother-founder of Rome eventually sought supremacy over the other, moved by *libido dominandi* rooted in *superbia*. They could not simultaneously share rule and obtain the highest glory, which each desired to possess unrivaled. Romulus prevailed in his

---

[4] For philosophic and political-theoretical reflections on hope, see Lamb (2018), Geach (2001), Marcel (2010), and Tinder (1999).

unholy quest: he slew Remus in a vainglorious thrust to possess "entire mastery" over the city (*CG* XV.5, 640). As Warner and Scott (2011, 860) have noted, Augustine's Romulus, much like Machiavelli's later rendition of Rome's founding father in the *Discourses*, is conspicuous for his desire to be superior and so to be *alone* in his dominion over others.

Although Augustine never speaks of *superbia* in his description of Cain's sins, what he does say about Adam and Eve's eldest son echoes Augustine's earlier depictions of this vice and its effects. In this regard, Cain presents us with a portrait in miniature of the earthly city. Before slaying Abel, Cain offered sacrifice to God, but his sacrifice was not pleasing to God because it was not "rightly divided" (*CG* XV.7, 643). The expression "rightly divided" Augustine interprets to mean that "although [Cain] gave something of his own to God, *he nonetheless gave himself to himself*" (*CG* XV.7, 643; emphasis added). Augustine's analysis continues:

[So] do all who follow their own will and not the will of God ... who live with a perverse and not a righteous heart, yet who still offer gifts to God. ... And this is the way of the earthly city: to worship a god or gods so that, with their aid, that city may reign in victory and earthly peace, not by the counsel of charity, but with lust for mastery. (*cupiditas dominandi*; *CG* XV.7, 644)

As the story is related in Genesis, before the fratricide occurs, God offers Cain an opportunity to repent of his pride and envy, admonishing him to recognize and reject his hatred of his brother while there is still time. "Be still; for when it [sin, waiting at your door] shall return unto thee, then thou shalt have the mastery of it" (*CG* XV.7, 645). Augustine interprets God's counsel to mean that when one, in silent stillness, examines one's conscience and takes responsibility for the sin one discovers, then one can repent and ask pardon before the cycle of pride and hatred spirals beyond control in yet worse ways.

In such a cycle Augustine finds afresh a distorted, vicious form of humility *qua* placing oneself beneath another: here in fact, beneath a vicious desire or urge, one that as evil has no real being in itself, and which therefore diminishes the moral being of the person who succumbs to it. "For a man will have the mastery of his sin if he does not place it over himself by defending it, but makes it subject to himself by repenting of it. Otherwise, he will indeed be its slave, and it will have the mastery of him, if he lends it his protection when it arises" (*CG* XV. 7, 645). Beyond recognizing and rejecting sin, Augustine understands God to be calling Cain, and with him all readers of scripture, to a watchfulness that detects temptations to sin, rejects inclinations to rationalize them, and finally restrains them by reason and free will, assisted by God's grace. "Do not suffer [sin] to do anything outwardly and, governed by the benevolent power of your mind, neither will it be moved inwardly" (*CG* XV.7, 646).

Augustine here calls his readers' attention to parallels between his interpretation of this passage from Genesis and the teachings of certain philosophers concerning prudent restraint of the passionate part of the soul by the "command of the mind, and restrained by reason from unlawful acts" (*CG* XV.7, 645–46). Had Cain followed God's merciful guidance, Augustine indicates, he would have changed his life to follow his virtuous brother's example, rather than seek "to rival" Abel in Cain's own arrogant "elation" (*CG* XV.7, 644).[5] Cain nonetheless neglected to call upon God's mercy, to receive his gracious counsel gratefully, and to hope in God's help to overcome his temptation and repent of his sin. This lack of hope Augustine considers of a piece with failures of faith and love. Cain does not believe God, and he does not really love God, although he offers God some produce of his labors in the false hope of appeasing God thereby or buying his future favor. From this failure to trust, believe in, and give one's heart above all else to one's make, comes an earthbound vision. From Cain's limited horizon, closed to transcendence, in turn comes the proud rebellion productive of the earthly city. In Cain's work and in much of his posterity, Augustine sees this earthbound city appear in a conventionally civic form. Cain, whose name means "possession," begets a son Enoch, whose name means "dedication." This latter name Cain gives to the community he eventually founds: denoting dedication to the city that lives for these sensibly perceptive goods above all else, trusting unwisely in its own ingenuity and willfulness (see *CG* XV.8, 647–49).

As we saw earlier, back in the fifth book of *The City of God*, Augustine is adamant that earthly, temporal, sensible goods such as peace and plenty *are* true goods. The citizenry of the earthly city is not wrong to recognize them as such and to seek them. Where it errs is in judging them to comprise the only true goods, or goods higher than those of the spirit that are not visible: justice, mercy, knowledge of God, right worship, and charity. They further err, in Augustine's estimation, in judging that by their own works – their own willing alone – they can secure these goods for themselves and

---

[5] *utique fratrem bonum mutatus imitari, non elatus debuit aemulari.* Dyson's translation, rendering *non elatus debuit aemulari* as "succumbing to pride and envy," seems to fall short in conveying the parallel and contrast Augustine intends between this phrase and the preceding *fratrem bonum mutatus imitari* [*debuit*].

their children. God indeed created the human will, and created it good, as we have also seen, but it is a finite, mutable good, created *ex nihilo*, and so not wholly to be trusted. "For the will, which is present in man's nature, can fall away [of its own power alone] from good to do evil; and it does this through its own free choice. ... It can also turn away from evil to do good; but it cannot do this without divine aid" (*CG* XV.21, 678–79). Thus, Augustine's rhetorical dialectic reveals to readers that, while seeking the temporal goods that all humans need and recognizing their true, if limited, goodness, people ought "not [to] place hope in [themselves], so that [they] may become ... citizen[s] of that other City and not of the one dedicated to this age and named after Cain's son. [They] must not, that is, place [their] hope in the transient course of this mortal world, but in the immortality of everlasting bliss" (*CG* XV.18, 671).

In contrast with Cain and his sons, Augustine's rhetorical dialectic recalls the righteous Abel, whose name means "lamentation," and his younger brother Seth, whose name signifies "resurrection." From Seth in turn came a son named Enos, who "hoped to call upon the name of the lord God" (*CG* XV.18, 670; quoting Genesis 4:26). In this humble acknowledgment of both human insufficiency and hope of fulfillment in God, Augustine sees the heavenly city embodied in a perennially relevant way for all wayfarers though time and space.

Noah: Humble Justice and Pilgrim Perfection

Readers of Genesis will recall with Augustine its chronicle of the tragic decline in human affairs from the times of Enoch and Seth down to the famous flood. Wickedness creeps into the lives of the descendants even of Seth and his righteous son Enos so pervasively in the end that God finds the family of one descendant alone – Noah – worthy of preservation. Augustine, near the close of his fifteenth book, lauds Noah as "that wise and just man" (*vir ille sapiens et iustus*; see *CG* XV.27, 692). In this Augustine echoes the praise he offered at the outset of this discussion:

We come now to Noah, who was a just man, and, as the Scriptures truly say, "perfect in his generations." He was not, indeed, perfect as the citizens of the City of God will be in that immortal state when they will be equal to the angels of God; but *he was as perfect as it is possible for a man to be during this pilgrimage*. God commanded Noah to make an Ark, in which he and his family ... were to be saved from the devastation of the Flood, together with the animals that went into the Ark in accordance with God's directions. Without doubt this [Ark] is a symbol of the City of God on pilgrimage in this world. (*CG* XV.26, 686–87; emphasis added)

In this description of Noah, Augustine's rhetorical dialectic returns to an early theme of book XV, highlighting for readers some traits of and reasons for humility. Noah believed God, gratefully received and preserved His gifts, and sought righteousness. For this he was counted as just, though not perfectly so. His perfection was that of the pilgrim on his way to perfection, an imperfect perfection. Noah's obedience to God's instructions to build, fill, and enter the Ark reflects his wise acknowledgment that his salvation was not in his own hands alone; rather, it principally rested with God, prompting humility and obedience. Yet Noah's virtuous humility spurred him to action, to resist the pulls of passivity and presumption. He did not wait for God to build the Ark for him, but set about working with his own mind, will, and manual skill. In believing God and following his word, Noah evinced virtuous humility joined with magnanimity. And yet even this "wise," "just," "perfect" Noah struggles with prudence and perhaps with moderation, as we sense after the flood in the story of his drunkenness and nakedness. He reacts to learning of one son's scornful treatment of him while he was in this shameful condition with a curse on his posterity, rather than with mercy and a more hopeful admonishment (see Genesis 9:20–27; CG XVI.1, 694).

This imperfect pilgrim-perfection, exemplified by Noah, comprises a trope framing book XV, the first of the histories of the two cities Augustine offers his readers. In chapter 5, Augustine emphasizes that vicious strife is present not only among the earthly city's citizens in this age. "[E]ven the carnal desires of two good men, who have, however, not yet achieved perfection, may strive, just as the wicked strive among themselves, until those who are being healed are finally brought to victorious health" (CG XV.5, 641). This gradual healing, begun in time and perfected in eternity, of the wounds of original sin and personal sins, is the work chiefly of God's grace. It requires of the wayfarer patience with others, willingness to forgive, and openness to accept correction and forgiveness gratefully from others, as from God himself. Over time, this merciful medicine becomes felt and noted within and among human beings. One cares more and more for truth and for "the preservation of peace, without which no one will be able to see God"; one thus finds in one's "own changed mind, a gentler ruler here; and, hereafter, when ... perfected in health and gifted with immortality, man will reign without sin in eternal peace" (CG XV.6, 642). Christ's kingship is participated in by all the citizens of the heavenly city: the saints do not check their agency at the gates of heaven, as it were, but rather hope to reign with God, as Augustine's rhetorical dialectic stresses in the latter books of *The City of God*.

Augustine's rhetorical dialectic in this regard, its compatibility with magnanimous truth-seeking and agency, presents a balanced, agency- and responsibility-enhancing vision of humility that is echoed some 1,500 years later by novelist and short-story writer Flannery O'Connor. "We hear a great deal about humility being required to lower oneself, but it requires an equal humility and a real love of the truth to raise oneself and by hard labor to acquire higher standards" (O'Connor, 1969, 189).

BOOK XVI: OUT OF ASSYRIA AND EGYPT

Book XVI sweeps across many centuries, starting from the eminent found- ers and foundations of the greatest ancient cities and empires, especially Assyria, its capital Babylon, and the great city of Nineveh. In the midst of these magnificent and powerful places and peoples a small shoot springs up almost imperceptibly, which will in time flower into the Hebrew nation. There is a beautiful, mysterious passage in which Augustine marks the dawn of the Hebrews and highlights their significance for all humanity:

But it is, in fact, undoubtedly true that they were named "Heberews," after Heber [who was "foremost" among the "descendants of Shem," son of Noah], and later, with the omission of one letter, Hebrews. The Hebrew language exists only among the people of Israel; and *it is in that people, and in the saints, and, in a shadowy and mysterious sense, in all mankind*, that the pilgrim City of God is embodied.[6] (*CG* XVI.3, 700; emphasis added; cf. XVI.9, 711; XVI.10, 713; and XVI.11, 714–15)

At the forefront of this section, in terms of the theme of pride and humility, is the contrast Augustine draws between Assyrian Babylon with its founder Nimrod and the tower he sought to build, and Abraham – born in Assyrian lands – with his pilgrim posterity. In recounting the biblical narrative of the Tower of Babel, Augustine's rhetorical dialectic depicts the story of human pride, a tale that in its essential features will be repeated in innumerable instantiations throughout history till its end.

The Tower of Babel

In chapter 11 of the book of Genesis, it is said that the people of the great city of Babylon, whose name means "confusion," planned to construct a tall tower "whose top may reach unto heaven; and … [to] make a name

---

[6] *Hebraei, quam linguam solus Israel populus potuit obtinere, in quo dei ciuitas et in sanctis peregrinata est et in omnibus sacramento adumbrata.*

[for themselves]," and gather to themselves for strength all people dwelling on the face of the earth. Augustine attributes the origin of this civic conspiracy to the founder and ruler of Babylon, "the giant Nimrod." Just as Babylon "took precedence over all [other cities] ... as a capital city," so also in Babylon Nimrod held pre-eminence over all other human beings. Nimrod is described in the book of Job as "a mighty hunter against the Lord" (Job 15:13). Augustine glosses this unholy epithet in political, as well as religious, terms: "[W]hat does this word mean, what is a 'hunter,' if not a deceiver, an oppressor, a slayer of earth-born creatures? Thus [Nimrod], with his peoples, began to build a tower *against the Lord: a tower which symbolizes his ungodly pride*" (CG XVI.4, 703; emphasis added).

Despite the very great power of this city and its first king and the vast extent of its future empire, Babylon "was not brought to the perfection which, in their proud ungodliness, its builders had intended"[7] (CG XVI.4, 702). The Lord God knew that all the inhabitants of the world then spoke one language, and that in this unified speech lay no small part of the power that humans would misuse. He opted to scatter them in the proud thoughts of their hearts (cf. Luke 1:51), preventing their mutual understanding and thereby precluding a monopoly of concerted civic action. Hence the famous confusing of speech, introducing a diversity of tongues among the children of Adam, Eve, and Noah. "What kind of punishment was imposed, then? Because the power of a ruler lies in his tongue, it was there that Nimrod's pride was condemned, so that he who refused to understand and obey God's bidding was himself not understood when he gave his bidding to men. Thus that conspiracy of his was dissolved" (CG XVI.4, 703). Each of Nimrod's subjects ceased to associate with those of their peers whose language she or he could no longer comprehend. Small groups with their own common languages formed clans and future political communities, going out from Babylon in search of space to establish themselves. "[S]o the nations were divided by their tongues, and scattered abroad upon the face of all the earth, as it pleased God. And God accomplished this in ways which are hidden from us, and which we cannot understand" (CG XVI.4, 704).

As Augustine's rhetorical dialectic will later note, regarding Babel's ostentatious political attempt to achieve and display excessive grandeur apart from God and even against him, "because of the *pride* shown in

---

[7] *quamuis perfecta non fuerit usque in tantum modum, quantum superba cogitabat impietas.*

building a tower to reach up to heaven, *the city, that is, the society, of the ungodly now appeared*" (CG XVI.10, 713; emphasis added).[8]

Abraham: "My Father was a Wandering Aramaean" (Deuteronomy 26:5)

A powerful foil for proud Nimrod, Babylon, and Assyria is found in Abraham and his faithful descendants. Writes Augustine in transition, "Let us now examine the progress of the City of God from the era beginning from father Abraham onwards" (CG XVI.12, 717). Abraham's own father, Terah, was first called by God to come with his household out of Assyria, where he had been persecuted for his fidelity to the one Creator-God, who had made his covenant with the human race through Noah. Augustine surmises that just as Noah's family was chosen to save the human race from perishing utterly from the earth, "so now only the house of Terah remained in the midst of the flood of superstition covering the whole world, as the place where the City of God was tended and planted" (CG XVI.12, 718). Terah left Ur of the Chaldeans, where he had been persecuted for refusing to follow false gods. With his household he went first into Mesopotamia and then to Haran (cf. Judith 5:5; CG XVI.13, 719).

Terah's son Abraham later heard God's call and command: "'Get thee out of thy country, and from thy kindred, and from thy father's house. ...' So Abram departed ... and Lot [his nephew] went with him ... when he departed out of Haran" (Genesis 12:1–4). Unlike the proud Nimrod, who seeks to stay in Babylon, establish his and his city's pre-eminence with a tall tower, and attract all the people of the world to settle and join with him and increase his city's strength, Abraham humbly departs even his adopted country and his father's house, dwelling in tents and traversing foreign fields. Augustine understands this second departure of the son of Terah (with the first being Abraham's departure from Assyria with Terah and all his household) to signify the removal not only of his body from his own land but also his mind and spirit from the hope of returning there again to possess it (CG XVI.15, 723). Whereas Nimrod fought against God and refused to listen or obey, Abraham hears, obeys, and follows. Nimrod sought to draw all peoples to himself and his city, while Abraham voluntarily parts ways even from his own nephew to assure

---

[8] For a study of *The City of God* focusing on Jerusalem and Babylon as antitheses and archetypes of the two cities, see van Oort (1991).

sufficient pastures for their flocks and to promote concord between their households, giving the younger Lot the choice of lands (*CG* XVI.20, 726–27; cf. Genesis 13:8f.). "[O]therwise," Augustine surmises, "human nature being what it is, quarrels might have arisen between themselves also." Abraham acts to "forestall such an evil" (726), even if in so doing he lessens the grandeur of what he might have termed "his own" family and his future polis.

That a great people could come from the humble faith of this wandering Aramean, Augustine's rhetorical dialectic recalls, God promised the aged Abraham and his wife Sarah a son. Both responded to this surprising news with laughter – with "astonished joy" and "joyful celebration." Fittingly enough, when "a son was born to Abraham by Sarah, according to God's promise … he gave him the name Isaac, which means 'laughter.'" As Sarah said after Isaac's birth, her laughter is meant not as a private boon but as a common good widely shared among humanity. "God hath made me to laugh, so that all that hear will laugh with me" (*CG* XVI.31, 744). Perhaps Sarah had no idea how widely, hopefully, and long her laughter would echo.

Into the Promised Land: From Isaac, to Moses, to Israel's Judges and Kings

Augustine's narrative runs quite rapidly after Abraham, through his son of the promise, Isaac, and his grandson Jacob; through Joseph's sojourn as a slave and then great official in Egypt; to the Chosen People's later enslavement, the Exodus, and the founding of the political community of Israel, ruled by God's law, judges, and eventually, kings. All this history transpires in just eleven chapters, emphasizing how God's people grew and embodied – albeit always imperfectly – the heavenly city on its pilgrimage. Many examples of Abrahamic humility emerge throughout this story, with Moses as perhaps their pinnacle.

In Augustine's description of Moses, we see a mixture of *grandeur et misère*, with an emphasis on the divine gifts that made Moses "so great a man" and so "wondrous" a leader (*CG* XVI.43, 761–62). Moses fled from Pharaoh after slaying an Egyptian who was oppressing his Hebrew brethren. On his own he was no match for Pharaoh's power. Yet God prepared him with great gifts of character and learning and endowed him with the courage to represent God before Pharaoh on behalf of the people of Israel. It is clear in Augustine's language in these passages that while God's agency in all this is pre-eminent, Moses's free cooperation with God's will is also indispensable. Augustine makes a similar point concerning the apostle Paul, in *On Grace and Free Will*, composed just after *The City of God*, writing near the end of his life in AD 428:

Certainly merit was found in the Apostle Paul, but while he was persecuting the Church, it was evil. Hence in his avowal, "I am not worthy to be called an Apostle because I persecuted the Church of God" (1 Corinthians 15:9). So it was while he possessed the evil merit that good merit was given to him in return for evil merit. That is why he went on to say: "But by the grace of God I am what I am." And, in order to show that there is also free will, he at once added: "And His grace in me has not been fruitless but I have labored more abundantly than all of them" (1 Corinthians 15:10). *He does, in fact, exhort man's freedom* also in others where he says to them: "We entreat you not receive the grace of God in vain." (*On Grace and Free Will* 1.5.12; quoting 2 Corinthians 6:1–12)

Moses and his successor Joshua led the people through the wilderness and into the Promised Land of Canaan. They went out from Egypt on pilgrimage and persevered in the passage to the Promised Land when their sins elongated their exile. All this was in response to God's promise to father Abraham. "[A]fter those two leaders [Moses and Joshua], when the people were ... established in the promised land, there were judges [and later kings]. Thus, God's first promise to Abraham now began to be fulfilled, in one people, the Hebrew nation ... Its fulfilment did not, however, yet extend to all nations and to the whole world" (*CG* XVI.43, 763). For this universal redemption to be made ready, God called the prophets to preach to the people, at the time of another "wandering," this time into and out of exile in Babylon. As from Israel will arise, in Augustine's estimation, a universal church, so also after Babylon's *exemplum* some 1,200 years later arises Rome. "Rome was founded as a second Babylon, as it were, in the West" (*CG* XVI.17, 724–25; cf. XVIII.22, 848).[9]

In book XVII, Augustine's rhetorical dialectic proceeds to chronicle the work of the prophets and their preaching to the people of God against pride and in favor of humility. Then, in book XVIII, Augustine returns his attention to the earthly city as it shows its presence in many political societies, not least in proud Rome throughout the long centuries of its republic and empire. It is to these segments of his long rhetorical dialectic that we now turn.

---

[9] Cf. also *CG* XVIII.2, 824, where Augustine describes Babylon as "the first Rome, as it were" and Rome "like a second Babylon." See also *Conf.* II.3.8, 28, in which Augustine describes himself in his youth as "walk[ing] the streets of Babylon," and his mother Monica then as "linger[ing] on [Babylon's] outskirts," with reference to their degrees of citizenship or residence, as it were, in the unrighteous earthly city at that time.

BOOK XVII: PRIDE AND HUMILITY IN
THE "AGE OF THE PROPHETS"

Although book XVI concludes with the reign of King David, Augustine's narrative there barely touches on this key moment of Israel's history and the preceding era of rule by judges. It is therefore not surprising that the story rewinds somewhat at the beginning of book XVII, back to the times of the great prophet and judge, "holy Samuel" (*CG* XVII.1, 765), and of King David, "a son of the heavenly Jerusalem" who "ruled in the earthly Jerusalem" (*CG* XVII.20, 812). Thence the narrative of book XVII continues into the stormy eras that followed the reigns of David and his son Solomon in Israel's history, up to the time of Jesus's birth. Augustine terms this long period of political consolidation and crisis, pilgrimage into and out of exile, self-rule and foreign subjection, and through it all, long waiting for the promised Messiah, as the "age of the prophets" (*CG* XVII.1, 765). This era in the people of God's history, on Augustine's account, ends with the restoration of the Temple after the Babylonian exile, in the times of the Jeremiah and of Malachi, Haggai, Zechariah, and Ezra. Then follow long centuries with little or no prophecy in Israel, up to the time of the advent of the Christ. This last period Augustine considers marked by at least six prophetic voices in Israel – women's as well as men's – around the time of Jesus's birth and at beginning of his public ministry (*CG* XVII.1, 765; XVII.24, 819–20).

From the vantage point of Augustine's rhetorical-dialectical defense of humility and his prosecution of vicious pride, book XVII boasts three key moments. The first chronicles events leading up to the birth and dedication to God of the prophet-judge Samuel. In this segment, Augustine offers a long interpretive discourse on the prophetic prayer of the holy woman Hannah, Samuel's mother. At the core of Hannah's song of praise and prophecy, Augustine finds an exaltation of godly humility, coupled with a hopeful interpretation of even the falls of the proud as divine summons to humility. It is in this chapter, comprising a lengthy meditation on the song of Hannah, that the terms *humilitas* and *superbia* and their cognates occur most often of all the chapters in books XV–XVIII, Augustine's segment on the history of the two cities.[10]

---

[10] On my count, in book XVII, chapter 4, *humilitas* and its cognates occur six times, and *superbia* and its cognates five times. Most other chapters in books XI–XVIII have no more than one occurrence of each.

The second highlight of book XVII, from pride and humility's vantage point, comes in Augustine's explication of the Davidic Psalms and in his commentary on David's person and legacy. David's life – manifesting both hubris and humility, but with the latter trait predominating and winning out in the end – is considered in contrast with the lives and legacies of David's son Solomon and of Rehoboam and Jeroboam, Solomon's heirs in a divided kingdom. The third key moment is found in the final two chapters of the book, treating the conquest of Israel by Assyria and the last of the prophets sent to the Chosen People before Christ according to Jewish and Christian canons. In at least three of these prophetic precursors to Christ found in the New Testament narrative, Augustine's Christian readers may recognize a profound kinship of spirit to Hannah of the Old Covenant, manifested in the incorporation of passages from Hannah's prophetic praise into their own canticles of hopeful humility against pride and presumption.

Hannah: The Prophetic Greatness of a "Little Woman"

Augustine's Hannah, mother of Samuel the prophet and judge, may be considered alongside his account in book III of the sister of the Horatii, in whose tears Augustine found more humanity than in all the rest of the Roman people. To the sorrow of this young Roman, readers of *The City of God* may juxtapose, now in book XVII, the rejoicing, or rather the *sorrow turned to joy*, of Hannah, "a little woman" and also a great prophet (*CG* XVII.4, 771). She had long been childless but prayed with faith to God, and in due time she gave birth to Samuel, who in his turn would become "a holy man of great renown." As in the weeping of the sister of the Horatii, Augustine witnessed truer humanity than elsewhere in the early annals of Rome, so in the prophetic prayer of Hannah when she comes to Shiloh to dedicate her weaned son to God, Augustine finds a truly prophetic expression of God's grace and his designs to heal sorrowing humanity, teaching humans ways to true justice and humility.

Augustine underscores that Hannah's very name means "God's Grace" (*CG* XVII.4, 771, 775). "Through her," writes Augustine, "there speaks, by the spirit of prophecy, the grace of God itself, from which the proud are estranged so that they fall, and by which the humble are filled so that they rise: the grace which, in the highest degree (*maxime*), resounds throughout her hymn" (*CG* XVII.4, 771–72). By harkening to Hannah's great prophetic prayer of thanksgiving and exaltation (1 Samuel 2:1, ff.; cf. Jeremiah 9, 23 f.), Augustine judges that readers of the Bible can learn much of great import about the "City of God itself" and its "King and Founder" (CG XVII.4, 771), which they will miss if they pass over her speech on account of her comparative physical and historical small-ness (cf. CG XVII.4, 770–79). Chapter 4, interpreting Hannah's canticle slowly, line by line, is the longest chapter of book XVII, and one of the longest of the entire *City of God*.

God is humanity's "only rock," and so Hannah exhorts her hearers to "'[t]alk no more so exceedingly proudly; let not arrogancy come out of your mouth'" (CG XVII.4, 772–73). Augustine notes that in this admo-nition, Hannah and through her God's Spirit address "the adversaries of the City of God, who belong to Babylon: who presume upon their own strength and glory in themselves and not in the Lord" (CG XVII.4, 773; cf. 771). God, through Hannah's humble, great-souled song of praise, reveals how he prepares things so that "the proud should fall and the humble rise" (CG XVII.4, 773), not indeed to condemn the proud for-ever, but to give them an opportunity for growth in self-knowledge and for conversion (CG XVII.4, 774). "[I]n another place (James 4:6) we read, 'God resisteth the proud and giveth grace unto the humble.' And this is the whole meaning of what she says, whose name means 'God's Grace'" (CG XVII.4, 775). As Augustine also indicates, Hannah's pro-phetic prayer connects knowledge of God and his justice, with a fuller human capacity and commitment to "[do] justice and righteousness 'in the midst of the earth'" (CG XVII.4, 779; see also 773). Reading Hannah's song in light of the New Testament, Augustine's commen-tary highlights its fulfillment in Christ, by whose humility we have been exalted, by whose poverty we are enriched, and by whose death we may hope for eternal life (CG XVII.4, 775–76).

Davidic Humility in Deed and Song

If all people are called upon to "do justice and righteousness," this injunc-tion is especially intended for those holding political office and in posi-tions of political rule. In a monarchic regime, such as Israel's from the time of King Saul, for the king to love and strive after justice holds great urgency for his own citizenry and neighboring peoples. Following the wis-dom of Hannah's prophecy, pride and arrogance need to be powerfully repressed at least as efficaciously as the inevitable pulls of a kingly regime toward tyranny and indifference to the needs of the common people.

Scripture lauds David, Israel's second monarch, as a man who greatly "loved his Maker" and attended willingly to God's worship, enriching it with his musical and poetic gifts (Sirach 47:8; *CG* VII.14, 802). As we have seen, to acknowledge and worship the Creator-God is the root of virtuous humility, as Augustine understands it. Thence David's desire to do God's will, which comprises working for "justice and righteousness 'in the midst of the earth'" (*CG* VII.4, 779, quoting Psalm 74:12). Yet David was far from flawless in fulfilling this noble mission of government. Although he was a prophet as well as a king (*CG* XVII.15, 803), he had need of other prophets, Nathan and Gad, sent to him by God to help him correct his course, at times dramatically (see 2 Samuel 12:1–13; 2 Samuel 24:11–13). With these prophetic rebukes and summons to repentance, David had opportunity to grow in righteous humility, expressed both in deed and in song, as in the Psalms.

With regard to the scriptural Psalms attributed to King David, Augustine surveys for his readers varying views on their authorship. Some scholars hold that David wrote none of them directly, others that he composed a few or many, and still others that David was the author of the whole psalter. Augustine concurs most closely with this last thesis, considering it likely that David wrote "all 150 of the psalms" (*CG* XVII.14, 802). The messianic and prophetic content of many of these psalms reveal to Augustine a deep humility on the part of their composer: a complete confidence in God, David's and Israel's rock; an acknowledgment that the promised messiah will be far greater than David himself and will partake eternally of the priesthood in "the order of Melchizedek" (*CG* XVII.17, 807); and indications that the Christ will suffer great humiliations on the path to redeeming His people (see, *inter al.*, *CG* XVII.14–19, 802–12). Such were some of the many aspects of and reasons for humility, expressed in the poetry of the great prophet-king David, as Augustine interprets the psalter.

As we have noted, Augustine's rhetorical dialectic emphasizes more than once, especially in books VI and VII, the importance of *living* in truth, not simply knowing or speaking truth, or even writing or singing it. Concerning the deeds of David that reflect virtuous humility, Augustine refers in general terms to the king's reactions to his biggest falls from "justice and righteousness." In alluding to David's most serious falls, Augustine likely has in mind David's adultery with Bathsheba and subsequent murder of her husband Uriah, sins committed while David was at ease in his palace instead of with his troops in battle, as was his duty (see 2 Samuel 11–12), as well as the hubris David expressed in the census he took of his great and growing people (see 2 Samuel 24). And yet when David realized his sinfulness, he did not despair, react with more *superbia*, or refuse to make reparation. Rather, as Augustine notes, David was "greatly praised by the Divine testimony because his sins were overcome by a piety so great, and a *penitence of such wholesome humility*" (*CG* XVII.20, 812; emphasis added). At this juncture, the reader of *The City of God* harkens back to book V, in which Augustine marvels at and approves of the humiliation Emperor Theodosius underwent voluntarily, doing public penance at the behest of church authority to atone for a serious breach of faith, justice, and mercy committed in his work of government. Like David, king under the Old Covenant, Theodosius, a Christian under the New Covenant, seems to have repented, "[doing] penance with ... humility" (*CG* V.26, 235). In David's case, however, Jewish and Christian readers have the added testimony of scripture to ratify the sincerity of David's humble repentance and its acceptability to God, whom in his pride the king had offended. In this limited but still relevant regard, Augustine's rhetorical dialectic suggests, David can serve as a model for political officials down through the ages, in a myriad of different regimes and governmental structures.

Kings Solomon, Rehoboam, and Jeroboam

Although Augustine does not use the words "pride" and "humility" in describing David's successors, first in the united kingdom and later in a house divided, his descriptions of their behaviors' and their reigns' respective political and religious effects reflect realities corresponding to virtuous humility and, most often, to vicious pride.

David began his reign well, but then fell seriously into sin more than once through pride. Still, David repeatedly returned humbly to God in penitence, and he ended his life well. His son Solomon likewise began admirably, as evinced in his famous prayer to God for wisdom unto just government (see I Kings 8:22–53).[11] Yet he ended his reign badly. Augustine's all-too-brief analysis of Solomon's failure alludes to an overconfidence born of long-lasting, far-famed prosperity, coupled with greater attention given to pleasing his numerous foreign wives than to pleasing the Lord his God. Solomon in his later years gives evidence of what Augustine understands as "living according to the flesh," acting according to human standards and for his own ease and glory more than

---

[11] For a contemporary reflection for a diverse political audience on Solomon's prayer for a wise or "listening heart" in order to perform his public responsibilities well, see Benedict XVI (2011).

for God and his glory, and so for the true good of human persons and polities in his care and under his leadership. Solomon lapsed into idolatry and set poor precedents for his people, establishing shrines to the divinities adored by the foreign nations of his wives and neglecting the cult of the only Creator-God and savior of Israel in the very temple that Solomon had built for him.

As a punishment for this hubristic and foolish disobedience, God's providence permitted the division of the kingdom of David after Solomon's death. Solomon's son Rehoboam ruled Judah, with its capital in Jerusalem. In the reduced kingdom of Israel, with its seat now in Samaria, Solomon's servant Jeroboam was the first to govern. Augustine notes that "it was not [the Jewish people's] religion which had been divided, but only their kingdom" (*CG* XVII.21, 817).

Due to manifestations of political pride in the behavior of both kings, as well as to the legacy of idolatry that Solomon had bequeathed to the people, this religious unity was soon under political assault. Things took this turn "when Rehoboam, like a tyrant, wished to persecute that divided part with war." In this he evinced *libido dominandi*, the lust for domination that is according to Augustine the clearest hallmark of political *superbia* (see Chapter 2). God, however, countered the king's speech with prophetic discourse, announcing to the people that he had effected this political division, and that they were not to use force to undo it if they wished to act justly. Augustine's rhetorical dialectic here is somewhat vague, but it seems that prophetic speech had such an impact on popular opinion that the people's ruler Rehoboam had no option other than to pursue peace (*CG* XVII.21, 817).

Rehoboam's designs to reunite the kingdom under his sole reign had not escaped his counterpart's notice. Jeroboam appears on Augustine's account to have concluded that God's deliverance to him of the rule of part of the people could not be relied upon to endure. He therefore did not believe God (*non credans deo*; *CG* XVII.22, 818).[12] In order to put his claim to rule beyond doubt, he sought and established a new civil religion, that of the regional divinity Baal, for his new people with their new capital. Jeroboam thus "instituted idolatry in his kingdom," writes Augustine, "and deceived the people with dreadful ungodliness" (*CG* XVII.22, 818). Once again, God sent prophets to admonish the king and the people, of

---

[12] Here I modify Dyson's (1998) translation of *non credens deo*, "he did not believe in God" (818).

whom a small but significant number remained faithful. The prophetic voice in Judah's and Israel's politics remained a bulwark against the complete dominion of political pride, at home or in exile. The exilic experience was likewise a pedagogy permitted by God as an antidote to pride and to bring his people back to trusting, magnanimous humility.

Elizabeth and Zachariah, Anna and Simeon, and Mary and John the Baptist

Of the six prophetic voices Augustine finds in scripture around the time of Jesus's birth and at the beginning of His public ministry – Elizabeth and Zachariah, Anna and Simeon, and Mary and John the Baptist – three offer canticles of praise to God, hymns that echo to varying degrees Hannah's humble canticle of praise and hopeful prophecy (*CG* XVII.24, 819–20). Augustine does not call his readers' attention to this fact explicitly, but he likely surmised that Christian readers would recognize this striking parallel, especially in the case of Mary, "the Virgin Mother of the Lord" (*CG* XVII.24, 820).

Mary's hymn of praise, sung to God as she greets her cousin Elizabeth, who is pregnant with John the Baptist, is popularly known by its first Latin word, "*magnificat*": "My soul *magnifies*," or "*proclaims the greatness* of the Lord, and my spirit finds joy in God my savior, because he has regarded the humility of his handmaid, for behold, all generations will call me blessed. He has scattered the proud in the conceit of their heart and has exalted the humble. He has filled the hungry with good things, while the rich he has sent empty away" (Luke 1:46–55). Echoing and announcing the fulfillment of Hannah's song of praise (1 Samuel 2:1–10), Mary's prophetic hymn, alluded to by Augustine at the close of this book (*CG* XVII.24, 820), expresses confidence in the goodness of humility and notes well the perils of pride. God chastises the latter, as Hannah's song implied in Augustine's interpretation, in order to be able to raise them up to true and higher heights by setting their personal and social lives on a much firmer foundation.

Despite the prophetic exaltation of humility that Augustine's history emphasizes again and again, in this segment and in other passages scattered throughout *The City of God*, his rhetoric concerning the Jews often reads in an arrogant key. At times his prose is balanced, and even highly laudatory, but at other times excessively harsh, denoting ignorance, pride, or at a minimum, rash judgment of unknown others and immoderation in speech. If Augustine were able to read his own work today, after the tragic era of pogroms and the Shoah, given his sensitivity to wrongful suffering and his emphasis on genuine dialogue, one hopes and suspects that he would revisit these aspects of his views and prose, recognize his errors, and reform his writing.[13]

BOOK XVIII: EARTHLY PROGRESS AND PROPHECY
UP TO THE COMING OF CHRIST

Book XVIII comprises the climax of Augustine's history of the two cities and their "progress" (*procursus*) together through time toward their appointed ends (*CG* XVIII.1, 821).[14] Its narrative ends with the advent and impact of Christ the Mediator, who triumphs over pride by perfect humility and offers humble exaltation to all those who are willing to share in his humiliation out of love for God and neighbor.

This book is framed by stark binaries, as was also the case at the outset of this segment of *The City of God* in book XV: *The City of God* versus the earthly city; and prophetic and divine humility versus political and philosophic pride. At times Augustine appears to forget what he has already and more charitably written and argued in the heat of rhetorical flourishes and exaggerated antitheses (cf. Kabala, 2020; Rist, 1994, 310–13). At the same time, portions of book XVIII's argument are expressed with complexity, nuance, and even moderation. Here a tension in Augustine's prose between persuasion and predestination comes to the fore, perhaps prompting perplexity in his readers. The rhetorical dialectic in book XVIII also shows some tension between its trope of political and poetic divinization of dead human beings as expressive of extreme *superbia*, and the pity evoked by Augustine's account of human ignorance and misery as motives for such divinization. Righteous *thumos* and merciful *pathos* point together toward fulfillment in Christ, the true and humble Mediator, who alone can heal humanity with the strength of the true God and bring those despairing to hope, fulfilling humanity's aspirations for what is good. As John Rist describes Augustine's ambition and ethos:

---

[13] See Fredriksen (2010), for an analysis of Augustine's thought regarding Judaism and the Jews. See also Cohen (1999, 19–71); and Cavadini (2007, 128, note 24).

[14] Augustine's word choice, *procursus*, literally means "*a running forth, running on*" (Charlton T. Lewis's *Elementary Latin Dictionary*, 1918, 654). It lacks the optimistic overtone of "progress" in contemporary English, though it does convey a rapid covering of ground. Augustine employs the related verb *concurro, concurrere*, to run together or to make haste (Lewis, 1918, 157–58), to describe the intertwined histories of the two cities in this world (see, e.g., *CG* XVIII.1: *currurerunt, cucurrisse, cucurrerit*).

Augustine was not only the man who saw through the idolatries of Greco-Roman antiquity; he was also himself, in every unguarded moment, an admirer of the classical hero – just as Plato, whose tradition he had found so vital a medium for his Christian psychology and theology, had been, while suspicious of the moral influence of the poets, an admirer of Homer and the "most Homeric" of the Greeks. For like the ancient thinkers almost to a [person] … Augustine lived by the inspiration of the Good, or the nearest he could come to it, and was impelled by it to do good at any cost. Imagine Hector, or Socrates, or Praxiteles, or Antigone, or Hipparchia, or Sappho inspired by the Christ-man, Jesus. (Rist, 1994, 312–13)

Augustine's rhetorical dialectic against pride and for humility in book XVIII has three major movements, following the structure of the history he offers in this book. First and at greatest length, Augustine describes and chastises the long tendency of the earthly city to fashion false divinities and to mandate their acknowledgment by means of impious laws and draconian penalties.[15] Second, Augustine turns to the salutary teaching of the so-called minor prophets, in biblical books of whose teaching both Jews and Christians consider canonical. These prophets extolled godly humility and rebuked civic hubris. Their discourse invited the People of God to learn from harsh experience, even from foreign humiliation and domination, to trust in the Lord more than in their unaided strength, and to return to the true God with a strong, agency-enhancing humility. Augustine will later extend this motif to refer to the church "preparing through her present humiliation for her future exaltation" (*CG* XVIII.49, 896). Third, Augustine discourses briefly on Jesus Christ as the fulfillment of these prophecies, emphasizing that Christ's humility, evinced by his free and loving acceptance of humiliation at the hands of the proud, paradoxically provides the strongest proof of his greatness and his capacity to exalt those who hope in him (cf. *CG* I, preface, 3). In this way, Augustine sets the stage for the final segment of *The City of God*, books XIX–XXII, treating the ultimate ends of the two cities in light of the universal human desire for happiness and fulfillment.

Clarifying by Contrast: Augustine's Introduction

Augustine introduces book XVIII by reviewing the plan and progress of *The City of God* thus far. After recapping the ordering and aims of books I–XIV, our author details afresh the structure and content of

---

[15] For studies of Augustine's thought on law, see Chroust (1973) and Dougherty (2013).

books XV–XVIII. In describing the progress or running-on (*procursus*) of the two cities through time (cf. inter al. *CG* I.35, 49; XVIII.1, 821), Augustine's rhetorical dialectic began in book XV with the early growth of the heavenly and earthly cities in the lives of the children of Adam and Eve and their descendants down to the time of Noah and the flood. Then in books XVI and XVII, the focus shifted to the heavenly city, as it was present in the persons and lives of patriarchs, prophets, and kings among the Chosen People. "I wrote in this way," Augustine explains, "because … I wished to present the history of that city [of God] more plainly, by describing its course, without the obstruction of that other city which is its opposite" (*sine interpellatione a contrario alterius civitatis ista*; *CG* XVIII.1, 821). Augustine now judges that he must backtrack to balance his narrative, chronicling the parallel course of the earthly city that becomes visible most clearly and most constantly in the greatest of the Gentile nations and rulers. Augustine's goal in this discourse is to illumine the nature of the heavenly city by juxtaposing it with its foil, and to that end his pen here brings the earthly city's past glories and follies to light once more. Thus, writes our author, "those who read may compare both cities and observe the contrast between them" (*CG* XVIII.1, 821), deciding to which to pledge loyalty.

Augustine considers Assyria in its vast ironclad empire, rather than the ancient Greek cities and empires, to be the greatest predecessor of Rome. Still, Augustine seems to consider a defense of this valuation necessary. Despite Assyria's superiority in the strength, breadth, and length of its dominion to that of the Greeks, Augustine notes that the Athenians in particular were deemed politically extraordinary and might seem Rome's true predecessor in imperial grandeur. Augustine follows Sallust in suggesting that the Athenians' daring civic deeds may have been magnified beyond their just measure by Athens's famed "writers of great genius" (*CG* XVIII.2, 823; quoting Sallust, *Catil.*, 8,7 ff.). The Athenians "acquired no small glory from literature and from her philosophers, because such disciplines were pursued there with exceptional vigor" (*CG* XVIII.2, 823). The Romans, moreover, trace their genealogy from the Greeks through the Latins, and Greek history is far better chronicled among Latin writers than is Assyrian. By contrast, Augustine gives imperial precedence to the Assyrians and considers them the key political precursors to the earthly empire he inhabits.

Augustine concludes this portion of his rhetorical dialectic by setting up his thematic in the coming chapters as follows:

Thus, we must give the names of Assyrian kings where necessary, in order to show how Babylon, the first Rome, as it were, pursues its course alongside the City of God on pilgrimage in this world; but the things which we must insert for the sake of comparing the two cities … must be derived rather from Greek and Latin history [given the paucity of historical material accessible to Augustine concerning Assyria], in which Rome herself is like a second Babylon. (*CG* XVIII.2, 824; cf. *CG* XVIII.2, 822)

Pride and Pathos in the Earthly City's Progress

As Augustine recognizes the heavenly city on pilgrimage in time by its chief mark – the search for and right worship of the one true God, in response to His free gifts of grace and charity – so here he continues to identify its foil, the earthly city, by its practice of creating false deities and encouraging or even ordering their worship. The advance of the earthly city on Augustine's account combines elements of what we would term scientific, technological, and artistic progress with religious regress. The earthly city's citizens and those of the heavenly city share the benefits of progress in the arts and sciences, as all human beings need to make use of knowledge and crafts to navigate together the "vicissitudes of time" (*CG* XVIII.1, 821). What sets the earthly city's citizens apart from their heavenly counterparts in human society is the former's progress – or rather regress – in divinizing and worshipping elements of nature, dead human beings, and even malicious spirits. For this reason, it is unsurprising that Augustine's history in book XVIII, chapters 2 through 24, emphasizes the recurring trope of false divinization in the Hellenic and Latin classical worlds, and the subsequent creation of cultural, political, and legal norms enforcing these divinities' cult. The first instance of which Augustine is aware occurred in the time of Abraham. In the Sicyonian kingdom, a man named Telxion ruled. "[His] reign was a time of such peace and happiness that, when he died, men worshipped him as a god, offering sacrifices to him and celebrating the games which they say were first established in his honor" (*CG* XVIII.2, 824). Varro notes the custom of offering sacrifice also at the tomb of the seventh Sicyonian monarch Thuriacus (*CG* XVIII.3, 825). In Argolis, a member of the royal family named Phegous was likewise worshipped after his death (*CG* XVIII.3, 825–26).

Augustine pauses here to inquire why one who was obviously a human being would be regarded posthumously as a divinity. He surmises that Phegous's promotion of religious shrines in his region of the empire, and especially his introducing a calendar based on months and years, explains the cult that arose in his honor after his death. "Wondering at these innovations of his, men who were still untutored believed, or wished to believe, that at his death he had become a god" (*CG* XVIII.3, 826). Augustine offers a parallel possible explanation of the famed Egyptian ruler-turned-goddess, Io, or Isis. "[B]ecause her government was both broad and just, and because she instituted many beneficial things, especially the art of writing, divine honors were accorded to her there after her death." So great was the reverence in which Isis was held that it was a "capital crime" for anyone to question her divine status (*CG* XVIII.3, 826; cf. XVIII.5, 827).

This pattern continued down through the centuries in Greece and neighboring dominions. Most often it was deceased monarchs who were enrolled with the gods, yet some private persons posthumously received divine honor as well. Such was the case of "Homogyrus ... the first to yoke oxen to the plough" (*CG* XVIII.6, 828). In the midst of the earthly city, there were other low moral marks besides that of false cult, such as the deeds of the Greek King Busiris around the time of Israel's exodus from Egypt. This notorious "tyrant ... was sacrificing his guests to the gods," adding deeply inhuman depravity to the worship of fabricated divinities (*CG* XVIII.12, 836).

The early Latins learned from the Greeks' ongoing divinization of their heroes before and after the Trojan War (*CG* XVIII.15–16, 840–41). Augustine laments that both Greeks and Latins continued to lower themselves, "serving dead men – who did not live truly even when they were alive" (*CG* XVIII.18, 845). Aeneas himself was divinized in Latium. There followed after him eleven monarchs who were not considered greater than human, and then a twelfth, Aventinus, who was divinized after his death. "After Aventinus, no one was made a god in Latium except Romulus, the founder of Rome" (*CG* XVIII.21, 847). There was no more room in the Pantheon, it seemed. Not even the great Numa, founder and extender of Roman civil religion, could find a place there (*CG* XVIII.24, 853).

In light of the first ten books of *The City of God* and Augustine's equation therein of the false divinization of daemons with a high degree of *superbia*, readers of book XVIII might project a similarly harsh critique onto its rhetorical dialectic concerning the pagan elevation of human beings to divine honor. Strikingly, this is not an emphasis or even an element of Augustine's narrative in book XVIII, nor generally throughout *The City of God* when he discusses civic-poetic divinization of deceased human beings. Instead, the compassion toward these all-too-human errors, or at worst, forms of flattery, with which Augustine evinces and seeks to evoke in his readers, predominates the bulk of book XVIII. Why does pride not now play a central role?

After the original sin of Adam and Eve, the history of human progress is one punctuated by violence, rapaciousness, darkness, and oppression. Within our shared human nature and its near-universal eagerness for prolonging life, diverse desires of individuals and nations arise and come into conflict with one another. As a result, some peoples are cruelly enslaved by their neighbors, while the victors are themselves enslaved by their own lust for domination (CG XVIII.2, 822; I, preface, 3). It is no exaggeration to describe the human condition after the Fall, as Augustine does repeatedly in *The City of God*, as a time marked by "tears ... aris[ing] from the infirmity of our human condition" (*CG* XIV.9, 599).

Still, human nature, created good and for good by the all-good God, is not wholly corrupted or destroyed. From time to time, individuals rule more justly in political communities than their predecessors, promote education and arts, advance science, and make better provision for the necessities and comforts of life for their people. Thus, here in book XVIII Augustine's narrative of the early pattern of divinizing dead men is largely one of the miserable human beings rejoicing to have their sufferings alleviated and their lives made for a while fuller and more secure, and praising their benefactors excessively in the hopes of prolonging their benefactions. Yet outside the ambit of redemption – of the families and people of the great patriarchs – and beneath the sacrifices and festivals in honor of these rulers and innovators, humans more deeply experience their condition as "without hope and without God in the world" (Ephesians 2:12).

In this circumstance, can one really blame cities, nations, and peoples for recalling and trying to hold on to the blessings they have received from remarkable benefactors? For recall, this is how Augustine describes at least the earliest known practice of raising dead men and women to the status of gods, or believing them to have been so exalted by the gods. Gratitude for periods of peace, for more common welfare, for agriculture, and for arts and letters seems at the root of this admittedly excessive honor, coupled with a sense or wish that perhaps if these honors are perpetuated in games and sacrifices, the benefits themselves will endure or recur. An ancient Latin epitaph laments: *In nihil ab nihilo quam cito recidimus.* (How quickly we fall back from nothing into nothing [Benedict XVI, *Spe Salvi* §2]). Augustine's metaphysics and his revealed theology support this tendency of unaided, sinful human life and being to recede toward nothingness, if not ever its completion in actual nonbeing. Should we not excuse and pity these efforts, more pathetic than proud, to prolong and enhance our fragile being? Outside Israel and its prophetic tradition, as we will see, on Augustine's reading only the greatest philosophers and some poets inspired by them, such as Virgil, seem able to find a substantive cause for hope of happiness beyond the grave.

Still, the divinization of select human beings cannot offer hope for eternal, full happiness to all their fellow humans, and since human beings are not God, to worship them constitutes a flawed form of humility. Augustine's rhetorical dialectic in the next chapters and segment of book XVIII will underscore Israel's prophets as indispensable divine pedagogues for all humanity. These prophets teach true, rather than false, humility by drawing salutary lessons from humiliation – personal and political – and by revealing gradually the mystery of divine humility as the sole effective antidote to the dominion of political-religious pride. This mystery is made fully manifest in the Incarnation of the Mediator and Redeemer.

Prophetic Pedagogies of Humility

In his conclusion to chapter 26 of book XVIII, Augustine writes:

Up to this time [the return of the captives to Jerusalem, under the reigns of Cyrus et al.] the people of Israel had had prophets; but ... the writings of only a few of them have been retained as canonical by the Jews and by ourselves also. When I brought my last book to a close I promised that I would present some account of these prophets in this present book, and I see that I must now do this. (*CG* VIII.26, 855)

In chapters 27 through 45, Augustine thus returns to the "age of the prophets," which his rhetorical dialectic took up in book XVII. He rejoins this hopeful era in the long centuries leading up to the birth of Jesus. Augustine's considerations in book XVIII focus on the twelve minor prophets (so called because of the short length of their writings), whose books are accepted as canonical by Jews and Christians, while he discourses on major prophets such as Isaiah. Augustine reads the prophetic writings in the context of increasing or more explicit universality. Earlier prophecies chiefly addressed and benefited the people of Israel, while these later ones redound more clearly to the admonition, consolation, and instruction of all nations (*CG* XVIII.27, 856). In this prophetic development, the merciful undoing of Babel's division among humanity is intimated (*CG* XVIII.33, 869; 34, 869; 42, 883–84; cf. XVIII.49, 897). Israel's history is chronicled alongside the founding and progress of Rome, with parallels and antitheses between them highlighted in Augustine's prose.

A recurring motif of this segment of book XVIII is the interplay among exaltation, pride, humiliation, and humility in history and the prophets' discourse on the meaning of historical events and trends. Glossing the prophecies of Habakkuk, Augustine writes:

> "He looked and the nations wasted away": that is, He had mercy, and made the people penitent. "The mountains were ground down by his violence": that is, the pride of those who were lifted up was ground down by the power displayed in His wonders. "The everlasting hills melted away": that is, were humbled for a time, that they might be raised up for all eternity. (*CG* XVIII.32, 864)

This message of a people humbled by long endurance of civic division, foreign conquest, captivity, and exile, and so prepared for exaltation according to truth and true being, is repeated many times in the prophets' works and in Augustine's interpretation. It is a message of hope for the People of God amidst political misfortunes and in times of crisis, and a call to moderation and humility in periods of prosperity.

In the Chosen People's history, the consequences of turning a deaf ear to the prophetic pedagogy of humility, the fruit perhaps of false self-sufficiency and desire for self-justification, were devastating: religiously, with lapses into idolatry and eventually a cessation of prophecy; and politically, with a worsening of affairs for Israel leading up to Alexander's and Rome's conquest and the eventual destruction of the Temple by the Romans. Writes Augustine, "After the Jewish people had begun to be without prophets, there is no doubt that their condition grew worse: and this at the very time when they hoped that it would improve, on the restoration of the temple after the captivity in Babylon" (*CG* XVIII.45, 888). The effects of civic ambition in Israel on the eve of the Roman occupation parallel those in Rome's own foundation and development.

> Hyrcanus [striving for the kingdom] sought Roman help against his brother. By that time, Rome had already subjugated Africa and Greece and commanded a broad empire ... yet it seemed as if she was not strong enough to support her own weight, and had, as it were, broken herself by her own greatness. ... She had proceeded to the Social War and, shortly afterwards, to the Civil Wars; and these had so diminished and exhausted her that the transformation of her commonwealth into a monarchical government (*ut ei mutandus rei publicae status, quo regeretur regibus*) was now imminent. (*CG* XVIII.45, 890)

Such was Rome's hidden weakness when Pompey, in league with Hyrcanus, entered Jerusalem and dared to profane the Holy of Holies in the Temple of the one true God (*CG* XVIII.45, 890).

Augustine's dialectic also indicates, and evokes rhetorically, the greatness and pedagogical advantages of prophetic discourse vis-à-vis philosophy. Given that authentic prophecy originates with God rather than with
human beings and is faithfully proclaimed by true and humble prophets,
the prophetic teaching of *The City of God* is more authoritative, more
coherent and unified, and also more ancient than the teachings of the
classical philosophers and the theological poets and sages who preceded
them (*CG* XVIII.37, 875–76 and XVIII.41, 879–83). As Augustine finds
a new Babylon in Rome with its imperial grandeur and desire for mastery, he sees echoes of Babylon even in the philosophical search for wisdom, in the dissension of disharmonious voices to which it gives rise, "for
'Babylon' means 'confusion,' as we remember having said already" (*CG*
XVIII.41, 882; cf. *CG* XVI.4, 703).

In his assessment of the philosophers here, specifically in declar-
ing them *all* to be citizens of the earthly city "because of their great
and manifold ungodliness," Augustine's rhetorical dialectic seems at
its most rigid and unstable (*CG* XVIII.41, 882). Indeed, he cannot go
more than a few sentences further in his harsh condemnation without
backtracking:

> Some of the philosophers were indeed able to perceive a certain amount of truth
> in the midst of all their false opinions, and they strove by painstaking discussion
> to persuade others that God made this world and that He Himself directs it by
> His most gracious providence. They spoke of the nobility of virtue; of love of
> country; of fidelity in friendship; and of good works and all the things that per-
> tain to decent morals. (*CG* XVIII.41, 882)

Does this not sound like a description of human beings apt for, if not
actually or fully partaking in, heavenly citizenship, as portions of his rhetorical dialectic in *The City of God* previously indicated?

The upshot of Augustine's occasionally harsh rhetoric and judgment in this book, whether directed at those Jews who lapsed into
idolatry, did not believe the prophets, or later failed to recognize the
Christ, or the pagan philosophers and their students and admirers,
seems to be a renewed warning to his readers against temptation to
glory in oneself or one's political community and in one's unaided
ability to know, merit, and attain happiness. Book XVIII's teaching in
this aspect appears as a prelude to the most famous book of *The City
of God*, book XIX, with its exploration of happiness or the last end
of human life, and the identification of this *telos* with "'peace in life
eternal,' or 'life eternal in peace'" (*CG* XIX.11, 933). We will consider
this crucial book in Chapter 8.

Augustine's rhetorical-dialectical response in book XVIII to political and philosophic self-sufficiency is to defend true prophecy's superiority to both. In Israel,

[T]hose prophets who were in accord with each other … were acknowledged and accepted … as the true authors of Holy Scripture. *These were their philosophers, that is, lovers of wisdom*, their sages, their theologians, their prophets, their teachers of probity and godliness. Whoever believes and lives according to their teaching believes and lives not according to men, but according to God. (*CG* XVIII.41, 882; emphasis added)

As Augustine noted earlier in *The City of God*, the philosophers' best discourses on wisdom, virtue, and goodness of life were passed over all too often by elites and common people alike who preferred myth, pleasure, and power. In writing of true human goods, the philosophers

[K]new not the end to which all these things are to be referred and the rule by which they are to be judged.[16] In that City of ours, however, it was by prophecy – that is, by the divine voice speaking through men – that such things were commended to the people: they were not inculcated by controversy and argument. And this was done so that anyone who came to know them should fear to despise that which was not the mere cleverness of man, but the utterance of God. (*CG* XVIII.882–83)

From "the Humility of [Christ's] Patience" to "the Splendor of His Power"

"Do you wish to grasp the exaltedness of God? Grasp first the humility of God" (Augustine, *Sermones*, PL 38.671). This famous passage from one of the Augustine's sermons, quoted earlier in this book, sums up as well Augustine's brief treatment, at the close of book XVIII of *The City of God*, of the advent and impact of Jesus the Mediator and the spread of His teaching "among all nations … beginning at Jerusalem" (*CG* XVIII.54, 906).

The human and divine paradox of the greatness of God's humility, and the need to see and embrace it through faith before understanding and embracing God's magnitude, is revealed through the advent of Jesus – the Mediator between God and humanity. Writes Augustine in transitioning

---

[16] Compare *CG* X.29, 435, where Augustine's rhetorical dialectic addresses Porphyry, and through him, his admirers and followers among Augustine's contemporaries: "You see after a fashion, though at a distance, and with clouded vision, the country in which we should abide." See also Augustine's paraphrase of Plotinus in *CG* IX.17, 382: "We must fly, therefore, to our beloved fatherland, where dwells both our Father and all else."

from the prophecies to their fulfillment, "[I]t would not be possible for the Gentiles to expect Him to come and do judgment in the splendor of His power ... had they not first believed in Him when He came to suffer judgment in the humility of His patience" (*CG* XVIII.45, 890–91). Having taken to his divinity a human nature, Christ "was first revealed to us as a man ...[,] and His Godhead ... was concealed" (*CG* XVIII.46, 891). Only by means of the life, suffering, death, and Resurrection of "the man Christ Jesus" do his divine nature and its depth of love become manifest to humans. Similarly, the lives of his apostles, the teaching of his evangelists, and the witness of his martyrs, who did "battle for the truth even unto death – not by force of arms, but by the mightier power of endurance" (*CG* XVIII.54, 906; cf. XVIII.49, 896 and XVIII.50, 897–98), reveal the power of Christ's humility and the strength of godly love.

The following pair of quotations from the closing chapters of book XVIII encapsulate its contents and indeed Augustine's rhetorical dialectic in this entire segment on the progress of the two cities. The second passage particularly points the way to the work's next and final segment, treating the two cities' final ends, preparing us to embark on the next portion of our journey through history, and beyond it, with the author of *The City of God*.

In this fashion, the Church proceeds on her pilgrimage in this world, in these evil days: a pilgrimage which began not simply in the time of the corporeal presence of Christ and His apostles, but with Abel himself, that first righteous man slain by his ungodly brother; and which extends from that time even to the end of this world, amid the persecutions of the world and the consolations of God (*CG* XVIII.51, 900).

Now ... let us bring this book to a conclusion. Thus far, we have depicted, to the extent that seemed sufficient, the mortal course of the two cities, the Heavenly and the earthly, which are mingled together from the beginning to the end. One of them, the earthly, has made for itself such false gods as it wished, from whatever source it chose – even creating them out of men – in order to serve them with sacrifices. But the other, the Heavenly, a pilgrim in this world, does not make false gods. Rather, that city is itself made by the true God, and is itself to be His true sacrifice. Both cities alike make use of the good things, or are afflicted with the evils, of this temporal state; but they do so with a different faith, a different hope, a different love, until they are separated by the final judgment, and each receives its own end, to which there is no end. And those different ends must be the next topic of our discussion (*CG* XVIII.54, 907–8).

8

The City of God XIX–XXII

Humility, Pride, Peace, and Participation

Books XIX–XXII form the final segment of Augustine's *City of God* and its rhetorical-dialectical defense of humility. This segment's progression follows along these lines: Book XIX offers a philosophic exploration of the *summum bonum* of humanity, arguing that it coincides with the last end of the heavenly city and its citizens. This book is justly famous for its focus on peace. Book XX explicates and aims to justify a Christian theological account of the last step on the path to the ultimate end: God's final judgment of each human being and the good or evil of his or her deeds. Augustine next elaborates, in book XXI, his understanding of the "last end" of the earthly city's citizens – the last end in terms of outcome, not true fulfillment, as those loving themselves to the contempt of God pass from judgment to eternal misery with the fallen angels. Finally, in book XXII, Augustine's rhetorical dialectic circles back around to the theme of book XIX, the nature and meaning of the *summum bonum*, the last end or ultimate *telos* of humanity.

In these final four books, Augustine repeatedly renews his emphasis on the essential role of the body, as well as of the soul, in human nature and its happiness. In defense of the body's potentiality for resurrection and eternal life, whether in bliss or in misery, Augustine offers readers of books XXI and XXII two memorable discourses on wonder and miracles. As John Cavadini aptly describes Augustine's critique of the philosophers on this score, Augustine questions the wisdom of philosophic "wonder management."[1]

---

[1] This phrase is quoted from a talk given by John Cavadini to the graduate seminar on Augustine and Contemporary Political Thought at the University of Notre Dame, April 13, 2015. See Cavadini (2012) for an argument to this effect, though without using this precise phrase.

Augustine's protest and plea here are summed up well by Shakespeare's iconic character Hamlet:

There are more things in heaven and earth, Horatio,
Than are dreamt of in your philosophy. (*Hamlet*, act 1, scene 5)

Even if the classical philosophers also dream of wonders from time to time and call their readers' and interlocutors' attention to the wonders of the world and human life, Augustine implies that they do not ascertain just how much in nature and human nature is truly wonderful, and that we cannot adequately explain. Humility excels at opening human minds and hearts to wonder. By contrast, pride resists wonder, explaining it away, rashly judging truly remarkable things and persons to be common and unexceptional, merely matter to be ignored, or worse, dominated and possessed.

Augustine's rhetorical dialectic in these four final books presents pride as a formidable – but not invincible – foe of just peace and equality among humans. Pride, including its political or philosophic instantiations, prevents people from embarking on the path to true happiness, humanity's *summum bonum*. The antidote to pride, flowing from humility, emerges in Augustine's narrative as *participation* – free and willing participation in God's being, wisdom, and love. Crucial to this participation are the recognition of humanity's creaturely status and the rejection of the pull toward autarchy or a false sense of self-sufficiency. Only in accepting happiness and peace *humbly*, via participation, as gifts of God, common goods rather than private property, is real *res publica* possible. Otherwise, human "community" is formed through domination, deception, and oppression, as in imperial forms of rule striving for universality by force, fear, flattery, and fraud. The peace of such regimes forms a veneer over violence and corruption, but falls short of healing people's or polities' deep wounds (Cavadini, 2012). Only participation in God's life, being, wisdom, and love can fulfill human life and society, Augustine will argue, endeavoring to bring his readers to desire and cling to this participation until it is perfected in the heavenly city's eternal peace and life.

BOOK XIX: PEACE, PRIDE, HUMILITY, AND HOPE

On virtually any reading of *The City of God*, book XIX is pivotal.[2] This chapter's interpretation of Augustine's classic work through the lens of

---

[2] For studies of social and political dimensions of book XIX of *The City of God*, see inter alia Busch (2019), O'Donovan (1995), and Ogle (2021, 144–81).

humility and pride is no exception. In book XIX, Augustine's rhetorical dialectic offers readers a crucial description of pride (*superbia*), reflects on the ways pride affects social and civic relationships, and considers how pride relates to true greatness and virtue. In a quieter manner, book XIX likewise reflects deeply on humility (*humilitas*) as it relates to the attainment of happiness, virtue, and peace.

This section of our eighth chapter focuses on humility and pride in book XIX under a three-part schema. First, the analysis follows Augustine's explication of the nature of happiness, or the universal *summum bonum* for human beings, personally and socially. The modes in which virtuous humility paves the way for perfect happiness hereafter, and, through hope, real though relative happiness in the present age, are recapped and analyzed. Second, this section highlights Augustine's description of pride as "a perverted imitation of God" (*CG* XIX.12, 936). On Augustine's account, human nature's yearning for peace is not erased or fully silenced in the proud person or polity. Yet the peace that results from the proud having their way, from their satisfied *libido dominandi*, scarcely merits the name peace when compared with the peace of a just "fellowship of equality under God" (*CG* XIX.12, 936). Third, this segment of *The City of God* elucidates the nature of the best way of life, according to Augustine, in dialogue with various philosophical schools, especially as the best way of life for human beings relates to charity, humility, and pride.

Happiness, Humility, and Peace

Book XIX begins Augustine's inquiry into the final ends of the two cities. These ends correspond respectively to a universal human *summum bonum* (highest good) for *The City of God* and its citizens and a *summum malum* (highest, or worst, evil) for human beings, for the earthly city and those who love to dwell there. Augustine's intentional interlocutors and audience continue to comprise both believers and nonbelievers in Judeo-Christian revelation. For the sake of those who do not share his faith, Augustine clarifies that in developing his rhetorical dialectic here, he will rely "not only ... upon divine authority, but ... [make] as much use of reason as possible" (*CG* XIX.1, 909). Once again, far along in our rhetorical-dialectical journey, we find Augustine deep in dialogue with the philosophers.

The inquiry into the ultimate good for humans either involves or relates to the question of the best way of life, if there is such, for humans to follow in order to reach happiness and attain this ultimate good. Even more centrally, the quest for the *summum bonum* rests upon consideration of human nature and the goods that correspond to it (*CG* XIX.2–3, 914–18). The Greco-Roman philosophers had by Augustine's day given close to 300 different accounts of the "final good" of humans, as Augustine gleans from Varro's *De philosophia* (unfortunately for us, not extant). All 300 accounts cannot be correct, of course, if indeed any one of them is completely so. Augustine nonetheless supposes there to be a measure, and in some cases, a good measure, of truth in each of them: "[T]hough [the philosophers] have erred in many different ways, nature itself has not permitted them to wander too far from the path of truth" (*CG* XIX.1, 909–10).

The philosophic schools described by Varro and their accounts of the happiness and the highest good for humans locate happiness in the primary goods of body or soul, or both body and soul. Philosophers, in turn, offer diverse accounts of each of these sets of goods and the modes of living that are conducive to them. Varro's own answer to the query regarding the essence of the *summum bonum* or happiness is a composite one. It consists of virtue, in Varro's view the sine qua non for human happiness, together with the other goods of soul and body that support virtue. Happiness is even more perfect when a person possesses "all good things without exception," those proper to soul and body, and external goods, even independent of whether they are required for virtue (*CG* XIX.3, 917).[3]

In Varro's account, which Augustine follows here, the diverse philosophic schools seem united in seeking happiness in this life (cf. *CG* I–V), and by their unaided human efforts (*CG* XIX.4, 918–19). Unsurprisingly for readers at this late stage of his argument, Augustine finds in these patterns evidence of philosophic pride (cf. *CG* XIX.4, 922, 924–25). In chapter 4, Augustine reviews each account of human good, focusing on the flourishing of body and virtues of soul. He endeavors to persuade readers of the fragility, imperfection, and insufficiency of each good, as we experience it in this life, for full happiness. True human wisdom and virtue, on Augustine's account, acknowledge their ultimate insufficiency to fulfill the human desire for happiness. They do not claim to overshadow or undo the suffering we experience in illness, injury, death, the

---

[3] Cf. *CG* XIX.10, 932: Here Augustine seems to approve aspects of Varro's "composite" theory of "our final happiness," as Augustine describes the natural human longings and multiple goods and their fulfillment in the eternal peace of the heavenly city.

struggle against vices, and our lapses or headlong falls into them. True virtues thus are *humble virtues*. They do not claim a power or a completeness that is not truly their own by nature; rather, they look upwards to the only one who is perfectly wise and virtuous, namely God. They seek their sufficiency and strength from God.

Humble virtue conduces to a real, though incomplete and imperfect, happiness here and now. Augustine describes this felicity as happiness in hope (*CG* XIX.4, 924), a happiness both possible and reasonable since through prophecy, grace, and the advent of the Mediator, God has promised perfect happiness to his people in the life to come. True human virtue thus opens itself to faith and hope. It contrasts with proud philosophic virtue, which "will no[t] believe in this happiness because [it] does not see it. Thus, [those philosophers] endeavour to contrive for themselves an entirely false happiness [*beatitudinem ... falsissimam*], by means of a virtue which is as false as it is proud"[4] (*CG* XIX.4, 924–25).

Another aspect of happiness or the final good, on which many philosophers concur, is that it is achieved through or comprised by a social life. Augustine evidently thinks highly of this conclusion and judges it true. "[T]his is a view of which we much more readily approve," he muses, in comparison with arguments for the immediacy and self-sufficiency of human happiness on some philosophic accounts (*CG* XIX.5, 925). A happy social life is for Augustine synonymous with friendship.[5] Society and friendship exist on at least four levels, or in at least four fora: the household; the city or political society; the world of human beings; and the universe, including society among humans and gods or angels (*CG* XIX.3, 917–18; cf. XIX.1, 913).

Augustine therefore endeavors to examine, albeit briefly, social life or friendship at each level, vis-à-vis happiness and its prospects in this life (*CG* XIX.5–9, 925–31). He concurs that there truly is, in human nature and temporal life, much conducing to human happiness in friendship and society, yet challenges that friendship can ever fully achieve its *telos* in the here and now. Augustine argues that friendship or society, not perfected by participation in God's life in eternity, cannot attain the security, permanence, depth, and freedom that by nature humans desire to find in such fellowship. Friendship is a true good – indeed, a great good. It is,

---

4 *quam beatitudinem isti philosophi, quoniam non videntes nolunt credere, hic sibi conantur falsissimam fabricare, quanto superbiore, tanto mendaciore virtute.*

5 For studies on friendship in Augustine's thought and life, see Burt (1999), Cassidy (1992), McFadden (2018), Paffenroth (2005), and von Heyking (2008).

however, never fully actualized or fully free from fear and misery in this life. To claim otherwise would be counterfactual – at best, wishful thinking, and at worst, deception of oneself and others.

Augustine's readers are led to reflect on his earlier conclusion:

> [T]rue virtues ... can exist only in those in whom there is true godliness; and these virtues do not claim that they can protect those in whom they are present against suffering any miseries. True virtues are not such liars. ... They do, however, claim that, though human life is compelled to be miserable by all the great evils of this world, it is happy in the hope of the world to come and in the hope of salvation. For how else could it be happy, seeing that it is not yet saved? (*CG* XIX.4, 924)

Humble virtues protect persons both from calling misery bliss and from despairing of ever reaching a safe haven of happiness. They open the soul to faith and hope and to the imperfect yet real joy humans can experience in temporal existence. With true faith and true hope, true happiness can begin to take real root and grow, if not yet to flower in perfect fullness.

In sum, virtuous humility frees the mind and heart of a person to discern what is and is not true happiness and to ascertain which paths among humans lead to the peak of fulfillment and which paths to a precipice.

Peace and the Problem of Pride

In the middle chapters of book XIX, Augustine's rhetorical dialectic famously puts forth a form of peace as the *summum bonum* of humanity and of the heavenly city (*CG* XIX.10, ff.). Human beings desire peace by nature, Augustine observes; what differs among them, and even within a single person at diverse moments of life, is the form of peace that is sought. Is it a just peace of fellowship with other humans? Is it peace of inertia and ease, or a cessation of violence and conflict, to follow times of turmoil and civic strife? Or is it peace of secure domination of the weak by the strong, for the advantage of the latter?

According to human nature, which, as we have seen Augustine emphasize repeatedly, is eminently social and fundamentally equal in all humans, what human beings should seek is "a just peace," peace as conducive as possible to the flourishing of all – peace of "a fellowship of equality under God" (*CG* XIX.12, 936). And yet, even when such forms of peace are approximated in this life, they are never perfect or fully secure. Our nature itself directs humans to hope for something better: a peace without risk of loss, damage, death, or betrayal; an endless peace of fellowship with God, within oneself, and with one's neighbors. This is what Augustine identifies as the core of happiness, the final good for humans – "eternal peace" (*CG* XIX.10, 932), "'peace in life eternal' or 'life eternal in peace.' For peace is so great a good that, even in the sphere of earthly and mortal affairs, we hear no word more thankfully, and nothing is desired with greater longing: in short, it is not possible to find anything better" (*CG* XIX.11, 933).[6] This universal *telos* is witnessed, Augustine considers, in even a "cursory" "examination … of human affairs and our common human nature" (*CG* XIX.12, 933).

Pride emerges in this segment of Augustine's rhetorical dialectic as a powerful foe of eternal peace and also of lesser forms of (imperfectly) just peace. Yet even vicious pride is, in a certain sense, *conquered by peace*: the wicked and prideful cannot help seeking some kind of peace, due to the power and perdurance of human nature, which even so strong a vice as pride cannot wholly undo. Augustine's central passage on pride and peace merits quoting for our consideration:

Even the most savage beasts … protect their own kind by a kind of peace. … How much more strongly, then, is man drawn by the laws of his nature, so to speak, to enter into a similarly peaceful association with his fellow men, so far as it lies within his power to do so? For even the wicked wage war only to maintain the peace of their own people. They wish to make all men their own people, if they can, so that all men and all things might serve one master; but how could that happen, unless they should consent to be at peace with him, either through love or fear? *Thus pride is a perverted imitation of God.*[7] For pride hates a fellowship of equality under God, and wishes to impose its own dominion upon equals, in place of God's rule. Therefore, it hates the just peace of God, and it loves its own unjust peace; but it cannot help loving peace of some kind or other. For no vice is so entirely contrary to nature as to destroy even the last vestiges of nature. (*CG* XIX.12, 936; emphasis added)

The peace sought and achieved in social and political life in this world is never, on Augustine's account, a perfect "tranquility of order," nor, *pace* Kant, could it be perfectible on a lasting basis by human means alone. The peace enjoyed by people in this world can be better or worse, more or less equitable, depending on the choice and quality of the loves

---

[6] Augustine's prose continues to the end of the chapter:

If I wish to speak at somewhat greater length on the subject [of peace], therefore, this will not, I think, be a burden to my readers. They will attend both for the sake of understanding the end of the City which is the subject of this discourse, and also for the sake of the sweetness of peace, which all men love. (*CG* XIX.11, 933)

[7] Literally, "pride perversely imitates God": *superbia perverse imitatur deum.*

on the basis of which a particular polity constructs its institutions and customs (*CG* XIX.24, 960). Augustine offers as a definition of *populus*, a nation or people, and of *res publica*, a republic or commonwealth that consists of a multitude of human beings "united by a common agreement as to what it loves" (*CG* XIX.24, 960).[8] He does not repudiate Cicero's account of a people and republic in *De re publica*, which Augustine interprets as requiring a sharing of advantage and "true justice" (*CG* II.21, 76–80). Rather, Augustine notes that this correct account is achieved in a full and lasting way only in the heavenly city, and so "a more practicable definition" is required when investigating and assessing politics in this world (*CG* II.21, 80; see also *CG* XIX.23–24, 959–61). The participant in, and student of, social and civic life can inquire into the agreed-upon objects of a people's love, and can judge them a better or worse people, according to the quality of those objects of their loves (*CG* XIX.24, 960).[9]

Seeking the most equitable peace possible is, in Augustine's view, the moderate, nonnegligible, and even noble goal of political life. Augustine suggests that true Christians and others seeking to love God above all things would be foolish and proud to despise temporal peace. He writes of and to the citizens of the heavenly city sojourning on earth, instructing them that *The City of God*

summons citizens of all nations and every tongue, and brings together a society of pilgrims [*perigrinam ... societatem*; literally, a pilgrim society] in which no attention is paid to any differences in the customs, laws, and institutions by which earthly peace is achieved or maintained. *She does not rescind or destroy these things ... [since] all tend towards the same end of earthly peace.* Thus, she preserves and follows them, provided only that they do not impede the religion by which we are taught that the one supreme and true God is to be worshipped. ... *Indeed, she directs that earthly peace towards heavenly peace ...* [:] a perfectly ordered and perfectly harmonious fellowship in the enjoyment of God, and of one another in God. (*CG* XIX.17, 946–47, emphasis added; cf. XIX.17, 945–46; XIX.26, 961–62)

Augustine's rhetorical dialectic in these passages proposes that through rightly worshipping the true God with our humanity, body and soul, in deed as well as desire, thought, and word, happiness in hope is possible

---

[8] On Augustine's understanding of "people" and "republic," see Adams (1971), Dodaro (2009), and Fortin (1973). On Augustine's view of love, its effects, and its objects in social and civic life, see Cary (2005, 3–34), Clark (2016), Fortin (1993), Gregory (2008), and Mitchell and Keys (2018).

[9] US President Joe Biden referred to these passages from Augustine's *City of God* during his inaugural address on January 20, 2021.

for people here and now, even in the most unjust and wretched circumstances. All deeds done for the sake of justice, love of neighbor, and deeper peace among human beings can be ordained ultimately toward the attainment of the fullness of perfect peace, and thus toward the ultimate end of humanity. Even amidst the most bitter disappointments and wrongful sufferings, some happiness and peace are possible, while in no way overlooking or denying the misery that accompanies them in this era (*CG* XIX.20, 950).[10] Imperfect and unjust peace likewise must have some vestige of genuine peace, some relation to "the order of things among which it has its being ..., [o]therwise it would not exist at all" or be recognizable as such (*CG* XIX.12, 936). In comparison with the perfect peace Augustine hopes for in eternal life, nevertheless, it remains a partial, deformed, and shadowy imitation. Thus, Augustine's rhetorical dialectic concludes, one "who has learnt to prefer right to wrong and the rightly ordered to the perverse, sees that, in comparison with the peace of the just, the peace of the unjust is not worthy to be called peace at all" (*CG* XIX.12, 936).[11]

The Best Way of Life and the *Summum Bonum*

As we have noted, Augustine's rhetorical dialectic in book XIX opens by recapping Varro's critical examination of philosophical schools' diverse positions on human nature and the highest good, and on the related query of the way of life best suited to help humans attain the *summum bonum* – the highest good attainable for them.[12] The possible ways of life are classically termed (1) contemplative or leisured, (2) active, and (3) mixed or combined. Varro, Augustine notes, held the highest good to consist of virtue together with the other goods essential for virtue and, if possible, all the true goods distinct from and not needed for virtue,

---

[10] Apuleius, as we saw earlier in Chapter 4, also emphasizes the misery that accompanies, to a greater or lesser degree, the imperfect human happiness possible this life, in *De deo Socrates* 4, 355.

[11] This passage evokes another, in book I of Augustine's much earlier dialogue *On Free Choice of the Will (De libero arbitrio voluntatis)*, and famously included by Dr. Martin Luther King, Jr., in his "Letter from a Birmingham Jail" (see King & Washington, 1986, 293): that an unjust law is, or seems to be, no law at all *(nam lex mihi esse non videtur, quae iusta non fuerit)*.

[12] Portions of an earlier version of this section were included in "Love's Labor Leisured: Augustine on Charity, Contemplation, and Politics" (Mitchell & Keys, 2018), a more extensive study of the theme of the best way of life in Augustine's thought and Augustine's reflection on and revision of classical ideals in this regard.

such as great strength of body or beauty of form (*CG* XIX.3, 916–18). Unsurprisingly, therefore, as Augustine himself notes in passing, Varro holds that the mixed way of life ("the combination of both" contemplation and action) is the best path to human flourishing, and that this life is necessarily a social one among friends at home, in civic affairs, and in the wider world (*CG* XIX.3, 917–18).

Later, in chapter 19 of book XIX Augustine's rhetorical dialectic returns to this question of the best way of life, to assess it afresh after having offered his own account of the *summum bonum* as "peace in life eternal," or "life eternal in peace" (*CG* XIX.11, 933). Augustine argues here that Christians are free to undertake any of the three classical ways of life without prejudicing their attainment of the *summum bonum*, so long as their faith remains firm and one's actions are coherent with one's faith. One might conclude from this discussion that Augustine presents his readers with a fourth way of life, one which can embrace and elevate any of the other three, and that he considers it to be unqualifiedly the best for humans: *vita caritatis*, the life of charity, of love of God and neighbor.

[I]t is, of course, important also that [a person] loves the truth and performs the duties of charity. For no one ought to live a life of leisure in such a way that he takes no thought ... for the welfare of his neighbor; nor ought he to be so active as to feel no need for the contemplation of God. (*CG* XIX.19, 948)

Whether one's defining activity is pursuing and contemplating truth, or working in public life for the well-being of household, city, or world, Augustine argues that seeking the good of others and aiming to share one's wisdom, learning, honor, and material goods with others must always be present, for the sake of one's neighbors, and ultimately for love of God.[13] "Thus, the love of truth (*caritas veritatis*) seeks a holy leisure (*otium sanctum*), while the impetus of love (*necessitas caritatis*) takes up a just business (*negotium iustum*)"[14] (*CG* XIX.19, 949). The love that is charity most deeply defines a life on the way to the *summum bonum*.

---

[13] Note also that Augustine explicitly indicates that Christians can continue as philosophers. "Hence, when philosophers become Christians, they are required to change their false doctrines; but they are not compelled to change their dress or their customary mode of life, for these are not an impediment to religion" (*CG* XIX.19, 948). There is no opposition between true faith and true philosophy. For accounts of Augustine's philosophic pursuits in Milan and Cassiciacum, see Brown (2000, 93–129), and Lancel (2002, 99–111).

[14] Here I modify Dyson's translation slightly, to parallel Augustine's tighter prose.

Charity is compatible with any upright activity, including philosophy, the first example Augustine gives in this important discussion.[15] The life defined and inspired by charity participates in the *summum bonum* even here and now, in an inchoate manner, precisely through the "love of God that has been poured into our hearts" (Romans 5:5); and that love of charity, Augustine holds, "weld[s]" together persons and lives according to friendship's "truest meaning" (*Conf.* IV.4.7, 58).

By Augustine's account, it is the primacy of charity, rather than the choice between philosophy and politics, or contemplation and action, which marks the best way of life. Humility as "the dwelling place" of charity (*Holy Virginity* 51, in Augustine, 1999, 207) again emerges as essential for human beings on their pilgrimage toward eternal peace. Humility prompts humans to think of activity – theoretical or practical – as a work of service for others. Philosophy must gladly share wisdom and teach others. Positions of honor and power in the city, the church, and the world must be seen as valuable for the good they enable one to do for individuals and for the broader community – household, city, or world (*CG* XIX.19, 948; cf. XIX.14 and 16). Thus, the classical tension between the active and contemplative lives is lessened, and ultimately, in the deepest sense, overcome, through the fusion of contemplation and love. Here in book XIX, Augustine applies this orientation of the active life explicitly to tasks of government in the church, as well as implicitly to office-holding in political society, which he engaged directly earlier (see *CG* IV.3, 147; V.24, 231–32). Significantly, he admonishes himself and his confreres in the episcopate against pride and vain ambition: "[A] bishop who takes delight in ruling rather than in doing good is no true bishop" (*CG* XIX.19, 949).

Humble love and a life of charity, by Augustine's account, help heal the divisions opened by pride within and among persons and groups on account of social and civic status, intellectual powers, or educational levels; they conquer or at least chasten *libido dominandi*, the lust for mastery. Virtuous humility encourages and inspires just loves among people, here and now, and these loves in turn impel humans toward

[15] The dress or manner of life adopted by whoever embraces the faith that leads to God does not matter to the Heavenly City, provided that these things do not contravene the divine precepts. Hence, when philosophers become Christians, they are required to change their false doctrines (*falsa dogmata*); but they are not required to change their dress or their customary mode of life, for these are not an impediment to religion. (*CG* XIX.19, 948)

life in society, conceived as a "fellowship of equality." In this way, the church – in its teaching and in its members when they are faithful to their call and the gift of God – stands to approximate and strengthen justice and promote a freer, more compassionate sense of global or universal human community than any earthly empire could achieve (cf. *CG* XIX.7, 928–29 with XIX.17, 947).

Augustine concludes book XIX with a recap of the ends of the two cities (*CG* XIX.26–28, 961–64) and with an admonition to humility regarding human virtue in this life. As a prelude to this portion of his rhetorical dialectic, Augustine argues that human virtues that look solely to themselves as exemplars and ends cannot be "true and honorable" virtues (*verae atque honestae … virtutes*; *CG* XIX.25, 961; cf. *CG* V.19, 225–26). Virtue must look up to, imitate, and worship the true exemplar of virtue, the one true God. Writes Augustine, appealing to pagan philosophers and statesmen alike:

> Some, indeed, suppose that the virtues are true and honorable even when they have reference only to themselves and are sought for no other end. Then, however, they are *puffed up and proud*, and so are to be adjudged vices rather than virtues. For just as that which gives life to the flesh is not something derived from the flesh, but something above it, so that which makes the life of man blessed is not something derived from him, but something above him. And this is true not only of man but of every heavenly power and virtue whatsoever. (*CG* XIX.25, 961; emphasis added)

Here Augustine appeals not only to his pagan compatriots but also to his fellow Christians. Christians ought not presume proudly and falsely that perfect virtue is theirs in this life. Only in the next life, when God will "be all in all" (1 Corinthians 15:28; *CG* XXII.30, 1179), may we rightly hope no longer to need forgiveness for offenses from God and neighbor. Until then, all should pray daily the Lord's Prayer ("Our Father"): "Forgive us our trespasses, as we forgive those who trespass against us" (Matthew 6:12, quoted in *CG* XIX.27, 962). Augustine's rhetorical dialectic on the last end of human life and the best way of life to reach it thus finishes with a reflection on this deeply human, humble petition:

> [P]eace in the full sense does not exist for as long as it is necessary to govern the vices. … Who can presume then that he is living in such a way that he has no need to say to God, "Forgive us our trespasses"? No one but an arrogant man would think such a thing: *not a truly great man, but one puffed up and swollen with pride*, who is with justice resisted by Him who bestows grace on the humble. For this reason, it is written: "God resisteth the proud, but giveth grace to the humble". (*CG* XIX.27, 963, emphasis added; cf. *CG* I, preface, 3)

BOOK XX: PRIDE AND THE PROBLEM OF EVIL,
HUMILITY, AND GOD'S JUDGMENT

In book XX of *The City of God*, Augustine moves from seeking and describing the last end of humanity – happiness understood as "peace in life eternal, or life eternal in peace" – to exploring and defending God's final judgment, by which human beings either come to enjoy that last end in its fullness, or fail forever to attain it. In this context, Augustine implicitly defends, in response to the vexed problem of evil, the need for and fittingness of such a final judgment administered by the only perfectly wise and just judge (cf. CG XX.1–2, 965–68). Augustine's rhetorical dialectic in this book describes the problem of evil, with help from the Psalms, as involving the exaltation and elation in this world of the proud, even as they trample on the right and dignity of the humble and lowly.

The antidote to unrepentant pride's apparent victory is its definitive judgment by the just judge – not an aloof, indifferent spectator, but one who humbled himself to "become our neighbor" (*CG* XX.29, 1037), Jesus Christ. As Augustine has emphasized again and again in *The City of God*, this most surprising, divine humility is best shown to us through God's assuming in Jesus a human body and soul and in Jesus's voluntarily suffering the death of the body (cf. *CG* XIII.2, 541, discussed in Chapter 6) in an unjust, humiliating manner. This humble judge enters into the very problem of evil, into the heart of evil, suffering its effects in solidarity with his human brethren and neighbors and bestowing on suffering a mysterious, redemptive value for the citizens of God's city.

That there will be a final judgment cannot be demonstrated by unaided reason, to say nothing of the senses. Augustine intimates, however, that the final judgment corresponds to the natural, eminently reasonable longing of the human heart for justice.[16] It is not *a priori* against reason to believe in a final retribution to each according to his or her works. Moreover, God, who is trustworthy, has promised in both the Old and New Testaments of "the Scriptures of His people" (cf. *CG* I, preface, 3) to vindicate justice at last. In the course of explicating throughout book XX what the scriptures teach concerning this last judgment, Augustine's rhetorical dialectic once again reminds readers of many motives for humility against pride on

---

[16] Augustine even opines that, had no sin ever been committed, God's judgment – perhaps not of a final but of an ongoing nature – would have been necessary for "the whole rational creation [being maintained] in eternal blessedness by persevering in its adherence to the Lord" (*CG* XX.1, 966).

epistemic, moral, and exemplary/theological grounds. The following sections of this chapter will elucidate these aspects of Augustine's long, rich rhetorical dialectic in book XX of *The City of God*.

Pride, Humility, and the Problem of Evil

As book XX approaches its end, Augustine quotes a passage from the prophet Malachi evoking pathos at the prosperity of the unjust: "And now we call the proud happy; yea, they that work wickedness are set up" (Malachi 23:14; *CG* XX.28, 1035). With this quotation, Augustine brings his readers back around to the beginning of book XX, which introduces the promised last judgment within the present problem of evil. From a perspective of faith-illumined reason, Augustine observes that God is always judging; that he is doing so "even now" (*CG* XX.1, 965); and that there will also be a universal final judgment. Augustine continues:

In this book, then, I shall speak, as far as God permits, not of those first judgments … but of the last judgment itself, when Christ will come from heaven to judge the living and the dead. For *that day is properly called the Day of Judgment because*, when it comes, there will *no longer be occasion for the ignorant to ask why this unjust man is happy and that just man is unhappy*. It will then become clear that true and full happiness belongs to none but the good, while all the wicked, and only the wicked, are to suffer deserved and supreme unhappiness. (*CG* XX.1, 966; emphasis added)

Augustine does not blame those who are ignorant concerning this vexed problem of the temporal prosperity of at least some – perhaps many – of the evidently unjust, proud, and cruel, while many of those striving after justice and equity languish and perish in misery. It is, he concurs, a "most difficult question" (*difficillimam quaestionem*), one pondered profoundly also in the scriptures' Psalms.

The psalmist says that the labor of solving this most difficult question, posed by the fact that the good seem to be wretched and the wicked happy, "was too painful for me, until I went into the sanctuary of God; then understood I their end" (Psalm 73:3, ff.). For in the last judgment, indeed, things shall not be thus. On the contrary, in the manifest wretchedness of the wicked and the manifest felicity of the righteous, a state of things very different from that which now prevails will appear. (*CG* XX.28, 1035)

On that day, "all the proud, yea, and all that do wickedly, shall be as stubble. … But unto you that fear my name shall the Sun of righteousness arise with healing in His wings" (Malachi 3:17, ff.; *CG* XX.27, 1034).

Even the humble people living on earth are sinners, in need of the healing God provides, and open and eager to receive it. By contrast, the proud refuse to receive healing and happiness from another, even from their Creator and Redeemer. Even while the temporal success of the proud poses a profound problem for humanity, the ultimate exaltation of the humble promised in Jewish and Christian scriptures provides a balm for the troubled mind and heart. As all Augustine's specific mentions of humility in book XX underscore, the exemplar of humility is not small-souled or insignificant, but rather the most truly great person to walk the earth, simultaneously human and divine (*CG* XX.29, 1037; XX.30, 1040–41; cf. XIX.27, 963). This exemplar, Christ, is king of the heavenly *civitas* and the perfectly just judge of all who live. Referring to judgment on literary works, J. R. R. Tolkien writes in a similar vein, paraphrasing poet Gerard Manley Hopkins: "[T]he only just literary critic is Christ, who admires more than does any man the gifts He Himself has bestowed" (Tolkien, *Letters*, 128).

In considering God's final judgment – both as a truth of faith corresponding to the righteous hope of humanity, and as a practical prospect to be prepared for – Augustine elaborates on the many motives humans have for adopting a humble attitude. Most of these we have seen before, indeed many times before (see, for instance, Chapter 5). Still, set now against the climax of history's drama, from the vantage point of faith and of reason open to faith, they take on special poignancy. These reasons for humility may be grouped under three headings: epistemological, moral, and exemplary/theological.

Epistemological Motives for Humility

Among the epistemological aspects of and motives for virtuous humility highlighted by Augustine in book XX, the central one highlights the weakness and limitations of the human mind vis-à-vis divine wisdom and providence. This in turn supports the reasonableness of faith, which Augustine understands as a lamp to light the path of life here below. Faith is not mere opinion, but true illumination, though for now enabling us to see as "through a glass darkly" (or, "in a mirror dimly"; cf. 1 Corinthians 13:12). We cannot know the ultimate divine judgment with the immediacy and clarity with which we perceive suffering here and now, especially the misery caused by human hubris and cruelty. Yet it is not contrary to reason to trust God to fulfill His promises – to consider that He is judging here and now, and that His word is not without effect.

Thus Augustine counsels Christians and those open to the gift of faith to "[learn] to bear" calmly the vicissitudes of fortune and "not to attach too much importance" to them (*CG* XX.2, 967). He continues this line of persuasion, with reference to the famous passage from Ecclesiastes that all is "vanity" (*vanitas*) except "a life of verity (*veritas*) under the sun's Creator" (*CG* XX.3, 969). The one Creator, moreover, is a provident father, not blind or indifferent to the needs of any of His children or ignorant of their true merits and worth, so often hidden from their fellow humans. "'For God shall bring into judgment every work' – that is, whatever a man does in this life – 'whether it be good or ... evil, with every despised person' – that is, *with every man who here seems to be contemptible, and is therefore not considered. For God sees even him, and does not disregard him*" (*CG* XX.3, 970, quoting Ecclesiastes 12:13ff.; emphasis added; cf. XX.6, 976). As Veronica Roberts Ogle argues (2021, 183), Augustine's *City of God* aims to move readers "to work for an earthly peace understood in light of *amor Dei* ..., in light of the needs of concrete human persons," none of whom should be regarded as negligible or superfluous.

Augustine continues on, to caution his readers against proudly presuming that their own virtue is, or will be, sufficient to pass this final test, or rashly resting assured of their citizenship in the heavenly city and their continuance in virtue until their earthly life's "twilight," when, as a much later poet has put it in an Augustinian vein, "we will be judged on love alone" (St. John of the Cross, *Dichos* 64). It is irrational to see oneself as the judge and arbiter of another's, or even one's own, just destiny. "[F]rom God nothing is hidden: not even any of those things which are yet to be. A man, however, sees a man only as he is at the present time – if, indeed, he can be said to see one whose heart he does not see" (*CG* XX.7, 981; cf. V.9–11, 198–206). Augustine continues pointedly: "He does not see even himself clearly enough to know what kind of person he will be in the future" (*CG* XX.7, 981–82).

A final aspect of human epistemological humility that Augustine underscores in light of God's promise of final judgment refers to the Christian teaching, present already in the Jewish scriptures, of the resurrection of the body of each human person. How can this be, once one's mortal flesh has disintegrated into dust? And what shall the righteous see, once resurrected and at home in the heavenly city, which will fill them with joy and efface fully all former sorrow (cf. Isaiah 26:19; 60:12ff; 65:17ff.; quoted in *CG* XX.21, 1014–16)?

Augustine argues, given divine omnipotence and omniscience, that readers ought not to trouble themselves too much about these things:

For the time being … with our inadequate powers of reasoning, we can only guess at how this is to come to pass; and we shall not be able to know until after it has happened. If we wish to be Christians … we must believe that the dead are to rise in the flesh when Christ comes to judge the living and the dead; and our faith is certainly not in vain merely because we are unable to comprehend perfectly how this resurrection is to be effected. (CG XX.20, 1013–14)

And again, speaking of the prophet Isaiah's hopeful passage, "And ye shall see, and your heart shall rejoice, and your bones shall rise up like an herb" (Isaiah 66:12ff.), Augustine notes:

The prophet does not tell us what we shall see; but what can he mean but God …? What can he mean but all those things which we believe in here, but do not yet see? For now, we only contemplate those things, and the idea which our feeble human capacity can form of them is incomparably less than the reality. … Here, ye believe; there, ye shall see. (CG XX.21, 1015–16)

Augustine's rhetorical dialectic again underscores that the weakness of human intelligence compared with divine wisdom and the need for faith in prophetic discourse ought not to discourage human inquirers from reasoning further. The obscurity of the meaning of prophetic texts, such as those we read in Isaiah, is intended to spur those capable, curious, and patient to seek greater, deeper understanding – even as it is a caution against expecting a clear vision of all spiritual realities, here and now. In "the usual prophetic style, figurative and literal expressions are mingled, so that a sober mind may, by useful and wholesome labor, arrive at the spiritual sense" (CG XX.21, 1016). The virtuous humility of the human mind is not an excuse for laziness or pusillanimity; rather, in the light of faith especially, this humility is a spur to confident study combined with lofty yet measured expectations.

Moral Motivations

The City of God, like the human race itself, is comprised of persons small and great in the eyes of human beings – people of every language and tongue, from nations well-known and unnoticed or forgotten (see inter alia CG XX.25, 1030). Augustine stresses repeatedly that none of them – persons or peoples – is disregarded by God. Christ, the just and merciful judge, cares for and looks for a right response from each human being. All will alike be judged, "the small and the great: 'And they were judged, every man, according to his works' (Rev. 20:13)" (CG XX.14, 999–1000).

In our all-too-human habit of overlooking and despising others, we see an aspect or effect of the moral misery that unites human beings. "'For', as the apostle says, 'all have sinned, and stand in need of the glory of God'" (Romans 3:23; *CG* XX.21, 1018). Thus, all humans are dependent on God's mercy – on God's glory – every day of their lives and through the final judgment. Augustine repeatedly refers to our parallel or shared experience of moral weakness and evil, as a motive for humility, faith, and hope, and for struggling not to set limits on our love of God and neighbor. He finds strong support in the Old and New Testaments for this humble stance in the face of human sinfulness: "'Ye that fear the Lord, wait for His mercy; and go not aside lest ye fall' (Ecclesiasticus 2:7); ... 'He that thinketh he standeth, let him take heed lest he fall' (1 Corinthians 10:22)" (*CG* XX.10, 992). And again, "For the time being ... it is not some feeble citizen of this [heavenly] city, but no less a person than John himself who cries out in his epistle, 'If we say that we have no sin, we deceive ourselves, and the truth is not in us'" (1 John 1:8; *CG* XX.17, 1004).[17]

Exemplar and Theological Motivations

The climax of book XX occurs in its pair of concluding chapters, in which Augustine's rhetorical dialectic highlights the humility of Christ the Mediator, who came first in lowliness and will come again in majesty to judge the living and the dead. With this finale, book XX harkens back once more to the preface of *The City of God*, in which the paradoxical greatness of lowly humility is proclaimed, opening Augustine's "arduous" argument (*CG* I, preface, 3). Jesus Christ is "at once ... God our goal, [and] man our way" (*CG* XI.2, 451). Jesus's human nature teaches and makes effective the renewal of our nature by grace. His virtues are the highest exemplars for human beings to imitate, keeping in mind that unlike Jesus, we are not God.[18]

Augustine's first mention of humility in book XX coincides with his first explicit mention of the humility of Christ the Mediator. Drawing on a moving passage from the prophet Malachi, Augustine reflects on the promised return of the prophet Elijah prior to the final judgment:

---

[17] Augustine prepares the way for this passage from the New Testament with quotations from the Hebrew Bible, from the Psalms composed by another great "citizen of the heavenly Jerusalem," King David, expressing his humility, contrition, and repentance. In chapter 24, Augustine asks of the philosopher Porphyry why he harshly criticizes Christian teaching concerning a final judgment and a renewal of the heavens and earth, while praising the piety of the Jewish people and prophets, which foretell the same events (*CG* XX.24, 1024–29; cf. XIX.23, 953–60).

[18] On "Christ and the Formation of the Just Society," see Dodaro (2004, 72–114).

Elijah will also turn the heart of a man to his neighbor: how can we better understand this than as the turning of the heart of a man to the Man Christ? For though, 'being in the form of God,' He is our God, yet, "taking upon Himself the form of a servant" [Philippians 2:7], *He humbled Himself to become our neighbor.* (CG XX.29, 1037; emphasis added)

This theme of the humility with which the Mediator comes to earth in human flesh and first reveals himself to humanity is continued in chapter 30, the concluding chapter of book XX. Jesus's final coming as judge will be heralded in "majesty" even as "[Christ] first came in his humility" (CG XX.30, 1040).[19] The grandeur of God's first people, Israel, Augustine considers, comes to fullest light when we reflect that God himself, in Christ, "received a body" of their "seed." The mysterious ennobling of humility and its compatibility with true greatness for now elude perfect human comprehension. Yet they come to light in human minds with and through faith, reflecting on Jesus's lowly human body and soul, with "reference to 'the form of a servant' in which the Most High humbled Himself" (CG XX.30, 1041). They further are nurtured in human hearts with reflection on Jesus's great-souled and humble identification of Himself with the lowest and least-regarded among His "brethren." As Jesus's own description of the final judgment stresses, the good or evil we do to any of our fellow humans is done not only to them but also in a real if mysterious manner, to their and our Creator, Redeemer, and Mediator (Matthew 25:34ff; CG XX.5, 974).

If God most high is thus humble out of love, how much should his human creatures value virtuous humility, not least of all when they are raised in the eyes of their fellow human beings to political or ecclesial posts or to philosophic prominence? Augustine's continual harkening back, throughout book XX, to the foreshadowing of the final judgment in both the Old and New Testaments, together with his particular emphasis on the prophetic texts of the Bible, seem intended for all his audiences: the pagan and philosophic, who through Porphyry praise the Jewish people and religion while reviling the Christian teaching; the political, who are more inclined to honor poet-prophet-kings like David than a carpenter crucified by a foreign imperial power; and the Christian, whose faith and hope are strengthened by Israel's prophetic testimony read in tandem with the New Testament texts. For all these readers, and others

---

[19] On this point see also chapter 24: "[Jesus Christ] 'shall come manifestly' to judge justly the just and the unjust, Who first came secretly, to be judged unjustly by the unjust ... [and Who] was silent before His judge" (CG XX.24, 1027; quoting Psalm 50:3ff.).

as well, Augustine's rhetorical dialectic presents an exemplar whose free and noble humility inspires hope in humans facing God's final judgment. If God seems to tarry in vindicating justice, one explanation lies in his great humility and mercy, yielding divine patience and perseverance in seeking human beings' conversion before their last judgment. Augustine quotes from the second epistle of the apostle Peter in this vein: "'[The Lord] is long suffering towards us, not willing that any should perish, but that all should come to repentance. ... Nevertheless we, according to His promise, look for new heavens and a new earth, wherein dwelleth righteousness'" (2 Peter 3:3, ff.; CG XX. 18, 1005–6).

HUMILITY AND PRIDE IN BOOK XXI: THESE
ARE DAYS OF MIRACLE AND WONDER[20]

Augustine's rhetorical dialectic in book XXI of *The City of God* explicates the last end of the earthly city: the society of those loving themselves to the contempt of God. As the reader will imagine at this juncture in Augustine's massive work, it is not a happy ending. Those who willfully live for themselves rather than for God and neighbor and die unrepentant experience an eternity of misery in company with the fallen angels.

Pride has much to do with this sad situation, rather obviously so. But where could humility find a place in this segment of Augustine's rhetorical dialectic? Humility enters explicitly into this discourse, in *the universal human need for mercy*: the last entreaties in vain of the damned, and especially, and hopefully, in requests for prayer and remembrance made by humble sinners sincerely seeking repentance in this life. Humility is in the background of other aspects of Augustine's defense of Christian teaching here, including his sustained argument, continued in book XXII, for recognition of the possibility of miracles and the rich humanity of openness to being in wonder. Humility is present too, in the response Augustine hopes to elicit from his readers to the miracle and wonder of mercy, especially in God's condescension and compassion in Christ, and the humble openness of the saints to the needs of their weaker brethren. In key passages, moreover, Augustine incorporates literary examples that his pagan readers can easily appreciate, softening with a measure of humility the harsh binaries of other segments of book XXI and reflecting his love of the classical tradition and liberal arts shared by pagans and Christians alike.

---

[20] Adapted from a phrase from Paul Simon's song "Boy in the Bubble" (1987).

Natural, Artistic-Inventive, and Miraculous Wonders

How can earthly bodies be resurrected postmortem, whether for bliss or affliction in the flesh? Does not the manifest impossibility of this Christian teaching undo whatever positive impact Augustine's rhetorical dialectic has thus far had on his readers? To answer this challenge, put forth by non-Christian philosophers especially, comprises Augustine's first challenge as he reaches out to pagan readers again near the climax of his magnum opus. He defends forms of intellectual and metaphysical humility through appeals to divine omnipotence, the rock on which his case rests. In this defense, he moves readers not only to humble openness to the miraculous as outside of the ordinary order of nature, but also to the true wonder of being and nature themselves, absent any extraordinary intervention of the Creator in the operations of the creatures he has created and sustains. Augustine also refers in passing to the marvels effected by human art and craft, at times so wonderful that they are mistaken for divine works.

A major trope in these chapters is the *wonder* of the ordinary, which we may miss due to over-familiarity. Augustine anticipates here a theme powerfully present in twentieth-century literary and political theory: the tendency of humans, from tedium or other causes of obfuscation, to ignore the amazing "ordinary."[21] Writes Augustine: "If we were to read or hear such a miraculous thing of some Indian mineral which we had no opportunity of experimenting with … at any rate, we should have greatly wondered at it. But we take no account of things which daily come before our eyes, not because they are really less wondrous, but because they are common" (*CG* XXI.4, 1050). A bit later, Augustine wonders at our human tendency to cease "to wonder because [many realities] are now familiar to us" (*CG* XXI.4, 1051).

Augustine's rhetorical dialectic in these chapters intimates that, with metaphysical modesty, epistemological humility, and reflection, human beings may yet realize that the world and all that is in it *are* truly wonderful; that "God Himself … created all the wonders of this world …

---

[21] For discussions of this theme, see Pippin (2003), and J. R. R. Tolkien's essay "On Fairy Stories" (Tolkien, 2001, 52–55). In a related vein, see David Brooks's "Fred Rogers and the Loveliness of the Little Good," the *New York Times*, July 5, 2018, reflecting on Mister Rogers's "respect for the dignity of each child," including those who seem weak or unexceptional, "that rises almost to the level of veneration." Brooks sees Rogers's attentiveness to and love for the "little" as exemplifying an ethos of "humble and earnest caritas," which we would do well to recover.

both the great and the small ...; and He it is Who has included them all in that greatest miracle of all, the world itself" (*CG* XXI.9, 1066). Indeed, the natures of things comprise many puzzling, surprising, wonderful properties for those with eyes and hearts open to see and not to explain them away with trite terms, such as "this is their nature," merely nature. Augustine mourns over our habit of stopping at this explanation, which he acknowledges is a true, "succinct," and in a certain sense "sufficient" answer to the question of why we observe wondrous properties in creatures. Yet it is not sufficient in an absolute sense, since we need also to ask who is the "author of all natures" and what he wills to do in and for them with his omnipotence (*CG* XXI.7, 1058). And when we observe portents that seem outside the order of nature, or even against it, Augustine cautions that they may be merely "contrary ... to nature *as we know it*" rather than outside of the realm of nature per se (*CG* XXI.8, 1061; emphasis added).

Augustine thus begs his skeptical, rationalist readers to open their minds to the possibility of recomposing and resurrecting human bodies long decayed by the same divine artist who first created them, that they might be reunited with their souls and sustained in eternal affliction or bliss. Even if this is contrary to nature "as we know it," it is not outside the order of possibility for God, who has worked many wonders through his prophets and foretold others that he later brought to fruition. "As far as the knowledge of nature is concerned, therefore, let not unbelievers make things dark for themselves. Let them not think it is impossible for something to occur in some object, though the exercise of divine power, which does not lie within their own human experience of that object. Even those things which are known to us most commonly in the natural order" – Augustine's example here is the uniqueness of each human being in appearance, within the similarities of our common species – "are no less wonderful, and would be a source of astonishment to all who consider them, if men were not accustomed to be amazed at nothing except what is rare" (*CG* XXI.8, 1062).

The Creator, moreover, has endowed his intellectual creatures, angelic and human, with powers to work wonders to the measure of their natures even after the Fall of Adam and Eve and of some angels. Fallen angels can deceive the ignorant by working wonders, even by presenting themselves to mortals in beautiful forms as if they were good and blessed. This they do according to their *superbia*, vicious pride, with its false claim to divinization and desire to dominate others. "[A]bove all, the demons possess the hearts of mortals, and are especially proud of this possession when they transform themselves into angels of light." Human beings likewise work wonders of art and invention,

contriv[ing] very many marvels ... called *mêchanêmata* by the Greeks: marvels so surprising that the ignorant suppose them divine. ... How much more, then, is God able to do such things? To the unbeliever they are unbelievable; but to His power they are easy, since it is He Himself Who has given their properties to stones and to all other things, and to men the skill by which they put them to marvelous uses. (CG XXI.6, 1056–57)

Humility before the Marvel of Mercy, Divine, and Human

Book XXI's rhetorical dialectic in many ways presents readers with Augustine's binaries at their most pointed: saved versus damned, pre-destined to life versus not so, faithful versus unfaithful, and even nature versus grace. At issue for Augustine is the need for proud human beings to humbly recognize the key roles of divine grace and genuine repentance in the history of salvation, personal as well as civic or ecclesial. Augustine stresses once again:

Sometimes, indeed, very obvious vices are overcome by other hidden vices, which are deemed to be virtues even though those who exhibit them are ruled by pride and lifted up by a kind of ruinous complacency. But vices are to be considered overcome only ... through the love of God, which is given by none save God himself, and only through the Mediator between God and man, the man Christ Jesus, Who became a partaker in our mortality that he might make us partakers in His divinity. (CG XXI.16, 1075–76)

Citizens of the heavenly city attribute their salvation to God, not to themselves. Those still on pilgrimage on earth hope for this salvation as a divine gift and endeavor to amend their hearts and lives in preparation for receiving it, initially and in its fullness. As Augustine has written else-where, in a sermon, "God made you without you ... [yet] he doesn't jus-tify you without you. ... [H]e justifies you with your willing consent to it" (*Sermons* 169.13). Grace is a gift, but one that must be received willingly by the one to whom it is offered. For this, knowing the truth is not enough: one must strive with all one's being to love it and to do it, and to repent as often as one is aware of failing in these regards. Receiving mercy hum-bly entails endeavoring to reform, to live more justly and mercifully by God's grace, and to persevere in His grace until the end of our lives. This is why Augustine rejects arguments that God will apply mercy to spare those who do not want to convert, even though holy men and women befriend and pray for them, and even though they themselves may have practiced compassion toward others. "Therefore, anyone who wishes to perform acts of mercy worthy of [forgiveness for] his sins must begin with himself. ... For if men refuse to forsake their habitual wickedness and amend their lives, they cannot be said to perform acts of mercy" (*CG* XXI.27, 1100). Mercy, like charity, may be said to begin at home: one should love one's neighbor *as oneself* (see Mark 12:31, Matthew 22:36–40).

Still, Augustine does hold out humble hope of salvation for those pilgrims who are willing, yet weak or inconstant, through the miracle of divine mercy and the derivative wonders of human compassion and friendship. Referring to what became known in the Catholic tradition as purgatory, a purification for souls after death to fit them for heaven, Augustine observes that "not all men who endure temporal punishments after death come into those everlasting punishments which are to follow after that judgment. As I have already said, some will receive forgiveness in the world to come for what is not forgiven in this" (*CG* XXI.13, 1072).

In addition to this merciful cleansing of the soul after its departure from the body, Augustine comments on the effect of friendship and deeds of service practiced by the imperfect toward holy women and men. Augustine marvels at a saying of Christ, which he interprets to reveal that some of these doers of mercy will receive justification in response to the prayers of those whom they have helped here below. Comments Augustine:

[T]hose who are thus received by those righteous men into everlasting habitations (Luke 16:9) are not possessed of a moral character[22] of their own sufficient to enable them to be redeemed without the intercession of the saints. Thus, it is especially true in their case that "mercy rejoiceth against judgment" (James 2:13). ... [Their] manner of life is not so good that it is of itself sufficient for the achievement of so great a blessedness if those who live it do not obtain mercy through the merits of those whose friendship they have won [by their deeds of sincere generosity and assistance]. (*CG* XXI.27, 1103–4)

Here, at the conclusion of book XXI, while contemplating this marvel of divine and human mercy comingled, Augustine's rhetorical dialectic bursts through the Christian-pagan binary in a beautiful manner. Unsurprisingly, the author of the *Aeneid* is once again his inspiration. "I often wonder[23] (or *marvel, am amazed*: *mirari autem soleo etiam*) to find in Virgil the same sentiment as that expressed by the Lord. ... For when that poet described the Elysian fields ... he put there not only those who

---

[22] Here I alter Dyson's rendering ("endowed with a moral character") of *his moribus praediti.*
[23] Here I alter Dyson's rendering, "I am often surprised," to emphasize the parallel between Augustine's reinvigoration of wondering and marveling in earlier chapters of book XXI. Augustine's verb is the same in both instances: *miror, mirari.*

had been able to arrive at that place by virtue of their own merits, but he also added 'those whose good deeds had made others mindful of them.' By this, he meant those who had served others, and thereby deserved to be remembered by them. It is as if they had used the words so frequently on the lips of the humble Christian when he commends himself to some saint and says, 'Remember me,' and tries to secure such remembrance by deserving it," by generosity coupled with repentance and amendment of his life (CG XXI.27, 1104, quoting *Aeneid* 6664; cf. Matthew 10:41 and Luke 23:42). One should not rashly or idly presume upon such mercy; rather, one should endeavor hopefully to receive and respond to it, living a life of participation in divine humility and charity. By noting parallels in pagan poetry and Christian belief about the afterlife, Augustine with humility acknowledges our common human condition and reflects with wonder on the appreciation by the pagans too of willing service and good deeds done to others.

TRUE DIVINIZATION AND THE *SUMMUM BONUM*: FROM PRIDE TO PARTICIPATION IN BOOK XXII

We contemporary pilgrims now come with Augustine, at last, to the final book of *The City of God*: book XXII. Augustine's rhetorical dialectic here returns to the theme of book XIX, the last end or *summum bonum*. Book XIX focused on the last end principally from a philosophic vantage point, moving thence to theological reflections on the divine prophecies in scripture that this desire of all people and nations would be fulfilled in God's own city. Now, in book XXII the rhetorical dialectic focuses on proving the possibility that the body can share with the soul in the final end, "eternal life in peace, or peace in eternal life," and on the nature of this ultimate peace, explicated much more fully in sacred scripture than in the philosophers' texts.

Book XXII contains just three explicit occurrences of pride (*superbia*) and none of humility (*humilitas*). The latter fact may be understood in light of Augustine's description of humility as the "dwelling place" of charity (*Holy Virginity* 51, in Augustine, 1999, 207). In this final book, Augustine describes and defends the fulfillment of charity, the eternal bliss of the heavenly city and its citizens. While the dwelling place is presupposed, it is here that the indwelling happiness brought about by love occupies his attention. The human body, as the humble vessel of the soul and human happiness, is likewise discoursed on extensively in its own wonderful potencies, as well as the divine omnipotence's predilection for it.

The framework of this exploration is rooted in the now familiar problem of pride and the promise of its definitive defeat and transcendence in the New Jerusalem, by means of the participation by angels and human beings in the divine life of fullness of being, wisdom, love, and bliss. Pride is once again the paradigm for our fallen nature and its lust for false forms of sufficiency. In book XXII's first chapter, Augustine refers to *superbia* in this manner: "[God the Creator] foreknew that, *in their pride*, some of the angels *would indeed wish to be self-sufficient* for their own blessedness, and hence would forsake their true Good" (*CG* XXII.1, 1107; emphasis added). Approaching the book's midpoint, Augustine contrasts virtuous humility with vicious pride, now with regard to the working of wonders and their meaning, truthful or falsified. "[T]he demons perform their wonders *with an impure pride like that with which they desire to be gods*; but the martyrs perform theirs – or rather, God performs them while they work with Him and pray – in order to strengthen the faith … [in] one God" (*CG* XXII.10, 1135; emphasis added).

The path to and nature of true felicity indeed involve divinization, as Augustine emphasizes in the book's concluding chapter. Yet true divinization is not to be desired or effected apart from God, but rather by participation in his free gifts of grace and glory.[24] As Augustine writes of the eternal Sabbath of the heavenly city:

True glory will be there. … True honor. … True peace. … The reward of virtue will be God Himself. … [And when God promises,] "I will be your God, and ye shall be my people" [Leviticus 26:12], what else was meant than, *I will be their sufficiency*; *I will be all that men honorably desire … common to all.* (CG XXII.30, 1178–79; emphasis added)

And again, close to the conclusion of *The City of God*:

Then shall we be still, and know that He is God: that He is what we ourselves desired to be when we fell away from Him and listened to the words of the tempter, "Ye shall be as gods" [Genesis 3:5], and so forsook *God, Who would have made us as gods, not by forsaking Him, but by participating in Him.* (CG XXII.30, 1181; emphasis added)

Augustine's framework for the concluding book of his long and arduous defense speech for *The City of God* thus underscores the fulfillment of virtuous humility, the path to true greatness, in the gift of sharing in God's own divine life, bliss, and sufficiency. This is not achieved by any human being's unaided powers, or by philosophy in itself, or by prideful

---

[24] On this theme in Augustine, see Meconi (2013).

civic self-assertion and elation. Rather, it is attained only as a common good, loved as such, with the other citizens of God's city, and as a gift received and rejoiced in, rather than as an accomplishment of one's own. The problems of peace and justice will be resolved definitively, together with all noble aspirations of the holy city and its members, in this final fulfillment. Augustine's *City of God* and its long rhetorical dialectic aim at nothing so much as eliciting a longing for citizenship in this city, removing the roadblocks to his readers' perception of it as a possibility for them – something they in fact deeply desire – and even to their glimpsing and experiencing it as an incipient reality in this *saeculum*.

The following sections of this chapter will treat key themes of Augustine's final book from the vantage point of humility and pride: God as artist and orator; a new discussion of miracles; providential designs for humanity and the human body; and the eternal life enjoyed by the heavenly city's citizens, vis-à-vis the teachings of scripture and some philosophers.

The Eloquence of the Divine Artist and Orator: Miracles in Chapters 1–10

Augustine opens his last book by recalling for readers the wonders of God's work of creation and providence. The "almighty Artist," as he calls the Creator in chapter 11 (*CG* XXII.11, 1137; cf. also XXII.19, 1148), brings beings into existence where none had been before, and creates a special marvel in human beings whose nature comprises body and soul, matter and spirit. If God could make such evident wonders, though we cease to think them wonderful when we have grown accustomed to them, why could he not likewise in heaven reunite now-glorified human bodies with the souls that had before death informed them? Might it not be merely philosophic or political pride that resists regarding as credible Christ's bodily Resurrection, Ascension, and promise of the resurrection of the body for all humans? (see *CG* XXII.4–5, 1111–15).

Further reflection on the spread of the Gospel in the opening chapters of the twentieth book leads Augustine to note God's surprising, humble, and tremendous eloquence, working chiefly through unlearned, untutored men, the original apostles and first disciples of Jesus. If what they preached, "the resurrection of our body to eternity," seems incredible, "the manner in which the world came to believe is itself even more incredible." Augustine pauses to elaborate and then will repeat this thought at least twice:

A few fishermen, uneducated in the liberal arts, completely uninstructed in the doctrines of their opponents, with no knowledge of grammar, not armed with dialectic, not adorned with rhetoric: these were the men whom Christ sent out with nets into the sea of this world. And in this way He caught all those fish of every kind, including – more wonderful still, because more rare – even some of the philosophers themselves. (*CG* XXII.5, 1113)

The humble condition of the human speakers of his word rendered God's eloquence working through them all the more grand: "The world has believed a small number of obscure, insignificant, untutored men precisely because the divine nature of what they proclaim is all the more evident in the testimony of such lowly witnesses. For the eloquence which made what they said persuasive consisted of miraculous works, not words" (*CG* XXII.5, 1114).

Augustine's rhetorical dialectic emphasizes three forms of miracles in the early evangelization of peoples: First, as we have seen, are the miraculous works – healings, conversions of heart with changes of life, and even raising the dead. Next comes the miraculous, or at least marvelous, wondrous fulfillment of the prophecies of testaments old and new. Finally, though far from least in Augustine's estimation, is the miracle of martyrdom for the sake of a kingdom that is not to be fulfilled in this world, and for a king who labored as a carpenter and whose citizens wondrously believe to have risen from the dead and ascended bodily into heaven.

In this regard, Augustine draws a sharp contrast between Jesus and Romulus, two founders who it was claimed ascended into heaven after their deaths. At first, a few, or perhaps even most, Romans were duped into believing in the apotheosis of Romulus because of their great love and admiration for him as their founder. Afterward, it was revealed to be a pious lie upheld for the exaltation of the *patria*. Rome imposed the cult of Romulus on most of its conquered peoples (with perhaps the only exception being the Jews). The denizens of the subject nations, however, worshiped Romulus out of fear of offending Rome, not from true faith or even from any love for the famed founder. Augustine observes that Romulus is not known to have had one single martyr – no one overcame the fear of death from faith in him and his saving power. How much more miraculous ought it to appear, then, that thousands of Christians, of both sexes and all ages and social and civic conditions, overcame the primordial human fear, fear of death, to hold fast to faith in and love for Christ, in the hope of sharing in His bodily Resurrection and glory? Add to this that they followed Christ's example in refraining from violent response to their persecutors, even to save their lives, out of love for God and neighbor, and the miracle of the Gospel's spread comes into still sharper relief (*CG* XXII.6, 1115–17).[25]

Augustine crafts a strong case that early Christian history ought to evoke humble wonder on the part of new hearers of the Gospel. Less convincing, perhaps, is his case that the very incredulousness of the Resurrection and Ascension of Christ in His human body, combined with the widespread growth of the faith in these incredible teachings, itself constitutes a motive of credibility. After all, entire pagan peoples believed some incredible teachings about a great multiplicity of divinities and their deeds, and Augustine shows no sign of taking this form of faith as an indicator of truth. Yet, if we read these claims together with his arguments that the eternal destiny of the human body is not irrational or impossible, even to unassisted human reason, his rhetoric regarding incredulity may be understood as a wakeup call, prompting readers to acknowledge that something profoundly new seems afoot with the Christian faith, perhaps even a *quid divinum*, a divine "something," that humans do well to consider with great care and humble openness. Augustine explains that Jesus came hundreds of years after Romulus was said to have lived, in a time when the peoples of the Roman empire were more enlightened and had ceased to believe in Romulus beyond acknowledging his centrality in the foundation of their polity, and recognizing the political utility of continuing to accord him superhuman honor. Thus, it is truly miraculous, or may reasonably be considered as such, that Jesus's Resurrection and Ascension could elicit faith leading to martyrdom in this later, more educated world. The fulfillment of prophecies and the working of miracles effected a *persuasion* for which that human speech and logic – much less poetic fiction – could not account (*CG* XXII.7, 1119; cf. I, preface, 3).

Augustine's next chapter, chronicling miracles he himself has witnessed or heard about from credible sources, exemplifies the childlike humility and wonder to which his rhetorical dialectic invites readers to reconsider and reclaim (*CG* XXII.8, 1120–34). Augustine pours heart and soul into this chapter, heedless of his dignity as a learned man and bishop and of the ridicule his faith-filled narratives might inspire in some worldly-wise readers. Toward the end of this lengthy chapter – perhaps the longest of *The City of God* – Augustine laments that he cannot pause longer, to record "all the miracles of which I have knowledge ...: a task

---

[25] On Augustine's thought on martyrs and martyrdom, see Dodaro (2005) and Kaufman (1994).

which the purpose of this work does not, after all, compel me to undertake" (*CG* XXII.8, 1130).

These postevangelical miracles lack the authority of church-confirmed canonical scripture, even as they lack revelation's universal promulgation. Nonetheless, they can serve to remind believers and unbelievers alike of God's power to work wonders in the human body, conducing also and especially to the health of the soul and so to the happiness of the whole human being and community. Augustine himself in this discussion is at his most personal, passionate, playful, pastoral, and childlike. His rhetoric is joyful and effusive. He emphasizes that these miracles themselves comprise common goods, shared by the local churches, families, and peoples. They are no just cause of worldly pride, for God works them without regard to the beneficiaries' social, civic, or intellectual status. Augustine recounts wonders worked on behalf of women and men, poor and rich, citizens and strangers (*CG* XXII.8, 1121–34). All are the work of the great God, who ordinarily works with and through coworkers from the human family. No human being should pride himself or herself for assisting in miracles; miracles are first and foremost marvels of God, performed for and conducing to his glory. Where pride seems present in those collaborating in God's miraculous interventions, Augustine implies, one should suspect demonic or human counterfeit rather than true divine intervention (see *CG* XXII.10, 1135). Yet God does count on humans to work with him and to tell of his works for the edification of others. To refuse personal, active participation in these tasks bespeaks not virtuous humility but smallness of soul, pusillanimity.

God "the Creator, the Wondrous Artist," and the Glorified Body

Chapter 11 is pivotal in Augustine's defense speech on behalf of the divine omnipotence regarding, and the wondrous destiny of, the lowly human body. Here Augustine's rhetorical dialectic again enters into the fray against philosophic pride, particularly Platonic objections to the resurrection and presence of human bodies in the heavenly realm. Augustine's strategy is both metaphysical or natural-theological and rhetorical or persuasive. In the former dialectical mode, he reminds readers at the beginning and end of, and indeed, throughout this segment, of the power of the "wondrous Artist," the Creator-God, and the irrationality of limiting the capacity of the Creator to recreate his human creatures, body and soul. In the latter, oratorical mode,

Augustine's approach is again familiar to readers: he reminds philosophers of diverse philosophic schools of some teachings they espouse,
such as the permanent presence of heavenly bodies (e.g., stars, planets)
thought to be ensouled in the heavens. If this is considered the case for
some bodies, and these of lesser dignity than human beings, why not
also human bodies? By this path, Augustine endeavors to remove roadblocks and to persuade his philosophical interlocutors that it is more
in accord with reason to be open to the possibility of divine revelation
to and salvation for the whole human being. An *a priori* rejection of
Christianity is not truly philosophic, a mark of love of wisdom; it is
rather foolish, and perhaps prideful, if Augustine's argument here is on
a solid path.

In the chapters that follow, Augustine confronts specific objections
and questions regarding the resurrection of the body and the glory promised it by the Mediator, Christ. In doing so, our author begins to paint
a moving picture of what the condition, life, and society will be for the
heavenly city's human citizens in that everlasting age to come, of which
we have no actual experience. Augustine does so by drawing on revelation and using his reason and imagination. The painting he produces
underscores afresh the union of greatness and humility, a theme he first
introduced in the preface to book I, and to which he has returned time
and again throughout the twenty-two books of *The City of God*.

The motives Augustine adduces in these chapters for a hopeful, magnanimous humility include the equality of human bodies in the final age
of the heavenly city. This radical equality does not entail uniformity: bodies may be smaller or larger, shaped one way or another, female or male,
older or younger, yet all will exhibit the fullness and beauty of humanity.
There will be no defect or deformity amidst all the redeemed heavenly
variety (see *CG* XXII.12–17, 1139–46). Augustine in this context explicitly defends the full humanity of the female body, which he notes in coun-
tercultural classical mode is not inferior to the male body. Female and
male bodies alike give expression to, and indeed with soul comprise, our
humanity's very nature, and so are equally good and capable of receiving
glory (*CG* XXII.17, 1144–46). Augustine similarly defends the humanity
of the unborn child who dies in utero. His or her tiny body may without
difficulty be raised up, nurtured, and perfected by the almighty Creator,
just as much as the body of a child who dies after spending time in the
sun's light (*CG* XXII.13–14, 1141–43).

This eschatological perfection and equality promised by God extends
also to human beings in comparison with the angels. Although angelic

natures are higher than human nature for being purely spiritual (*CG* XI.13, 376; XI.15, 379), in the heavenly city the body will not be any obstacle for humans in sharing the same "immortality and felicity" of the holy angels (*CG* XXII.17, 1145; see also XI.13, 467), who enjoy constant, full union with God, participating in his divine being, happiness, wisdom, and joy. And as Augustine's rhetorical dialectic intimated earlier in *The City of God*, while the angels are, simply speaking, superior in nature, human nature is perhaps even more wondrous than angelic for uniting matter and spirit in a manner known fully to God alone.

As Augustine's rhetorical dialectic continues into chapter 18, it underscores the oneness of the heavenly citizens in the church, the Body of Christ, in which we are brought to perfection in union with Christ the head. It is in this community, this society of the Redeemer with the redeemed, that human fullness is at last attained. The acknowledgment that our perfection requires union with God and others is a motive for humility as well.

Chapter 19 returns with passion to Augustine's trope of the goodness of nature, his defense of nature, and nature's Creator-God. Nothing in our human nature will be destroyed or diminished in its heavenly fulfillment. On the contrary, it will be restored, ennobled, and rendered more beautiful. He develops this argument with an analogy from the human art of bronze-casting: "If an artist has for some reason made a flawed statue, he can recast it and make it beautiful, removing the defect without losing any of the substance. ... And *if a man can do this, what are we to think of the Almighty Artist?*" (*CG* XXII.19, 1148; emphasis added). Some lines from a poem by J. R. R. Tolkien capture well Augustine's rhetorical dialectic here, stressing that the eternal destiny of the heavenly citizens does not alter all that is true being and good in their humanity: "Salvation changes not, nor yet destroys/garden or gardener, children or their toys./Evil it will not see, for evil lies/not in God's picture, but in crooked eyes,/not in the Source, but in malicious choice,/not in sound, but in the tuneless voice" (Tolkien, 2001, 90).

Augustine's reflection on the beauty of the heavenly citizens' bodies includes a profound reflection on the beauty of the wounds of the martyrs. As Christ humbly kept marks of His wounds after His Resurrection, with no lessening of His form but rather enhancing it with the marks of a great love, stronger than death (see John 15:13; Song of Songs 8:6), so perhaps the bodies of the martyrs may have gentle yet clear marks of their sufferings, such as scars, but no missing limbs or deep deformity. These would be true battle scars, earned in a nonviolent, humble, and great-souled struggle for justice and love. Each of these signs will comprise, Augustine imagines, "a badge of honor, and the beauty of [the martyrs'] virtue – a beauty which is in the body, but not of the body – will shine forth in it" (CG XXII.19, 1150).

Augustine's rhetorical dialectic in this segment of the final book of *The City of God* closes with a reaffirmation of reason and faith regarding the divine power to effect a real resurrection and glorification of the human body, developed once again in dialogue with the philosophers. Even if the matter of one's body has entirely been dispersed and altered beyond all human hope, God's wisdom and power more than suffice to render this promised miracle credible. Appealing to philosophic and patriotic Romans in one note, Augustine cites an authority to be considered with care:

So great a Roman author as Cicero, wishing to define God as accurately as he could, said, "God is a mind, unbound and free, remote from all materiality and mortality, perceiving and moving all things, and itself endowed with eternal movement" (*Tusc. disp.*, I, 27, 66). He found this definition in the doctrines of the greatest philosophers. Let me ask, then, in their own terms, how can anything either lie hidden from Him Who perceives all things, or irrevocably escape Him Who moves all things? (CG XXII.20, 1150)

Humbly to acknowledge God's power and goodness and greatly to hope in his promise regarding our future condition and happiness represent for Augustine true human wisdom, truest *philosophia*.

Final Happiness, Faith, and the Philosophers

In this final segment of the final book of his magnum opus, Augustine acknowledges with intellectual humility that he is incapable of describing the final end, vis-à-vis either the condition of the human body in glory, or the activity of the citizens of the heavenly city in its fullness. He has had, after all, no "experience," no direct vision of this condition or this way of life, this activity. Nonetheless, he ventures a description indirectly, "infer[ring] from the blessings which God bestows upon good men and bad alike in this most troublous life how great will be that joy which we certainly have no power to describe, because we have not yet experienced it" (CG XXII.21, 1153).[26] The glorified body will be the fully humble

---

[26] Cf. also CG XXII.29:

And yet, to tell the truth, I do not know what the nature of that occupation, or rather that rest and repose, will be. After all, I have never seen it with my bodily sight; and if I should say that I had seen it with my mind – that is, with my intellect – how great, after all, is our intellect, and how can it comprehend so excellent a condition? (1171)

body, docile to its soul, which will be in its turn perfectly united to the divine wisdom and will (*CG* XXII.21, 1152–53; XXII.24, 1165–66). The life, activity, and repose of the citizens of God's heavenly city will be one of full freedom, where the good that each longs by nature and by grace to partake in and to do encounters no obstacle, internal or external (XXII.30, 1179–80). It will be a life of praise, thanksgiving, fellowship, and joy. In that life, humans will have overcome definitively the many false or distorted forms of love that open a Pandora's box and flood the world with evil. Among these evils is of course *superbia*, pride, the fruit of excessive love of oneself, which Augustine now names for a final time in *The City of God* (*CG* XXII.22, 1153).

How is pride conquered and humility vindicated, once and for all? As we have seen, this triumph comes about by God's grace, seconded by humans' free response. The fruit of this grace is true, truly human divinization: participation by women and men in God's life, sharing in the peace of God that "'passeth all understanding' apart from His own" (*CG* XXII.29, 1172; Philippians 4:7). Augustine's rhetorical dialectic continues, "Because, in our measure, we are made partakers of His peace, we know the perfection of peace in ourselves, among ourselves, and with God, insofar as it is in us to achieve such perfection" (*CG* XXII.29, 1172).

God's peace in us will be so great that we will not only celebrate the eternal Sabbath rest; according to Augustine, we will *be* that very Sabbath rest of God, personally and in communion with our fellows. It is in this full participation that humility, justice, and charity are perfected, and pride and its lust for domination definitively disappear:

We ourselves shall become that seventh day, when we have been filled up and made new by His blessing and sanctification. Then shall we be still, and know that He is God: that He is what we ourselves desired to be when we fell away from Him and listened to the words of the tempter, "Ye shall be as gods," and so forsook God, Who would have made us as gods, not by forsaking Him, but by participating in Him. For what have we done without Him, other than perish in His wrath? But when we are restored by Him and perfected by His greater grace, we shall be still for all eternity, and know that He is God, being filled by Him when He shall be all in all. (*CG* XXII.30, 1181; cf. *CG* XIV.13. 610; XV.7, 645)

Augustine's swan song to the grandeur of humble participation in the life of the God who is love, as always, includes a plea to and persuasion for philosophic readers. He resounds here a key theme of his long rhetorical dialectic, that it is not against reason for philosophers to share Jews' and Christians' hope in the resurrection of the body and its share in the eternal perfection of humanity. Once again, Augustine refers to passages in the writings of Plato, Porphyry, Labeo, and even Varro, which singly and especially together tend to congruence in this natural, human hope, divinely ratified in prophetic writings backed by miracles, for eternal happiness *as human beings*, body and soul together (*CG* XXII.26–28, 1167–71). Augustine recalls implicitly in these passages his poignant agreement with many philosophic schools that the happy life spent seeking and loving wisdom is a social life (*CG* XIX.5, 925): no one philosopher has grasped all the truth, but taken together, their best insights may check error and further a fuller vision of the human heart, and even offer a glimpse of the goodness of its maker, the almighty artist. In philosophic interdependency on a human level, and ultimately in the dependence of human wisdom on divine wisdom for its fulfillment, the reader of Augustine's rhetorical dialectic grasps again the necessity and beauty of humility.

By the end of book XXII, the many strands of Augustine's long defense speech for humility against pride have been woven together in a beautiful tapestry by the author of *The City of God*. The divine summons to citizenship in the heavenly city has been extended to all, including those who admire the works of the philosophers of diverse schools, particularly the Platonic. It extends also to patriotic intellectuals inspired by Cicero (Roberts, 2016), with calls to those so gifted to continue serving civic and ecclesial communities in this age, encouraged by the hope of a future age in which our failures will be amended, our wounds will be healed, and our personal and common happiness will be finally, fully attained through a free gift of grace, humbly received. Augustine looks for this fulfillment humbly and hopefully, alongside his patient readers, as he concludes *The City of God*:

For what other end do we set for ourselves than to reach that kingdom of which there is no end? It seems to me, then, that, with the Lord's help, I have now paid my debt in bringing this huge work to a close. May those who think it too small or too large forgive me; let those who think it is enough not thank me, but join with me in giving thanks to God. Amen. (*CG* XXII.30, 1182)

Conclusion

We have come at last to the end of our long, rhetorical-dialectical journey in *The City of God*, having participated in its debates and witnessed Augustine's vigorous defense of humility (*humilitas*) and prosecution of pride (*superbia*). What have we learned, and why might it matter?

First, we have grasped how Augustine's *apologia*, his defense speech, for humility is multifaceted, comprising personal/experiential, political/historical, epistemological, moral, and theological elements. More than that, it is, anagogically (*mistice*) speaking, inherently civic. Humility is a signature trait of the citizens of the heavenly city – the city of God – in whatever land they may find themselves, not a quality of existentially isolated individuals. At the same time, while on pilgrimage through this world, even those inspired to seek and strive to be faithful to this transcendent civic allegiance do not possess perfect *humilitas*. The two – earthly and heavenly – cities' seeds still vie for ascendency in all human beings, and so Augustine's masterwork constitutes a call for a free, ongoing, personal struggle for humility against pride. Virtuous humility is exemplified in the heavenly city's founder, the Creator-God, and revealed in human form through his Son Jesus. Humility's foil, vicious pride, reaches its terrible *telos* in the diabolic founder of the earthly city. Whoever possesses the virtue of humility participates in it as a gift from God and a pledge of deeper humanity. It is a share in the common good – a gift, as well as a responsibility. Humility, as Augustine understands and presents it, undergirds and inspires fruitful human agency in political, scientific, artistic, philosophic, and ecclesial-theological affairs; it does not, as might at first glance appear, check or oppose honest human effort. Most of all, humility provides a welcome home for charity (*caritas*), love of

God and neighbor, which this world needs as desperately in our day, and I would venture, in any day spent under the sun, as in Augustine's.

Augustine's humility asks each of us to recall our "created-ness," beginning with the fact that we neither created ourselves nor are our own foundation, though we are responsible agents, and, contra Cain, both our own and our fellows' keepers (see Genesis 4:9). Each of our lives is a gift, and Augustine understands that philosophic reflection can appreciate this "given-ness" – at least to an imperfect degree. If our lives are gifts, if our origin, bond of unity, and end transcend our individuality without undoing it, and if the Son of God accepted a humanity like ours and died to save us, then politics and philosophy must be works of service – public and pedagogical. Those who are leaders in the political sphere, meant to foster peace and justice, must perseveringly resist the desire to dominate and the pull toward prideful false forms of divinization. The philosophic realm, while remaining true to its mission of truth-seeking, should not ignore the pre- or nonphilosophic majority of humanity, but rather should emphasize what we share and seek to communicate truth to all who will listen.

Augustine's humility has, as we have seen, positive implications for ecology, and also for what Pope Benedict XVI has called "human ecology" (2011). If Augustine is correct, humility leads reason to recognize that all natures are good, and that nothing and no one is evil per se, without significance and value for the universal *res publica* and for our human family. Humility requires politicians and philosophers alike to listen to nature – to being's voice – and to find there echoes of the voice of the Creator and Redeemer. In these echoes, Augustine himself discerned an ongoing summons to seek, to strive, and to struggle to accept the gift of grace, which nature sorely needs. In our world, wounded by war, oppression, prejudice, and pandemic – and pulled apart by political polarization and a scholarly culture of "canceling" rather than engaging – Augustine's humility holds out hope for rapprochement and peace, for listening, for understanding, and for an honest response in open dialogue, even when we cannot agree. Perhaps Augustine has made his case well and persuaded some of us, as he has this author, that though vicious pride is still present in our lives and hearts, lowly humility possesses a lasting, true *virtus*, an excellence or power that attracts us for good, if we will but be still and hear and see it.

Bibliography

Adams, Jeremy D. *The Populus of Augustine and Jerome: A Study in the Patristic Sense of Community.* New Haven, CT: Yale University Press, 1971.

Ambrose, Saint. *Letters 1–91.* Translated by Mary Melchior Beyenka. Washington, DC: The Catholic University of America Press, 2001.

Apuleius. *Apologia Florida; De Deo Socratis.* Translated by Loeb Classical Library and edited by Christopher P. Jones. Cambridge, MA: Harvard University Press, 2017.

Aquinas, Thomas. *Summa Theologiae.* Translated by Fathers of the English Dominican Province. Allen, TX: Christian Classics, 1981.

Arendt, Hannah, Joanna Vecchiarelli Scott, and Judith Chelius Stark. *Love and Saint Augustine.* Chicago: University of Chicago Press, 1996.

Aristotle. *Nicomachean Ethics.* Translated by Martin Ostwald. New York: Macmillan, 1999.

Aristotle. *The Politics.* Translated by Carnes Lord. Chicago: University of Chicago Press, 1984.

Augustine. *Against the Academics: St. Augustine's Cassiciacum Dialogues*, vol. 1. Translated and edited by Michael P. Foley. New Haven, CT: Yale University Press, 2019.

Augustine. *Confessions*, 2nd ed. Translated by Frank J. Sheed and edited by Michael P. Foley. With an introduction by Peter Brown. Indianapolis, IN: Hackett, 2006.

Augustine. *On Christian Belief.* Translated by Matthew O'Connor and edited by Boniface Ramsey. With an introduction by Michael Fiedrowitz. Brooklyn, NY: New City Press, 2005.

Augustine. *On Order [De Ordine].* Translated and introduction by Silvano Barruso. South Bend, IN: St. Augustine's Press, 2007.

Augustine. *Opera Omnia CAG: Corpus Augustinianum Gissense*, Electronic ed. Edited by Cornelius Mayer. Charlottesville, VA: InteLex Corporation, 2000.

Augustine. *Treatises on Marriage and Other Subjects: St. Augustine.* Translated by Charles T. Wilcox et al. and edited by Roy J. Deferrari. Washington, DC: The Catholic University of America Press, 1999.

Augustine. *The City of God against the Pagans*. Translated and edited by R. W. Dyson. Cambridge, UK: Cambridge University Press, 1998.

Augustine. *Sermons*. Translated by O. P. Edmund Hill. Hyde Park, NY: New City Press, 1992.

Augustine. *The Trinity*. Translated and introduction by O. P. Edmund Hill. Edited by John E. Rotelle. Brooklyn, NY: New City Press, 1991.

Baldwin, Barry. "Apuleius, Tacitus, and Christians." *Emerita* 52, no. 1 (1984): 1–3.

Balmaceda, Catalina. *"Virtus Romana": Politics and Morality in the Roman Historians*. Chapel Hill: University of North Carolina Press, 2017.

Balot, Ryan K. "Truth, Lies, Deception, and Esotericism: The Case of St. Augustine." In *Augustine's Political Thought*, edited by Richard J. Dougherty, 173–99. Rochester, NY: University of Rochester Press, 2019.

Bathory, Peter Dennis. *Political Theory as Public Confession: The Social and Political Thought of Augustine of Hippo*. New Brunswick, NJ, and London: Transaction, 1981.

Baumann, Notker. "Pride and Humility." In *The Cambridge Companion to Augustine's Confessions*, edited by Tarmo Toom, 208–26. Cambridge, UK: Cambridge University Press, 2020.

Beatrice, Pier Franco. *"Quosdam Platonicorum Libros*: The Platonic Readings of Augustine in Milan." *Vigiliae Christianae* 43, no. 3 (1989): 248–81.

Benedict XVI [Joseph Ratzinger]. "The Listening Heart: Reflections on the Foundations of Law" (Address to the Bundestag, September 22, 2011). www .vatican.va/content/benedict-xvi/en/speeches/2011/september/documents/hf_ben-xvi_spe_20110922_reichstag-berlin.html.

Benedict XVI [Joseph Ratzinger]. *Spe Salvi: On Christian Hope* (2007). www .vatican.va/content/benedict-xvi/en/encyclicals/documents/hf_ben-xvi_enc_20071130_spe-salvi.html.

Berchmann, Robert M. *Porphyry against the Christians*. Leiden, the Netherlands, and Boston, MA: Brill, 2005.

Bergel, Lienhard. "The Horatians and the Curiatians in the Dramatic and Political-Moralist Literature before Corneille." *Renaissance Drama* 3 (1970): 215–38.

Bobb, David J. "The Humility of True Religion: Augustine's Critique of Roman Civil Religion." In *Civil Religion in Political Thought: Its Perennial Questions and Enduring Relevance in North America*, edited by Ronald Weed and John von Heyking, 66–92. Washington, DC: The Catholic University of America Press, 2010.

Boone, Mark. *The Conversion and Therapy of Desire: Augustine's Theology of Desire in the Cassiciacum Dialogues*. Eugene, OR: Pickwick Publications, 2016.

Brooke, Christopher. *Philosophic Pride: Stoicism and Political Thought from Lipsius to Rousseau*. Princeton, NJ: Princeton University Press, 2012.

Brookes, Edgar H. *The City of God and the Politics of Crisis*. London and New York: Oxford University Press, 1960.

Brown, Peter. *Augustine of Hippo: A Biography*. Berkeley: University of California Press, 2000.

Brown, Peter. *Power and Persuasion in Late Antiquity: Towards a Christian Empire*. Madison: University of Wisconsin Press, 1992.

Brown, Peter. "Saint Augustine and Political Society." In *City of God: A Collection of Critical Essays*, edited by Dorothy F. Donnelly, 17–36. New York: Peter Lang, 1995.

Bruno, Michael J. S. *Political Augustinianism: Modern Interpretations of Augustine's Political Thought*. Minneapolis, MN: Fortress Press, 2014.

Burleigh, John H. S. "Introduction to St. Augustine: The City of God." *Scottish Journal of Theology* 4, no. 2 (1951): 214–16.

Burleigh, John H. S. *The City of God: A Study of St. Augustine's Philosophy*. London: Nisbet & Co., 1949.

Burnell, Peter. "The Problem of Service to Unjust Regimes in Augustine's City of God." In *City of God: A Collection of Critical Essays*, edited by Dorothy F. Donnelly, 37–50. New York: Peter Lang, 1995.

Burns, Paul C. "Augustine's Use of Sallust in the *City of God*: The Role of the Grammatical Tradition." In *History, Apocalypse, and the Secular Imagination: New Essays on the City of God*, edited by Mark Vessey, Karla Pollmann, and Alan Fitzgerald, 105–14. Bowling Green, OH: Philosophy Documenta, 1999.

Burns, Paul C. "Augustine's Use of Varro's *Antiquitates Rerum Divinarum* in his *De Civitate Dei*." *Augustinian Studies* 32, no. 1 (2001): 37–64.

Burt, Donald. *Friendship and Society: An Introduction to Augustine's Practical Philosophy*. Grand Rapids, MI: Eerdmans Press, 1999.

Busch, Peter. "On the Use and Disadvantage of History for the Afterlife." In *Augustine and History*, edited by Christopher T. Daly, John Doody, and Kim Paffenroth, 3–30. Lanham, MD: Lexington Books, 2008.

Busch, Peter. "Peace in the Order of Nature: Augustine, Giles, and Dante." In *Augustine's Political Thought*, edited by Richard J. Dougherty, 53–73. Rochester, NY: University of Rochester Press, 2019.

Button, Mark. "'A Monkish Kind of Virtue?' For and Against Humility." *Political Theory* 33, no. 6 (2005): 840–68.

Byers, Sarah Catherine. "Augustine and the Philosophers." In *A Companion to Augustine*, edited by Mark Vessey, 175–87. Malden, MA, and Oxford: Wiley-Blackwell, 2012a.

Byers, Sarah Catherine. *Perception, Sensibility, and Moral Motivation in Augustine: A Stoic-Platonic Synthesis*. Cambridge, UK: Cambridge University Press, 2013.

Byers, Sarah Catherine. "The Psychology of Compassion: Stoicism in *City of God* 9.5." In *Augustine's City of God: A Critical Guide*, edited by James Wetzel, 130–48. Cambridge, UK: Cambridge University Press, 2012b.

Camus, Albert. *Christian Metaphysics and Neoplatonism*. Translated by Ronald D. Srigley. Columbia: University Press of Missouri, 2007.

Carlson, John D. "Defending the Secular from Its Secularist Critics: Albert Camus, Saint Augustine, and the New Atheism." *Soundings: An Interdisciplinary Journal* 97, no. 1 (2014): 50–74. https://doi.org/10.5325/soundings.97.1.0050.

Cary, Phillip. *Augustine's Invention of the Inner Self: The Legacy of a Christian Platonist*. New York: Oxford University Press, 2000.

Cary, Phillip. "United Inwardly by Love: Augustine's Social Ontology." In *Augustine and Politics*, edited by John Doody, Kevin L. Hughes, and Kim Paffenroth, 3–34. New York and London: Lexington Books, 2005.

Cassidy, Eoin. "The Recovery of the Classical Ideal of Friendship in Augustine's Portrayal of *Caritas*." In *The Relationship between Neo-Platonism and Christianity*, edited by Thomas Finan, 127–40. Dublin, Ireland: Four Courts, 1992.

Catapano, Giovanni. "*Nobilissimus philosophus paganorum/falsus philosophus*: Porphyry in Augustine's Metaphilosophy." *Studia greco-arabica* 8 (2018): 49–66.

Catherine of Siena. *The Dialogue*. Translated and introduction by Suzanne Noffke. Mahwah, NJ: Paulist Press, 1980.

Cavadini, John C. "Ambrose and Augustine *De Bono Mortis*." In *The Limits of Ancient Christianity: Essays on Late Antique Thought and Culture in Honor of R. A. Markus*, edited by William E. Klingshirn and Mark Vessey, 232–49. Ann Arbor: University of Michigan Press, 1999.

Cavadini, John C. "Ideology and Solidarity in Augustine's *City of God*." In *Augustine's City of God: A Critical Guide*, edited by James Wetzel, 93–110. Cambridge, UK: Cambridge University Press, 2012.

Cavadini, John C. "The Darkest Enigma: Reconsidering the Self in Augustine's Thought." *Augustinian Studies* 38, no. 1 (2007): 119–32.

Chase, Michael. "*Omne corpus fugiendum?* Augustine and Porphyry on the Body and the Post-Mortem Destiny of the Soul." *Chora. Revue d'etudes anciennes et medievales* 2 (2004): 37–58.

Chroust, Anton-Hermann. "The Fundamental Ideas in St. Augustine's Philosophy of Law." *American Journal of Jurisprudence* 18, no. 1 (1973): 57–79.

Cicero, Marcus Tullius, and John Edward King. *Tusculan Disputations*. Cambridge, MA: Harvard University Press, 1927.

Clair, Joseph. *Discerning the Good in the Letters and Sermons of Augustine*. Oxford: Oxford University Press, 2016.

Clark, Gillian. "Augustine's Porphyry and the Universal Way of Salvation." *Bulletin of the Institute of Classical Studies* 50, no. S98 (2007): 127–40.

Clark, Gillian. "Augustine's Varro and Pagan Monotheism." In *Monotheism between Pagans and Christians in Late Antiquity*, edited by S. Mitchell and P. van Nuffelen, 181–201. Leuven, Belgium: Peeters, 2010.

Clark, Gillian. "*Caritas*: Augustine on Love and Fellow-Feeling." In *Hope, Joy, and Affection In The Classical World*, edited by Ruth R. Caston and Robert A. Kaster, 209–25. Oxford: Oxford University Press, 2016.

Clark, Gillian. *Monica: An Ordinary Saint*. Oxford: Oxford University Press, 2015.

Cohen, Jeremy. *Living Letters of the Law: Ideas of the Jew in Medieval Christianity*. Berkeley: University of California Press, 1999.

Connolly, William E. *The Augustinian Imperative: A Reflection on the Politics of Morality*. Newbury Park, CA: SAGE, 1993.

Cooper, Julie E. *Secular Powers: Humility in Modern Political Thought*. Chicago: University of Chicago Press, 2013.

Courcelle, Pierre. "Review of Edgardo de la Peza, *El significado de 'cor' en San Agustín*." *Latomus* 23, no. 3 (1964): 624.

Crosson, Frederick J. "Esoteric versus Latent Teaching." *Review of Metaphysics* 59, no. 1 (2005): 73–93.

Crosson, Frederick J., Michael J. Crowe, and Nicholas Ayo. *Ten Philosophical Essays in the Christian Tradition.* Notre Dame, IN: University of Notre Dame Press, 2015.

Crouse, Robert. "*Paucis mutatis verbis*: St Augustine's Platonism." In *Augustine and His Critics: Essays in Honor of Gerald Bonner*, edited by Robert Dodaro and George Lawless, 37–50. New York: Routledge, 2000.

Curbelié, P. *La Justice dans La Cité de Dieu.* Paris: Institut d'Études Augustiniennes, 2004.

Den Boer, Willem. "A Pagan Historian and His Enemies: Porphyry against the Christians." *Classical Philology* 69, no. 3 (1974): 198–208.

Digeser, Elizabeth DePalma. *A Threat to Public Piety: Christians, Platonists, and the Great Persecution.* Ithaca, NY: Cornell University Press, 2012.

Digeser, Elizabeth DePalma. "Christian or Hellene? The Great Persecution and the Problem of Identity." In *Religious Identity in Late Antiquity*, edited by Robert M. Frakes and Elizabeth DePalma Digeser,36–57. Campbellville, ON: University of Toronto Press, 2006.

Dodaro, Robert. "Augustine's Revision of the Heroic Ideal." *Augustinian Studies* 36, no. 1 (2005): 141–57.

Dodaro, Robert. *Christ and the Just Society in the Thought of Augustine.* Cambridge, UK: Cambridge University Press, 2004.

Dodaro, Robert. "Ecclesia and Res Publica: How Augustinian Are Neo-Augustinian Politics?" In *Augustine and Postmodern Thought: A New Alliance Against Modernity?*, edited by Lieven Boeve, Mathijs Lamberigts, and Maarten Wisse, 237–71. Louvain, Belgium: Peeters, 2009.

Dodaro, Robert. "Eloquent Lies, Just Wars and the Politics of Persuasion: Reading Augustine's *City of God in a Postmodern World*." *Augustinian Studies* 25 (1994): 77–137.

Dodaro, Robert. "The Role of Neoplatonism in St. Augustine's *De Civitate Dei*." In *The City of God: A Collection of Critical Essays*, edited by Dorothy F. Donnelly, 403–14. New York: Peter Lang, 1995.

Dodaro, Robert. "The Secret Justice of God and the Gift of Humility." *Augustinian Studies* 34, no. 1 (2003): 83–96.

Dodds, Eric Robertson. *Pagan and Christian in an Age of Anxiety: Some Aspects of Religious Experience from Marcus Aurelius to Constantine.* Cambridge, UK: Cambridge University Press, 1991.

Donnelly, Dorothy F. *The City of God: A Collection of Critical Essays.* New York: Peter Lang, 1995.

Dougherty, Richard J. "Law." In *The Oxford Guide to the Historical Reception of Augustine*, vol. 3, edited by Karly Pullman,1281–83. Oxford: Oxford University Press, 2013.

Dougherty, Richard J., ed. *Augustine's Political Thought.* Rochester, NY: University of Rochester Press, 2019.

Dunnington, Kent. *Humility, Pride, and Christian Virtue Theory.* Oxford: Oxford University Press, 2018.

Earl, Donald C. *The Political Thought of Sallust*. Amsterdam: Adolf M. Hakkert, 1966.

Enos, Richard Leo and Roger Thompson, eds. *The Rhetoric of Saint Augustine of Hippo: De Doctrina Christiana and the Search for a Distinctly Christian Rhetoric*. Waco, TX: Baylor University Press, 2008.

Escrivá, Josemaría. *Furrow*. London and New York: Scepter, 1987.

Evangeliou, Christos. "Porphyry's Criticism of Christianity and the Problem of Augustine's Platonism." *Dionysius* 13, no. 51 (1989): 51–70.

Farrell, James M. "The Rhetoric(s) of St. Augustine's Confessions." *Augustinian Studies* 39, no. 2 (2008): 265–91.

Figgis, John Neville. *The Political Aspects of St. Augustine's City of God*. London: Longmans, Green, and Co., 1921.

Fitzgerald, Allan D. "Christ's Humility and Christian Humility in The *De Civitate Dei*." *Mayéutica* 40, no. 90 (2014): 241–61.

Foley, Michael P. "A Spectacle to the World: The Theatrical Meaning of St. Augustine's Soliloquies." *Journal of Early Christian Studies* 22, no. 2 (2014): 243–60. https://doi.org/10.1353/earl.2014.0024.

Foley, Michael P. "Cicero, Augustine, and the Philosophical Roots of the Cassiciacum Dialogues." *Revue Des Études Augustiniennes* 45 (1999): 51–77.

Foley, Michael P. "The Other Happy Life: The Political Dimensions to St. Augustine's Cassiciacum Dialogues." *Review of Politics* 65, no. 2 (2003): 165–83.

Foley, Michael P. "The Quarrel Between Poetry and Philosophy in the Early Dialogues of St. Augustine." *Philosophy and Literature* 39, no. 1 (2015): 15–31. https://doi.org/10.1353/phl.2015.0012.

Fortin, Ernest. "Augustine and the Hermeneutics of Love: Some Preliminary Considerations." In *Augustine Today*, edited by Richard John Neuhaus, 35–59. Grand Rapids, MI: Eerdmans, 1993.

Fortin, Ernest. "Augustine and the Problem of Christian Rhetoric." In *The Rhetoric of Saint Augustine of Hippo: De Doctrina Christiana and the Search for a Distinctly Christian Rhetoric*, edited by Richard Leo Enos and Roger Thompson, 219–33. Waco, TX: Baylor University Press, 2008.

Fortin, Ernest. "The Patristic Sense of Community." *Augustinian Studies* 4 (1973): 179–97.

Fredriksen, Paula. *Augustine and the Jews: A Christian Defense of Jews and Judaism*. New York: Doubleday, 2008.

Geach, Peter. *Truth and Hope*. Notre Dame, IN: University of Notre Dame Press, 2001.

Gilson, Etienne. *The Christian Philosophy of Saint Augustine*. New York: Random House, 1960.

Gregory, Eric. *Politics and the Order of Love: an Augustinian Ethic of Democratic Citizenship*. Chicago: University of Chicago Press, 2008.

Hagendahl, Harald. *Augustine and the Latin Classics*, 2 vols. Stockholm, Sweden: Gothenburg, 1967.

Hammer, Dean. *Roman Political Thought: From Cicero to Augustine*. Cambridge, UK: Cambridge University Press, 2014.

Harding, Brian. *Augustine and Roman Virtue*. London: Continuum, 2008.

Harding, Brian. "The Use of Alexander the Great in Augustine's *City of God*." *Augustinian Studies* 39, no. 1 (2008b): 113–28.

Havel, Václav. *Living in Truth: Twenty-Two Essays Published on the Occasion of the Award of the Erasmus Prize to Václav Havel*. Edited by Jan Vladislav. London and Boston, MA: Faber and Faber, 1990 [1986].

Herdt, Jennifer. *Putting on Virtue: The Legacy of the Splendid Vices*. Chicago: University of Chicago Press, 2008.

Herdt, Jennifer. "The Theater of the Virtues: Augustine's Critique of Pagan Mimesis." In *Augustine's City of God: A Critical Guide*, edited by James Wetzel, 111–29. Cambridge, UK: Cambridge University Press, 2012.

Heyking, John von. "The Luminous Path of Friendship: Augustine's Account of Friendship and Political Order." In *Friendship and Politics: Essays in Political Thought*, edited by Richard Avramenko and John von Heyking, 115–38. Notre Dame, IN: University of Notre Dame Press, 2008.

Heyking, John von. *Augustine and Politics as Longing in the World*. Columbia, MO, and London: University of Missouri Press, 2001.

Hundert, Edward J. "Augustine and the Sources of the Divided Self." *Political Theory* 20, no. 1 (1992): 86–104.

Hunink, Vincent. "Apuleius, Prudentilla, and Christianity." *Vigiliae Christianae* 54, no. 1 (2000): 80–94.

Jacobitti, Edmund E. "Community, Prereflective Virtue, and the Cyclopean Power of the Fathers: Vico's Reflections on Unexpected Consequences." *Historical Reflections/Réflexions Historiques* 22, no. 3 (1996): 495–515. http://search.proquest.com/docview/1306693360/.

Jacobson, Norman. *Pride and Solace: The Functions and Limits of Political Theory*. Berkeley: University of California Press, 1978.

Jones, David Albert. *Approaching the End: A Theological Exploration of Death and Dying*. Oxford: Oxford University Press, 2007.

Kabala, Boleslaw Z. "Augustine and Contemporary Republicanism: On Speech as Domination." *Political Research Quarterly* 73, no. 1 (2020): 15–26.

Kabala, Boleslaw Z., Ashleen Menchaca-Bagnulo, and Nathan Pinkowski, eds. *Augustine in a Time of Crisis*. London: Palgrave Macmillan, 2021.

Kaufman, Peter Iver. *Augustine's Leaders*. Eugene, OR: Cascade Books, 2017.

Kaufman, Peter Iver. "Augustine, Martyrs, and Misery." *Church History* 63, no. 1 (1994): 1–14.

Kennedy, George A. *Classical Rhetoric and Its Christian and Secular Tradition from Ancient to Modern Times*, 2nd ed. Chapel Hill: University of North Carolina Press, 1999.

Kenney, Peter John. *Contemplation and Classical Christianity: A Study in Augustine*. Oxford: Oxford University Press, 2013.

Kenney, Peter John. *Mystical Monotheism: A Study in Ancient Platonic Theology*. Hanover, NH: Brown University Press, 1991.

Kenyon, Erik. *Augustine and the Dialogue*. Cambridge, UK: Cambridge University Press, 2018.

Keys, Mary M. "Augustinian Humility as Natural Right." In *Natural Right and Political Philosophy: Essays in Honor of Catherine Zuckert and Michael Zuckert*, edited by Ann Ward and Lee Ward, 97–113. Notre Dame, IN: University of Notre Dame Press, 2013.

Keys, Mary M. "Books 6 & 7: Nature, Convention, Civil Religion, and Politics." In *The Cambridge Companion to Augustine's City of God*, edited by, David Vincent Meconi,SJ., 102–21. Cambridge, UK: Cambridge University Press, 2021.

Keys, Mary M. "The Power and Peril of Names: Rhetoric, Politics, and Philosophy in Augustine's *City of God*." In *The Oxford Handbook of Rhetoric and Political Theory*, edited by Keith Topper and Dilip Gaonkar. Oxford: Oxford University Press, forthcoming.

King, Martin Luther, and James Melvin Washington. *A Testament of Hope: The Essential Writings of Martin Luther King, Jr.*, 1st ed. San Francisco: Harper & Row, 1986.

Kries, Douglas. "Echoes and Adaptations in Augustine's *Confessions* of Plato's Teaching on Art and Politics in the *Republic*." In *Augustine's Political Thought*, edited by Richard J. Dougherty, 152–72. Rochester, NY: University of Rochester Press, 2019.

Kries, Douglas. "Reason in Context: Augustine as Defender and Critic of Leo Strauss's Esotericism Thesis." *Proceedings of the ACPA* 83 (American Catholic Philosophical Society, 2010): 241–52.

Klauck, H. "Nature, Art, and Thought: Dio Chrysostom and the *Theologia Tripertita*." *The Journal of Religion* 87, no. 3 (2007): 333–54.

Kundmueller, Michelle M. "Augustine, Shakespeare, and Tolkien on the Identification and Excellence of Humility in Politics." *Perspectives on Political Science* 47, no. 4 (2018): 210–17. doi:10.1080/10457097.2017.1324685.

L'Arrivee, Robert A. "The Roots of Islamic Political Philosophy: a Comparative Study of Al-Fārābi's Virtuous City and Political Regime" (doctoral dissertation). Notre Dame, IN: University of Notre Dame Press, 2015.

Lamb, Michael. "Between Presumption and Despair: Augustine's Hope for the Commonwealth." *American Political Science Review* 112, no. 4 (2018): 1036–49.

Lancel, Serge. *St. Augustine*. Translated by Antonia Nevill. London: SCM Press, 2002.

Lavere, George J. "Camus' *Plague* and Saint Augustine's *Civitas Terrena*." *Proceedings of the PMR Conference* 10 (1985): 87–98.

Lavere, George J. "The Problem of the Common Good in St. Augustine's *Civitas Terrena*." *Augustinian Studies* 14 (1983): 1–10.

Lawler, Peter Augustine. "Esotericism and Living in the Truth." *Perspectives on Political Science* 44, no. 3 (2015): 199–203.

Lawler, Peter Augustine. "Tocqueville on Pantheism, Materialism, and Catholicism." *Perspectives on Political Science* 30, no. 4 (2001): 218–26.

Lewis, C. S. [Clive Staples] *The Complete C. S. Lewis Signature Classics*. San Francisco: Harper San Francisco, 2002.

Lieberg, Godo. "The *Theologia Tripertita* as an Intellectual Model in Antiquity." In *Essays in Memory of Karl Kerényi*. Translated and edited by Edgar C. Polomé, 91–115. Washington, DC: Institute for the Study of Man, 1984 [1982].

Livy. *The Early History of Rome: Books I–V of The History of Rome from Its Foundations*. Translated by Aubrey de Sélincourt. London: Penguin Books, 2002.

MacCormack, Sabine. *The Shadows of Poetry: Vergil in the Mind of Augustine*. Berkeley: University of California Press, 1998.

MacIntyre, Alasdair C. *Dependent Rational Animals: Why Human Beings Need the Virtues*. Chicago: Open Court, 1999.

MacIntyre, Alasdair C. *Whose Justice? Which Rationality?* Notre Dame, IN: University of Notre Dame Press, 1988.

Marcel, Gabriel. *Homo Viator: Introduction to the Metaphysic of Hope*, updated ed. South Bend, IN: St. Augustine's Press, 2010.

Markus, Robert A. *Christianity and the Secular*. Notre Dame, IN: University of Notre Dame Press, 2006.

Markus, Robert A. "*De Civitate Dei*: Pride and the Common Good." In *Collectanea Augustiniana. Augustine: Second Founder of the Faith*, 245–59. New York: Peter Lang, 1990.

Markus, Robert A. "Response" to Gerard O'Daly: "Augustine's Critique of Varro on Roman Religion." In *Religion and Superstition in Latin Literature*, edited by Alan H. Sommerstein, 77–80. Bari, Italy: Levante Editori, 1994.

Markus, Robert A. *Saeculum: History and Society in the Theology of St. Augustine*. Cambridge, UK: Cambridge University Press, 1988 [1970].

Marshall, Stephen. "Taking Liberty Behind God's Back: Mastery as the Central Problem of Slavery." *Polity* 44, no. 2 (2012): 155–81.

McFadden, Robert E. "A Tale of Ciceronian Christians: Spiritual Exercises and Friendship in the Cassiciacum Dialogues of St. Augustine" (doctoral dissertation). Notre Dame, IN: University of Notre Dame, 2018.

McInerney, Joseph J. *The Greatness of Humility: St. Augustine on Moral Excellence*. Eugene, OR: Pickwick Publications, 2016.

Meconi, David Vincent, SJ, ed. *The Cambridge Companion to Augustine's City of God*. Cambridge, UK: Cambridge University Press, 2021.

Meconi, David Vincent, SJ, ed. *The One Christ: St. Augustine's Theology of Deification*. Washington, DC: The Catholic University of America Press, 2013.

Melzer, Arthur M. *Philosophy between the Lines: The Lost History of Esoteric Writing*. Chicago: University of Chicago Press, 2014.

Melzer, Arthur M. "On the Pedagogical Motive for Esoteric Writing." *Journal of Politics* 69, no. 4 (2007): 1015–31.

Melzer, Arthur M. "Rousseau and the Problem of Bourgeois Society." *The American Political Science Review* 74, no. 4 (1980): 1018–33. https://doi.org/10.2307/1954321.

Menchaca-Bagnulo, Ashleen. "Deeds and Words: *Latreia*, Justice and Mercy in Augustine's Political Thought." In *Augustine's Political Thought*, edited by Richard J. Dougherty, 74–104. Rochester, NY: University of Rochester Press, 2019.

Mitchell, Colleen E., and Mary M. Keys. "Love's Labor Leisured: Augustine on Charity, Contemplation, and Politics." *Pensando il lavoro* II, no. 5 (Edited by Giorgio Faro [EDUSC], 2018): 315–32.

Mitchell, Stephen, and Peter van Nuffelen, eds. *One God: Pagan Monotheism in the Roman Empire*. Cambridge, UK: Cambridge University Press, 2010.

Mortley, Raoul. "Apuleius and Platonic Theology." *The American Journal of Philology* 93, no. 4 (1972): 584–90.

Nagle, John Copeland. "Humility and Environmental Law." *Liberty University Law Review* 10, no. 3 (2016), 335–69.

Nunziato, Joshua S. *Augustine and the Economy of Sacrifice: Ancient and Modern Perspectives.* Cambridge, UK: Cambridge University Press, 2020.

O'Connor, Flannery. *Mystery and Manners: Occasional Prose.* Edited by Sally Fitzgerald and Robert Fitzgerald. New York: Farrar, Straus & Giroux, 1969.

O'Daly, Gerard. *Augustine's City of God: A Reader's Guide.* Oxford: Clarendon Press, 1999a.

O'Daly, Gerard. "Thinking Through History: Augustine's Method in the *City of God* and Its Ciceronian Dimension." *Augustinian Studies* 30, no. 2 (1999b): 45–57.

O'Daly, Gerard. "Augustine's Critique of Varro on Roman Religion." In *Religion and Superstition in Latin Literature*, edited by Alan H. Sommerstein, 65–75. Bari, Italy: Levante Editori, 1994.

O'Donovan, Oliver. "Augustine's *City of God* XIX and Western Political Thought." In *The City of God: A Collection of Critical Essays*, edited by Dorothy F. Donnelly, 135–50. New York: Peter Lang, 1995.

O'Donovan, Oliver. *The Desire of the Nations: Rediscovering the Roots of Political Theology.* Cambridge, UK: Cambridge University Press, 1996.

O'Meara, Dominic. *Platonopolis: Platonic Political Philosophy in Late Antiquity.* Oxford: Oxford University Press, 2003.

O'Meara, John J. *Charter of Christendom: The Significance of The City of God.* New York: Macmillan, 1961.

O'Meara, John J. *Porphyry's Philosophy from Oracles in Augustine.* Paris: Études Augustiniennes, 1959.

Ogle, Veronica Roberts. *Politics and the Earthly City in Augustine's City of God.* Cambridge, UK: Cambridge University Press, 2021.

Ogle, Veronica Roberts. "Therapeutic Deception: Cicero and Augustine on the Myth of Philosophic Happiness." *Augustinian Studies* 50, no. 1 (2019): 13–42.

Ogle, Veronica Roberts. "Sheathing the Sword: Augustine and the Good Judge." *Journal of Religious Ethics* 46, no. 4 (2018): 718–47. https://doi.org/10.1111/jore.12242.

Oort, Johannes van. *Jerusalem and Babylon: A Study into Augustine's City of God and the Sources of His Doctrine of the Two Cities.* Leiden, the Netherlands, and Boston, MA: Brill, 1991.

Paffenroth, Kim. "Friendship as Personal, Social, and Theological Virtue in Augustine." In *Augustine and Politics*, edited by John Doody, Kevin L. Hughes, and Kim Paffenroth, 53–65. Lanham, MD: Lexington Books, 2005.

Peza, Edgardo de la. "El significado de 'cor' en San Agustín." *Revue des études augustiniennes* VII, no. 4 (1961): 339–68.

Peza, Edgardo de la. *El significado de "cor" en San Agustín.* Paris: Études Augustiniennes, 1962.

Pieper, Josef. *About Love.* Chicago: Franciscan Herald Press, 1974.

Pippin, Robert. "The Unavailability of the Ordinary: Strauss on the Philosophical Fate of Modernity." *Political Theory* 31, no. 3 (2003), 335–58.

Plato. *The Republic*, 2nd ed. Translated by Allan Bloom. New York: Basic Books, 1991.

Rachlin, Howard. *The Escape of the Mind.* Oxford: Oxford University Press, 2014.

Rickaby, Joseph. *St. Augustine's City of God: A View of the Contents.* London: Burns, Oates & Washbourne, 1925.

Rist, John. *Augustine: Ancient Thought Baptized.* Cambridge, UK: Cambridge University Press, 1994.

Rist, John. "On the Nature and Worth of Christian Philosophy: Evidence from The *City of God.*" In *Augustine's City of God: A Critical Guide,* edited by James Wetzel, 205–24. Cambridge, UK: Cambridge University Press, 2012.

Rist, John. "Plotinus and Christian Philosophy." In *The Cambridge Companion to Plotinus,* edited by Lloyd P. Gerson, 386–413. Cambridge, UK: Cambridge University Press, 1996.

Rist, John. *Plotinus: The Road to Reality.* Cambridge, UK: Cambridge University Press, 1967.

Roberts, Veronica. "Augustine's Ciceronian Response to the Ciceronian Patriot." *Perspectives on Political Science* 46, no. 2 (2016): 113–24.

Rotelle, John E., ed. *The Works of Saint Augustine: A Translation for the 21st Century.* Charlottesville, VA: Inte Lex Corporation, 2001.

Rousseau, P. "Language, Morality, and Cult: Augustine and Varro." In *Transformations of Late Antiquity: Essays for Peter Brown,* edited by P. Rousseau and M. Papoutsakis, 159–75. Burlington, VT: Ashgate, 2009.

Ruokanen, Miikka. *Theology of Social Life in Augustine's* De Civitate Dei. Göttingen, Germany: Vandenhoeck & Ruprecht, 1993.

Russell, Jeremiah, and Michael Promisel. "Truth, Lies, and Concealment: St. Augustine on Mendacious Political Thought." *Review of Politics* 79, no. 3 (2017): 451–73.

Russell, Robert. "The Role of Neoplatonism in St. Augustine's *De Civitate Dei.*" In *The City of God: A Collection of Critical Essays,* edited by Dorothy F. Donnelly, 403–13. New York: Peter Lang, 1995.

Sallust. *The Histories.* Translated by Patrick McGushin. Oxford: Oxford University Press, 1992.

Schmidt, Victor. "Is there an Allusion to the Christian Eucharist in Apuleius, Met. 9, 14–15?" *Latomus* 62, no. 4 (2003): 864–74.

Schott, Jeremy M. *Christianity, Empire, and the Making of Religion in Late Antiquity.* Philadelphia: University of Pennsylvania Press, 2008.

Simmons, Michael Bland. *Universal Salvation in Late Antiquity: Porphyry of Tyre and the Pagan-Christian Debate.* Oxford: Oxford University Press, 2015.

Smith, Gregory Bruce. *Political Philosophy and the Republican Future: Rediscovering Cicero.* Notre Dame, IN: University of Notre Dame Press, 2018.

Smith, James K. A. "An Emigré Spirituality: Camus, Augustine, and the Hope for Home in an Age of Mass Migration." *Soundings: An Interdisciplinary Journal* 103, no. 1 (2020): 35–51. https://doi.org/10.5325/soundings.103.1.0035.

Smith, Warren S. "Apuleius' 'Metamorphoses' and Jewish/Christian Literature." *Ancient Narrative* 10 (2012): 47–87.

Solzhenitsyn, Aleksandr. *The Solzhenitsyn Reader: New and Essential Writings, 1947–2005.* Edited by Edward E. Ericson, Jr., and Daniel J. Mahoney. Wilmington, DE: ISI Books, 2006.

Strauss, Leo. "On a Forgotten Kind of Writing." *Chicago Review* 8, no. 1 (1954): 64–75. https://doi.org/10.2307/25293010.

Tarrant, Harold, Danielle A. Layne, Dirk Baltzly, and François Renaud, eds. *Brill's Companion to the Reception of Plato in Antiquity*. Leiden, the Netherlands, and Boston, MA: Brill, 2018.

TeSelle, Eugene. "Looking for Home: Travel As Metaphor in Augustine." *Annali d'Italianistica* 14 (1996): 103–20.

TeSelle, Eugene. "Porphyry and Augustine." *Augustinian Studies* 5 (1974): 113–47.

Tinder, Glenn. *The Fabric of Hope: An Essay*. Atlanta, GA: Scholars Press, 1999.

Thompson, Samantha E. "What Goodness Is: Order as Imitation of Unity in Augustine." *The Review of Metaphysics* 65, no. 3 (2012): 525–53.

Tolkien, J. R. R. *The Silmarillion*, 2nd ed. New York: Houghton Mifflin Company, 1999.

Tolkien, J. R. R. *Tree and Leaf*. London: Harper Collins, 2001.

Torchia, N. Joseph. "St. Augustine's Treatment of *superbia* and its Plotinian Affinities." *Augustinian Studies* 18 (1987): 66–80.

Van Ophuijsen, Johannes M., ed. "The Continuity of Plato's Dialectic: An Afterward." In *Plato and Platonism*, ed. Johannes M. van Ophuijsen, 292–313. Washington, DC: The Catholic University of America Press, 1999.

Versfeld, Marthinus. *A Guide to The City of God*. London and New York: Sheed and Ward, 1958.

Versfeld, Marthinus. *St. Augustine's Confessions and City of God*. Cape Town, South Africa: The Carrefour Press, 1990.

Vessey, Mark, Karla Pollman, and Allan D. Fitzgerald. *History, Apocalypse, and the Secular Imagination: New Essays on Augustine's City of God*. Bowling Green, OH: Philosophy Documentation Center, 1999.

Virgil. *Aeneid*, 2nd ed. Translated by K. W. Gransden and S. J. Harrison. Cambridge, UK: Cambridge University Press, 2004.

Ward, Keith. "The God of the Philosophers and the God of Abraham, Isaac, and Jacob." *The Journal of Jewish Thought and Philosophy* 8, no. 2 (1999): 157–70. https://doi.org/10.1163/105369999790232105.

Warner, John M., and John T. Scott. "Sin City: Augustine and Machiavelli's Reordering of Rome." *Journal of Politics* 73, no. 3 (2011): 857–971.

Wegemer, Gerald B. *Young Thomas More and the Arts of Liberty*. Cambridge, UK: Cambridge University Press, 2011.

Wetzel, James, ed. *Augustine's City of God: A Critical Guide*. Cambridge, UK: Cambridge University Press, 2012.

Weithman, Paul. "Pride in a Time of Crisis." In *Augustine in a Time of Crisis*, edited by Boleslaw Z. Kabala, Ashleen Menchaca-Bagnulo, and Nathan Pinkowski, 247–58. London: Palgrave Macmillan, 2021.

Wood, Neal. "Sallust's Theorem: A Comment on 'Fear' in Western Political Thought." *History of Political Thought* 16, no. 2 (1995): 174–89.

You, Zhuoyue. "Lust, Confusion, and Solidarity in St. Augustine's *City of God*" (doctoral dissertation). Notre Dame, IN: University of Notre Dame, 2021.

Zuckert, Catherine H. *Plato's Philosophers: The Coherence of the Dialogues*. Chicago: University of Chicago Press, 2009.

Index

CPSIA information can be obtained
at www.ICGtesting.com
Printed in the USA
JSHW022016240723
45309JS00001B/13